The STORY of GOD

The STORY of GOD

Wesleyan Theology and Biblical Narrative

Michael Lodahl

Beacon Hill Press of Kansas City
Kansas City, Missouri

Copyright 1994
by Beacon Hill Press of Kansas City

ISBN 083-411-4798

Printed in the
United States of America

Cover design: Paul Franitza and Mike Walsh

10 9 8 7 6 5 4 3 2 1

To Janice,

partner in covenant

Contents

Acknowledgments   9

Part I. How God's Story Gets Told: Foundational Doctrine   13
1. Scripture: "The Oracles of God"   16
2. Tradition: Passing It On   25
3. Reason: Thinking It Over   31
4. Experience: Making the Story Your Own   40

Part II. The Beginning of God's Story: The Doctrine of Creation   49
5. The God Who Creates   51
6. The Universe as Creation   63
7. Humanity: The Creature in the Creator's Image   67

Part III. The Tragedy of God's Story: The Doctrine of Sin   73
8. Human "Response-ability" and Sin   75
9. Sin and Human Solidarity   80
10. Human Sin and Divine Persistence   86

Part IV. The Jewish People in God's Story: The Doctrine of Covenants   90
11. Noah: God's Commitment to Creation   93
12. Abraham: God's Calling of a People   99
13. Moses: God's Gift of a Way to Walk   104
14. David: The Quest for Kingship   111
15. The Prophets: The God of Partnership   118

Part V. A New Twist in God's Story: The Doctrine of Christ   125
16. A Covenantal Context for Christ   127
17. Jesus Christ, "Truly Man": Spirit Christology   134
18. Jesus Christ, "Truly God": Logos Christology   144
19. Jesus Christ, Resurrected One   153
20. Jesus Christ, Crucified Lord   158

Part VI. Living in God's Story: The Doctrine of the Church   166
21. Pentecost: Reversing Babel   168
22. Sacraments: Acting the Story   176
23. Salvation in Christ   184
24. Scriptural Holiness   192
25. The Praxis of Christian Existence   199

Part VII. The End of God's Story: The Doctrine of Last Things   205
26. What Do You Expect? A Lesson from John the Baptist   208
27. The Coming of the Kingdom   212
28. Death, Resurrection, and Immortality   220
29. Human Responsibility and Divine Judgment   227
30. The End of God's Story   234

Appendix   238

Bibliography (For Further Reading)   243

Subject Index   246

Index of Persons   249

Index of Scripture References   251

Acknowledgments

If John Wesley was correct in asserting that "the gospel of Christ knows of no religion, but social; no holiness, but social holiness," then certainly it is also true that Christian theology is best understood and practiced not as a lonely, individualistic quest. Rather, theology involves an ongoing, lively, and enlivening conversation among people of faith, whose brainstorms, probing questions, and support for one another provide a nurturing context for striving to comprehend the mysteries of God.

So many people have joined with me in the theological conversation represented by this book! My colleagues in the Division of Philosophy and Religion at Northwest Nazarene College are constant sources of stimulation, support, and good humor, and offered insightful comments on some of the earliest manuscript drafts. In particular, Division Chairperson Ralph Neil pushed me to transform a pipe dream into a real book by taking the initiative in helping me secure a research and writing grant from NNC's Faculty Enhancement Fund. To him and to Dr. Ken Watson, who established the fund several years ago to enrich the scholarly efforts of NNC faculty members, I offer my thanks.

I also wish to thank my student assistants, Catherine Schamber and Tim Flynn, who helped me during the two years of writing, for their tireless editorial efforts and seemingly endless barrage of questions that helped me sharpen many of the ideas explored in this book. At a later stage, good friend John Wesley Wright read the manuscript with a critical and insightful eye, offering priceless suggestions for its improvement. I trust that these three will recognize those passages where their insights and challenges have made their way into my head and heart, and thereby into the text. Thank you, friends.

I am grateful, too, for all the lively minds and hearts I have had the privilege to teach the past few years in Theology 201, Survey of Christian Thought. Those fine young people were asked to work with a manuscript-in-progress in various stages of "(in)completion," and their creative and thoughtful contributions to class discussions have been invaluable. It would not be enough to say that this book was written *for* them; more exactly, it has been written *with* them.

Finally, there is one whose love, support, understanding, and encouragement have sustained me through the hard and long work of writing this book. To her, my partner in the often precarious adventure of living, I dedicate this halting, stuttering attempt to tell the story of God.

All the oracles of God, all the Scriptures . . . describe so many scenes of divine providence. It is the beautiful remark of a fine writer, "Those who object to the Old Testament in particular, that it is not a connected history of nations, but only a congeries of broken, unconnected events, do not observe the nature and design of these writings. They do not see that Scripture is the history of God."

—John Wesley, "On Divine Providence"

PART 1

HOW GOD'S STORY GETS TOLD: FOUNDATIONAL DOCTRINE

"In the beginning God . . ." (Gen. 1:1).

Most people in English-speaking cultures recognize those words as the opening phrase of the Bible. But often the significance of the words eludes us. It is a happy circumstance that the Bible begins the way it does, for it gives us the feeling of an adventure about to get under way—a story about to be told.

Human beings are storytellers. We love to tell stories, and we love to listen to them. We tend to understand our own individual lives in terms of a story—with a beginning; important characters; a plot; twists, turns, and surprises with each new chapter; and an anticipated ending that will help make sense of the whole. And hearing someone else's story often sheds new light upon our own. We become characters in others' stories, and sometimes they become characters in ours.

Perhaps, then, it is no surprise that a growing number of Bible scholars and theologians are arguing for the importance of seeing the Bible as an overarching story (with many and various little stories along the way, to be sure) and of understanding that the primary task of *theology* (Gr., **theos** = God, **logos** = word; discourse about God) is to unravel and make sense of the biblical story, that is, to "tell the story" afresh in a new age filled with its own questions and anxieties. The style of religious thinking that attempts to be attentive to the biblical story, especially as it impinges upon and even profoundly shapes our own individual stories, is usually called "narrative theology."

The book you hold in your hands represents an attempt to present narrative theology on an introductory level—not simplistic, yet communicating narrative theology to people who are not professional theologians. This book is also an attempt to show how the various

13

doctrines, concerns, and issues of theology become closely related to one another as they are gleaned from both the Bible and everyday experience and are woven into the grand Story that Christians have told for two millennia. In other words, this book is an introduction to Christian theology, set within the style and concerns of narrative thinking.

Now, back to those opening words in Genesis: "In the beginning God . . ." This phrase suggests a couple of important considerations for us. The first is that the story Genesis is about to tell is *the story of God.* Certainly many characters fill the pages of Scripture but this opening phrase tips us off to a basic understanding of the Story as being first and finally God's. Sometimes God will seem to slip behind the scenes, but the Story remains His own throughout.

As many people have indicated in the past, an important implication of this point is that the Scriptures as a whole show little concern for attempting to prove the existence of the leading Actor. God is simply *assumed* and proclaimed from the very beginning of the Story. Nonetheless, as we begin the task of theology, we should keep in mind that we human beings are profoundly limited in our knowledge and understanding of this Character. But if we take the Bible's opening phrase seriously, we will first believe that everything in the universe— and the universe itself of course—is here because there is One who desires it to be. Such a conviction, in fact, strongly suggests that the notion of a story, with author, plot, and direction, is a fitting analogy for this universe and its Creator.

This belief in God the Creator is, in itself, of considerable significance. For one of the competing stories told today about our universe and ourselves is that our being here is a blind accident, sheerly a matter of deaf-and-dumb luck. In that version of the story of our life together in the universe, there really is no story except whatever small ones we might happen to generate along the way. But ultimately nobody will remember those measly stories, and we will someday fade (or perhaps explode) into a finale that will put an end to the meaningless charade. In contrast to this secularist story of our world and ourselves, the words "In the beginning God" place the events and actions of our lives into the context of a meaningful setting, a grander Story, in which a character called God is the primary Actor. But we must hasten to add that while the Bible simply assumes the reality of this Actor, theologians generally have not felt at liberty to make the same assumption without providing some rationale for their belief—and in chapter 3 we will consider some of the attempts they have made to establish ample reasons for believing in the Story's primary Character.

There is one other consideration that the opening phrase of Genesis might suggest to us. The proclamation that God operates "in the beginning" and, in subsequent verses in Genesis 1, during the first through sixth "days" of creation, reminds us of a critical aspect of narrative. Stories happen *in time,* with sequence; beginnings and ends and all the in-betweens provide the stuff of stories. Stories do not happen all at once; they go somewhere and take time getting there. To recognize that, in the Bible, God appears in time-full narrative is to understand God *historically.* This Actor in the Story truly does *act* in history, and though we will have much more to say concerning this idea in pages to come, it is an important primary consideration. Time and duration, direction and goal are inevitable factors in the story of God, and, for that matter, in the way God's story gets told.

If we keep these two considerations from Genesis' opening in mind—that God is the primary Character, and that this Character operates timefully, on a day-to-day, moment-by-moment basis—we are well on our way into a narrative introduction to theology. Perhaps one other factor would merit our attention, and that is the *reader* of the story—you. One of the strengths of the approach of narrative theology is that, when it is effective, it challenges the reader to locate himself or herself in the story. When God walks through the garden calling out to Adam, "Where are you?" the question is intended as much for the reader as for Adam. Jesus, of course, in this regard was a master of narrative theology; one example among many is His parable of the compassionate Samaritan, which ends not with "and they lived happily ever after," but with the question, "Which of these three do you think proved to be a neighbor . . . ?"—and with the challenge to "go and do likewise" (Luke 10:36, 37, margin).

The point is: to undertake the task of theology seriously is to become *involved,* to locate oneself in God's story. This does not mean that the theologian, professional or otherwise, never has any doubts about the story itself; in fact, having questions and asking them with utter seriousness is virtually a requirement for the task! Indeed, as we enter the world of theology, we must allow our minds to *wonder*—to ask and to seek and to knock—as we wander through the great events and scenes of the biblical story. We have it on good authority that the person who goes at it that way will get an answer, at least every now and then.

1

Scripture: "The Oracles of God"

In these introductory chapters we shall attempt to understand "How God's Story Gets Told." In many ways, it is the same way anyone's story gets told—except that this is a very old story, told over a considerable length of time with many tellers, twists, and complications, and with a rather unobtrusive main Character who seems not to be overly concerned that we get the Story "just right" in every detail. Certainly there are many believers in the Story who are convinced that God has given *them* (or, more likely, their denomination or religious movement) all the right details, but there are an awful lot of absolutely convinced Christians who disagree deeply with one another—and God has not done anything overwhelmingly obvious to settle the arguments! All of this makes for the complicated task of theology.

Christian theologians generally agree on this, however: no matter how complicated the job of telling God's story might get, we have a common starting point in the Bible. The Scriptures, then, provide the primary Source for theology, or thinking about God. Amazingly enough, it is in this vast collection of Hebrew literature, written in various styles and genres and collected over several centuries, that Christians encounter the story of God, the loving Creator and Redeemer of the world. No wonder Christians have been heard to sing,

> *Tell me the old, old story Of unseen things above—*
> *Of Jesus and His glory, Of Jesus and His love.*
> *Tell me the story simply, As to a little child;*
> *For I am weak and weary, And helpless and defiled.*

> *Tell me the story slowly, That I may take it in—*
> *That wonderful redemption, God's remedy for sin.*
> *Tell me the story often, For I forget so soon.*
> *The early dew of morning Has passed away at noon.*

16

Tell me the old, old story. Tell me the old, old story.
Tell me the old, old story Of Jesus and His love.

—KATHERINE HANKEY

It may not be classic poetry, but the simple words of this 19th-century hymn bespeak the power of the biblical story to offer encouragement, strength, and even transformation to its hearers.

But why? Whence does this Story derive its power? Part of its power rests quite simply in its story line: it is a basic conviction of the biblical writers that God acts in—and interacts with—human history to bring about His saving purposes. In other words, according to biblical faith, God reveals himself through certain events in history, events in which He is actively laboring to lead human beings to a saving relationship with himself, a relationship which indeed has as its ultimate goal the redemption of the entire created order (Rom. 8:18-25). In the Jewish biblical tradition, the events in which God is particularly remembered and celebrated as a saving God for the people of Israel are the Exodus from Egypt and the subsequent establishment of the Sinai covenant, all through the human leadership of Moses. (This is what Jews still celebrate in the Passover observance.) For Christians, a parallel cluster of saving events centers around the life and ministry of Jesus of Nazareth, particularly His death and resurrection. (This is what Christians still celebrate in the observance of baptism and the Lord's Supper.) Christians "love to tell the story . . . Of Jesus and His love" precisely because that story, like no other, tells of a loving God who acts for our salvation.

Thus, in both Judaism and Christianity, faith is centered in eventfulness, in time and place and history. The approach to religious belief taken in the Bible stands in tension with the more philosophical and meditative modes of Asian religion, and with the classical Greeks' more speculative quest for eternal truth untouched by historical change and challenge.

But if we say that biblical faith has to do with historical events—and this has become increasingly a commonplace observation among theologians in our century—we find ourselves faced with another problem. What do we mean by the word *history?* Do we mean simply everything that has ever happened? Does history include every event, no matter how small? If it does, then it is obvious that history is beyond our capacity to grasp. Not every event is accessible to us, and for that matter, not every event is important to us. Such considerations begin to reveal to us the inevitability of perspective and of value commitments when it comes to this slippery thing we call history. For example, if you were asked to give your life history, you would not even try to recount every little thing that ever happened to you and every little thing you ever did. We can't even recall all those little things, which are not nearly so important as some of the more memorable, life-changing events, persons, and activities that most profoundly make us who we are.

History is a little like that, except, of course, on a much larger scale. Histories are shaped by the perceptions and memories shared by communities (nations, tribes, religious denominations), and usually written by one person representing such a community (the historian), in which a pattern or succession of events is selected *and interpreted* to tell that people's story from a particular perspective and for a particular reason. For example, most Americans would agree that Gen. George Custer is an important figure in American history. But how does he fit? In the years immediately following the Battle of Little Bighorn, Custer was celebrated as a Christlike figure who "gave his life" to open the gates of paradise, as it were, for westward-peering settlers. In the early 20th century, he was still celebrated as a hero and patriot, if not quite so obviously in religious categories. Then came the 1960s and early 70s, the age of the antihero, and Custer generally was belittled as a self-glorifying buffoon. Most recently, Custer has been interpreted as a pawn of the U.S. government. American historians are still arguing about how most adequately to interpret Custer's significance. What is crucial to recognize is that, in each case, America's perceptions of General Custer are made to fit into the larger story Americans are telling about themselves and their country. We find the same phenomenon in the ongoing argument about what should and should not be in high school history textbooks; most recently the controversy has swirled around the amount and kind of attention Martin Luther King, Jr., and the civil rights movement in America should receive.

The critical point, finally, is that history and story are tightly related. Any person's or people's history involves the selection and interpretation of actions and events in such a way as to tell a story; history and story are both *narrative* whereby light is shed and meaning is evoked. An important implication of this is that there are many histories—as many as there are viewpoints from which to tell the human story. Various cultures, peoples, and religions all have their histories—all tell their stories—from divergent and sometimes warring perspectives.

Further, this insight into the nature of history (histories) has important implications for our understanding of the Bible; recall that our reason for these reflections on history was the observation that biblical faith is rooted in historical events, and a conviction that God is at work for our salvation in those events. In the Bible, then, we might say that its various writers interpreted the events of their cultural histories in such a way as to affirm God's active presence. A wonderful example of this is found in Exodus 14, where the great event of Jewish liberation and salvation is recounted. According to the text, "Moses stretched out his hand over the sea; and the Lord swept the sea back by a strong east wind all night, and turned the sea into dry land, so the waters were divided" (v. 21). First of all, we have to set aside that famous motion picture scene of Charlton Heston at the banks of the sea, with the waters rolling back in a matter of minutes. Exodus tells us that "a strong east wind [blew] all night," which means that the biblical story itself recognizes the natural element in the story. The *event,* if you will, was the blowing of the wind; the *interpretation,* which truly made the occurrence history for the believing Hebrew, was that "the Lord swept the sea back by a strong east wind all night." Later, when the Hebrews were safely on the other side, Moses composed a hymn that was even more poetic in its interpretation:

> Thy right hand, O Lord, is majestic in power,
> Thy right hand, O Lord, shatters the enemy. . . .
> And at the blast of Thy nostrils the waters were piled up,
> The flowing waters stood up like a heap;
> The deeps were congealed in the heart of the sea.
>
> (Exod. 15:6, 8)

The Hebrew prophets, of course, acted similarly by interpreting Israel's national and international fortunes (and misfortunes) as the activities of God, often as Yahweh's chastisement upon the people for their unfaithfulness and idolatry. Such events could, of course, have been interpreted simply from the perspective of power politics: were the Babylonians God's punishment for Israel's sins, or were the Babylonians simply power-hungry conquerors? But throughout the Scriptures, Israel's history is interpreted as the arena for the *story of God.* And the same process continued when the apostles proclaimed Jesus to be the Christ; they were, like the prophets before them, affirming that in specific events in Israel's history, God was acting in behalf of human salvation. Jesus himself inspired His followers to such interpretations when He asked them questions like, "Who do people say that the Son of Man is?" and "Who do *you* say that I am?" (Matt. 16:13, 15, italics added). And the fact that people were interpreting Jesus' identity in many ways means that it was not particularly obvious who He was. Peter's response of faith, "You are the Messiah," was hailed by Jesus as an evidence of divine revelation (vv. 16-17), but it was none the less one interpretation among many. ("Some say John the Baptist; and others, Elijah; but still others, Jeremiah, or one of the prophets" [v. 14]. I have a feeling the disciples mentioned only the more favorable interpretations that were floating around.) The upshot of this is that the four Gospels we carry in our Bibles are *a kind of history* in the sense we have been talking about history; they are stories of Jesus rooted in particular events in His life and ministry, but also told from a certain perspective (faith in Him) and for particular reasons (especially to inspire faith in Him). They are, like most of the rest of the Bible, *theological* history, or theology told in historical-narrative event.

Let me offer an illustration. There is no question that the central event in which Christian faith is grounded is Jesus' resurrection from the dead. Christians throughout the centuries have affirmed unreservedly that the Resurrection *truly happened* in historically datable, first-century Palestine. In the early years of the Christian movement, the apostle Paul put it this way: "I delivered to you as of first importance what I also received, that Christ died for our sins according to the Scriptures, and that He was buried, and that He was raised on the third day according to the Scriptures" (1 Cor. 15:3-4). It is clear that Paul, along with the Early Church as a whole, saw God's raising of the crucified Jesus as *the* event in history that brings salvation to us: "If Christ has not been raised, then our preaching is vain, your faith also is vain. . . . and if Christ has not been raised, your faith is worthless; you are still in your sins" (vv. 14, 17). This is God's decisively saving act in history—raising Christ "on the third day."

However, if one reads the four Gospel accounts of the Resurrection closely, one finds a great deal of latitude in the way this central historical event is narrated. For instance, the gospel of Mark, believed by many to have been the earliest of the Gospels, says that when the women came to Jesus' tomb on the first day of the week, they were greeted by "a young man sitting at the right, wearing a white robe" (16:5). Matthew, on the other hand, says it was "an angel of the Lord" (28:2), while Luke says it was "two men . . . in dazzling apparel" (24:4), and John mentions "two angels in white" (20:12).

All this detail perhaps would not be important if Mark's "young man sitting at the right, wearing a white robe" did not sound so very much like an intentional contrast to another nameless "young man" (also unique to the Gospel of Mark) who, at the site of Jesus' arrest in Gethsemane, flees into the night in humiliation and nakedness, his bedrobe torn away from him by the mob that has come to arrest Jesus (14:51-52). Tradition has surmised that this fleeing "young man" was indeed Mark, the Gospel's author. Generally it has been assumed, too, that the "young man" at the tomb was an angel, but Mark could have used the specific word for angel if that is what he had meant. Rather, the text specifically mentions a "young man," *sitting confidently and fully clothed,* in radical contrast to the young man who fled in fear and fully naked! One might easily suspect the author of actually placing *himself* in the Resurrection narrative, although he was not actually and literally there—precisely because it would mean that he, too, is a witness to Jesus' resurrection, an event that transformed his fear and humiliation before the powers of this world to a confidence and assurance that only Jesus' resurrection brings.

It would not make the Resurrection any less a historical event if we in fact surmise that this "young man" whom we traditionally have called Mark actually placed himself *in the story* as a literary device. The moral of the story would be that you cannot believe in Jesus' resurrection "from a distance." To believe is to become a witness, a transformed witness; *you too* may sit confidently and victoriously beside the empty tomb! You too may enter the ongoing story of Jesus' life-changing resurrection power.

And there are other interesting divergences in the Resurrection accounts. Why is it that only Matthew mentions the resurrection, along with Jesus, of "the saints who had fallen asleep . . . coming out of the tombs after His resurrection," entering Jerusalem and "appear[ing] to many" (27:52-53)? Might it be because of Matthew's deeply Jewish mind and his desire to spread the gospel specifically among fellow Jews, who believed in a general resurrection of God's saints at the end of time? And why is it that only Luke tells in careful detail the story of Jesus' walk with the despairing disciples on the Emmaus road, and how those same disciples returned to Jerusalem with burning hearts and the compelling news that He had been "recognized by them in the breaking of the bread" (24:35)? Might it be because Luke was attempting to say something about the profound meaning of the Lord's Supper and of Christ's continuing resurrection presence in the Church's meal of broken bread and outpoured wine?

And why is it that only John tells us of the appearance of the resurrected Jesus in the midst of His fearful disciples, cowering behind closed and locked doors, confused and disoriented by the Crucifixion—and His breathing on them and saying to them, "Receive the Holy Spirit" (20:22)? Might it be because John was attempting to say something about the relationship between the resurrected Christ and the gift of the re-creating Holy Spirit upon the Church that would echo Genesis, the first creation, when God "breathed into his nostrils the breath of life; and man became a living being" (Gen. 2:7)? In every case we find unique accents in the telling of the great historical event of Jesus' resurrection—accents that do not merely report facts but also give us *theology* through narrative.

History is story, story is narrative, and narrative is profoundly rooted in the Bible. The Bible as "the history of God," in John Wesley's words, is stuffed with stories and stories within stories. There is the overarching story of God, the Creator and Redeemer, within which we read the four stories of Jesus (Gospels), *within which* we read more stories (Jesus' parables). Telling a story, in fact, was the most common method for teaching theology among Jewish rabbis, and it remains a prominent Jewish teaching style even today. The novels of Chaim Potok (e.g., *The Chosen, My Name Is Asher Lev*) and Nobel prize winner Elie Wiesel's literary works (e.g., *Night, Dawn*) are prominent examples.

In a sense, then, the entire Bible is a story, with a beginning (creation), a crucial turn in the plot (human sin), and an anxiously anticipated end ("a new heaven and a new earth"). It is theological narrative, with countless little stories within that great narrative, countless characters, infinite twists and turns, but one basic plot: that the God who revealed himself in Israel's history did so that He might finally reach and redeem all peoples. As Christians, we affirm that this is a process begun in Abraham and fulfilled in Jesus Christ.

It is the Christian belief, then, that the biblical story is rooted in history—in a particular history of a particular people, Israel, as it has been interpreted by prophets (in the Old Testament) and apostles (in the New Testament). God's Story is comprised of a series of interpretations of historical events as the arena of His presence and activity. But no historical event, as I have tried to show, is sheer facticity without also the element of human interpretation; this means that even the events of biblical history were and are open to interpretations other than those the Bible offers. An assumption the biblical writers appear to share is that God exists and is working actively in human affairs to bring about salvation. Of course, not all people share that assumption. Other interpretations are possible.

To be a Christian includes, then, believing that the Bible is not simply one interpretation, among others, of human history and existence. To be truly Christian is to affirm that the biblical story of God, of the world, and of humanity is far more adequate and authentic than, say, the Marxist, Buddhist, secularist, or Muslim stories. To be a Christian means to believe that the biblical interpretations of history are *inspired* (*in-spire* = breathe into), that the human writers of the Scriptures were given unique direction and insight by God in order to interpret correctly God's presence and activity in historical events. In short, it is to believe in *revelation*, such that the Bible yields more than simply a human perspective on the events it describes.

Inspiration does not at all necessitate the idea of a word-for-word dictation from God to the biblical writer; in fact, the Bible's own evidence tends strongly to indicate otherwise. Inspiration most obviously refers to the living presence of God's Spirit (Gr., **pneuma** = breath, air in motion) offering divine insight to the writer to interpret God's activity without negating or undoing the writer's real humanity. Matthew gives us a stunning example of this divine-human interactive process in a narrative briefly alluded to earlier in this chapter: Peter's confession of Jesus as the Christ. To Peter's words, "Thou are the Christ [the Messiah], the Son of the living God," Jesus responded, "Blessed are you, Simon . . . , because flesh and blood [i.e., human resources] did not reveal this to you, but My Father who is in heaven" (16:16-17). Matthew is then careful to emphasize that it was *from that time* of Peter's confession that Jesus began to tell His disciples of His impending suffering in Jerusalem. But Peter—the very same Peter who acknowledged Jesus' Messiahship and whose confession was recognized by Jesus as having been inspired by God—pulled Jesus aside and told Him to quit talking nonsense! "God forbid it, Lord! This shall never happen to You" (v. 22). It would appear that Peter's rebuke of Jesus was grounded in his ideas about what a Messiah is and does—ideas he shared with most of his fellow Galilean Jews.

The central point is that although Peter received divine inspiration as to the identity and calling of Jesus, he understood and incorporated that moment of divinely breathed insight in the only way he could: within his own historical, social, intellectual context. God had revealed a central truth to Peter, in fact *the* central confession in Christian faith, but that did not give Peter infallible insight into God's purposes and activities. Peter remained Peter—human and fallible, and yet a vessel in and through whom God could work and speak. Perhaps this incident from the Gospels provides a clarifying model of the inspiration of the writers of Scripture.

As we have noted, in Israel's history it was the prophets who were believed to be "in-spired" or in-breathed by God; in the earliest years of the Church, it was the apostles, through the inspiration of the Spirit, who have given us reliable interpretations of God's reconciling act in Christ. I have always liked the definition I learned from my first teacher in theology: "Inspiration is the operation of the Holy Spirit upon the writers of the Bible in such a way that their writings become the expressions of God's will."[1]

But inspiration also has a lesser (but no less important) meaning as the enlightening work of the same divine Spirit in our *own* spiritual understanding. Though more will be said on this subject in chapter 4 under the category of experience, it is worthwhile here to point out

---

1. A. E. Sanner, "Survey of Christian Thought" (Lecture presentation at Northwest Nazarene College, Nampa, Idaho, Spring 1975).

that, especially in the Reformation traditions of Christian faith, inspiration can refer to the insight we are given into the Scriptures, so that, as we interpret them with care, we may receive God's guidance and a lively sense of His activity in the story of our own lives and in our behalf. It is the belief of many Christians, then, that they too, through the inspiring and enlivening presence of God, have become a part of God's story. In the words of John Wesley, the 18th-century evangelist whose story we will hear in the following chapter, "The Spirit of God not only once inspired those who wrote [the Bible], but continually inspires, supernaturally assists those that read it with earnest prayer."[2]

---

2. John Wesley, *Explanatory Notes upon the New Testament* (London: Epworth Press, 1952), 794.

2

Tradition: Passing It On

One of the important ways in which God's Story gets told is in the telling from one generation to the next. Each generation of believers finds itself compelled to reinterpret and retell the Story of God for itself and its contemporaries, and yet each generation also depends profoundly upon its inheritance from those who have gone before in the faith. For it is not enough simply to hand the Bible over to our children; rather, we tell and live and grapple with God's Story anew in every age, and also bequeath to our successors the same process of telling and living and grappling. This process is called *tradition.*

Tradition is necessary because, as we saw last chapter, the act of interpretation is an inevitable aspect of human existence. The Bible is a vast collection of writings united, in the main, by the conviction that God is actively laboring for the redemption of His fallen creation. This is, as we have seen, a particular *interpretation* of human life and history that, for the Christian, is believed to be inspired by God. But not only is it the case that the Bible offers an interpretation of human existence, but also it is clear that the Bible itself must always be interpreted by its readers. The various biblical books were all written within specific historical contexts, but those same books are also read by us within our specific historical contexts. The Scriptures are read, understood, and applied by people who live in particular places and times, facing particular challenges and questions. It is inevitable, therefore, that interpretations and applications of Scripture will vary according to the varying historical and social circumstances of any given community of believers. This ongoing dynamic relationship between the Church and its Scripture is, again, what we mean by tradition, particularly as that relationship is passed down from one generation to the next.

To tell God's story well, we must recognize the important role tradition plays in both our hearing and our telling. The traditions that surround and nurture us provide the "lens" through which we read, understand, and apply the Bible. Tradition is not only something we inherit, as a body of historically accumulated interpretation of Scripture, but also something we may contribute to through preaching, teaching, writing, testifying, and even simply living (if we live well). The tradition that has shaped you includes the sermons you have heard, the Sunday School lessons you have endured, the books and Bible commentaries you have browsed, the pastors or other Christian leaders you have watched in the acts and virtues of day-to-day living, and even the theology class lectures you have dreaded. Tradition is the inevitable reality of being a limited, finite creature living in history and within specific communities, including not only religious denominations but also the cultural, ethnic, and political dimensions of communal life. We are born into traditions of faith and of language, of thought and of practice. We are not absolutely determined by our traditions, but we are profoundly shaped by them.

Christian faith is richly diverse in its number of historical traditions, not unlike a mighty river with its many tributaries. There are three main streams that feed this river: Roman Catholicism, Orthodoxy (Greek and Russian), and Protestantism. Although we will have occasional opportunity to speak about specific aspects of each of these three, the particular Christian tradition that forms and informs the book in your hands is a tributary of the Protestant stream. The subtitle of this book suggests that it is the Wesleyan tradition—that is, the interpretation of Protestant Christian faith derived primarily from the teachings of John Wesley (1703-91)—that will provide our "lens" for reading and telling the story of God.

John Wesley and his brother Charles were two of the most visible figures in the great revival of evangelical Christian faith in England during the 18th century. Though John was born into an Anglican home and remained a minister in the Church of England (Anglican) all his life, he believed he had been led of God to sow the seeds of a religious movement within Anglicanism. The followers of this movement were called Methodists, who would "spread scriptural holiness throughout the land." Thus, an important contribution of the Wesleyan tradition to Christian faith has been a concern for understanding and promoting a doctrine of "holiness of heart and life." Since this is the tradition that provides the basis for the present book, it may be helpful to look at it more closely.

It is crucial to keep in mind that for Wesley this "scriptural holiness," or "Christian perfection," was in essence the holiness (or wholeness) of loving God with our whole beings and loving our neighbors as ourselves. It was a perfection "in love" that had to do not with abstract or legalistic ideas of absolute perfection, but the relative perfection of relationships "perfected" by love. Wesley said it this way: "Christian perfection . . . is nothing higher and nothing lower than this: the pure love of God and man—the loving God with all our heart and soul and our neighbor as ourselves. It is love governing the heart and life, running through all our tempers [emotions], words and actions. I ask no more. I'm interested in no other sort of perfection or holiness."[1]

Wesley, then, was in a profound sense saying nothing at all new; he simply had rediscovered and reemphasized the very heart of Jesus' own teachings and doings. Each of the Synoptic Gospels (Matthew, Mark, and Luke; **syn** = together with; **optic** = to see) tells in differing narratives the absolute importance Jesus attached to the commandments of Moses to love God and to love one's neighbor (Matt. 22:34-40; Mark 12:28-34; Luke 10:25-37; cf. Deut. 6:4-5 and Lev. 19:18, 34). These dual commands were for Jesus the greatest of all God's commandments, the linchpin for "the whole Law and the Prophets" (Matt. 22:40), the fulfillment of which is life eternal. This is the perfection for which human beings are created: *to love* as God, whom Wesley called "the great ocean of love," has loved us. Wesley simply believed that such a humanly loving life was indeed possible by the energizing, transforming power of God's love for us. Such a life is rooted and grounded in the fundamental biblical truth that "God *is* love" (1 John 4:8, 16, italics added). This truth will, in fact, provide the key for much of what we shall say about God throughout this volume.

There are three specific characteristics of Wesley's understanding of the life of love for God and neighbor, or *sanctification,* that are crucial to our appreciating the contribution the Wesleyan tradition has made to historic Christian faith.

First, holiness is *personal* or *experiential.* That is, it has to do with that profound dimension of who we are as persons in relationship to others. Commenting on 1 John 4:19, Wesley wrote, "'We love Him, because He first loved us'—and we cannot know his love to us till his Spirit witnesses it to our spirit."[2] Holiness is not a thing or an "it," but first of all a *relationship* in which we can stand, by grace, before God. Wesley was convinced by the New Testament that God's great demonstration of love has occurred in a particular historical event, in that "while we were yet sinners, Christ died for us" (Rom. 5:8). At the same time, Wesley argued, it is not enough to believe in the events of Christ's death and resurrection, or even to believe that He loves us; we need the Holy Spirit, God himself in presence and power, to impress upon our deepest selves the reality of that sacrificial love. As we shall see more clearly in chapter 4, Wesley was influenced profoundly by Paul's teaching that "the Spirit Himself bears witness with our spirit that we are children of God" (8:16).

---

1. *John Wesley,* ed. Albert C. Outler (New York: Oxford University Press, 1964), 288.
2. Ibid., 214.

The Wesleyan tradition, following Wesley not as a guru but as a guide, has then placed great emphasis upon the personal quest for, and personal experience of, God. One of the dangerous ironies of tradition is that it too often becomes a way of living and thinking that is simply inherited and passed on without much personal involvement, commitment, or experience. But inherent within a truly Wesleyan tradition will always be a component that is restless with a status quo mentality. Generally, new and vital religious movements eventually cool and harden into inflexible institutions, and while denominations within the Wesleyan tradition are not at all immune to this hardening process, they always carry within themselves at least the potential for breaking out into a fresh openness to God's transforming presence. "And we know by this that He abides in us, by the Spirit whom He has given us" (1 John 3:24). Of course this verse is in every Christian's Bible, regardless of denomination or tradition, but the Wesleyan tradition has been characterized by a particular persuasion that such conscious awareness of God's presence in human life is constantly to be expected and can actually be experienced.

Second, holiness is *loving*. As already mentioned, Wesley's vision of what human existence could be was sustained by the simple biblical declaration that "God is love" (1 John 4:8, 16). His brother Charles penned it well in his hymn "Come, O Thou Traveler Unknown," a poetic piece of narrative theology derived from the biblical story of Jacob's nocturnal wrestling match with God:

> 'Tis Love! 'Tis Love! Thou diedst for me!
> I hear Thy whisper in my heart.
> The morning breaks, the shadows flee;
> Pure, universal Love Thou art.
> To me, to all, Thy mercies move;
> Thy nature and Thy name is Love,
> Thy name is Love.

Correspondingly, there was for the Wesleys no higher human goal than to be bathed, immersed, baptized in the love that God is. To be filled with God's love meant that there was no room for sinful attitudes or actions, for sin is essentially lovelessness, a lacking of love for God and others. Thus, in response to the God whose "nature and . . . name is Love," John Wesley too waxed poetic:

> O grant that nothing in my soul
> May dwell, but Thy pure love alone!
> O may Thy love possess me whole.
> My joy, my treasure, and my crown.
> Strange flames far from my heart remove!
> My every act, word, thought, be love.

It is no accident, then, that one of the truly fine theologians in the relatively brief history of the Church of the Nazarene, Mildred Bangs Wynkoop, called her book on Wesleyan thought *A Theology of Love,* for that is truly what Wesley taught. Not only is God "the great ocean of love," but also we, said Wesley, are created simply "to exist and to love." The perfection to which God calls us is precisely a *perfection in love* (1 John 4:18). If the God who is love created us to love Him and others, then we are perfect—we are being and doing what we were created to be and to do—when we love. This love is manifested in a practical concern for the spiritual, physical, and emotional needs of others—a concern that deeply characterized John Wesley throughout his life.

Third, holiness is *expansive.* By this, I mean that the Wesleyan tradition, with love for God and others burning at its center, entails an acceptance of, and openness toward, those of differing traditions within the Christian faith. Holiness was not, for Wesley, a narrowing, constricting way of life that encouraged a superiority complex. Holiness is not "holier than thou."

Wesley's vision of the universal love of God is what pushed him to claim the whole world as his parish. He was no narrow sectarian, thinking that he and his Methodists had a corner on truth or on love! One of his most famous sermons, in fact, is titled "Catholic Spirit," in which he sought common ground with Christian believers whose opinions and worship practices were unlike his own—and he sought that common ground in the love of God.

> "Is thine heart right, as my heart is with thy heart? . . . If it be, give me thine hand" (2 Kings 10:15 [KJV]). I do not mean, "Be of my opinion." You need not. I do not expect or desire it. Neither do I mean, "I will be of your opinion." I cannot; it does not depend on my choice. I can no more think than I can see or hear as I will. Keep you your opinion; I, mine, and that as steadily as ever. . . . Let all opinions alone on one side and the other: only, "give me thine hand." . . . "If thine heart is as my heart," if thou lovest God and all mankind, I ask no more: "Give me thine hand." . . . [and] love me with a very tender affection, as a friend that is closer than a brother, as a brother in Christ.[3]

Wesley's catholic or universal spirit, which he called the spirit of love, was such that, in fact, he often reported in his journal with great delight that Roman Catholics frequently attended the Methodist preaching services and generally were not opposed to his ministry. His most striking contribution to an ecumenical spirit in theology is his

---

3. Ibid., 99-100.

1750 tract, *A Letter to a Roman Catholic,* in which familiar themes are sounded:

> . . . Does your tender love to all men, not only the good but also the evil and unthankful, approve you the child of your Father which is in heaven? . . . This, and this alone, is the old religion. This is true, primitive Christianity. O when shall it spread over all the earth? When shall it be found both in us and you? . . .

> O brethren, let us not still fall out of the way. I hope to see *you* in heaven. And if I practice the religion above described, you dare not say I shall go to hell. You cannot think so. None can persuade you to it. . . . Then if we cannot as yet *think alike* in all things, at least we may *love alike.* Herein we cannot possibly do amiss. For of one point none can doubt a moment: God is love; and he that dwelleth in love, dwelleth in God, and God in him (1 John 4:16).[4]

Wesley's understanding of holiness, then, encourages a Christian faith that is catholic or universal, rather than narrow and exclusivist, in its attitude toward other traditions. Wesleyan tradition at its best is profoundly open to learn and benefit from others, and to share its insights and particular accents with others. If historically and sociologically the tendency (temptation?) for religious traditions is to isolate themselves in robes of self-righteousness or superiority, the Wesleyan tradition has—and should nurture—a built-in expansive openness to other Christian traditions. Catholicity characterizes the Wesleyan holiness tradition at its best. This will have important implications for us as we proceed in this Wesleyan theology grounded in biblical narrative, for it will mean that, precisely because it is Wesleyan, it will be open to hear and to learn from voices in other theological traditions.

---

4. Ibid., 497, 498.

3

Reason: Thinking It Over

We have been considering the roles of the Bible and tradition in the task of theology, or the telling of God's story. But we are able to do something we would describe as "considering" only because of the human ability to think, to reflect, to *reason*. John Wesley lived in an era and a culture (18th-century Europe) that emphasized and even celebrated the human capacity for reason, and the confidence Wesley shared with his contemporaries in our ability to use our heads is an important dimension of the Wesleyan theological tradition. All of us desire to make sense of our lives, experience, and beliefs, and this desire is rooted in our reasoning abilities.

Our ability to doubt, too, is a function of reason. We have already seen that the story of God as told in the Scriptures involves a particular interpretation of events in history that are, in fact, open to alternative readings. The looming possibility of seeing things differently, of believing otherwise, means that even the most deeply committed Christian can entertain doubts. Theologians generally have been sensitive to the possibility of doubting—some people think overly sensitive!—and thus have, through the centuries, attempted to use the reasoning capacity to establish rationally justifiable grounds for belief in the God narrated in the biblical story.

These attempts, traditionally called "proofs" for God's existence, have not always been well received even by fellow believers. For some, it is enough to have the Story, and one cannot go beyond simple faith in the main Character, God. After all, the Bible seems simply to assume the reality of God, with little or no concern for establishing that assumption on rational grounds. Others have criticized that to argue for God's reality outside of appeal to the power of the Story of God is to conjure an anemic philosophical deity who bears little or no resemblance to our main Character. "The God of Abraham, the God of Isaac and the God of Jacob, not of philosophers and scholars," wrote the famed mathematician Blaise Pascal (1623-62), and many have since echoed his sentiments.

On the other hand, while the Bible does not offer rational arguments for faith, there are occasional hints in Scripture that it may be humanly possible and permissible to do so. The Psalmist's declaration, "The heavens are telling of the glory of God; and their expanse is declaring the work of His hands" (19:1), certainly makes an appeal to the beauties of nature as a basis for belief in God's reality. The apostle Paul states even more explicitly that "since the creation of the world [God's] invisible attributes, His eternal power and divine nature, have been clearly seen, being understood through what has been made" (Rom. 1:20). Such passages as these are often cited as providing biblical support for a belief in *general revelation,* or the belief that God the Creator and Sustainer of all the world purposely leaves evidences of His presence and power in the created order that are accessible to anyone who pays attention.

Certainly such passages, and others like them, do point to the possibility of finding hints of Deity in creation. But it should also be kept in mind that both of these biblical authors wrote from within the perspective of the history of God's saving acts, or what is called *special revelation,* so that nature already had for them the accents of the Redeemer's presence. Nonetheless, their words encourage us to explore the possibility of offering some rational justification for faith in the God of the biblical story. They remind us, after all, that human beings are thinking creatures, and to think hard and intentionally about what one usually takes by faith is never a bad idea.

The arguments for God's existence that we shall explore briefly are classic examples of a style of thinking about God called *natural theology,* because those who employ it are committed to restricting their evidence to the world of nature around and within us. Natural theology by definition does not have recourse to the Bible to provide evidence for God's existence. As we have already suggested, this style of thinking often stands in tension with *revealed theology,* which is discourse about God that begins with the testimony of Scripture. Simply put,

General revelation	*is to*	natural theology
(God's existence revealed in creation)		(human discourse about this God)

as

Special revelation	*is to*	revealed theology
(God's character revealed in historical acts of Scripture)		(human discourse about this God's saving works)

Often a decisive wedge is driven between natural and revealed theology. But if we believe in God and believe that He is one, then we will affirm that God is not only Redeemer and Savior (as emphasized in revealed theology) but also Creator and Sustainer (as recognized in natural theology); hence, we will be open to the possibilities of both styles of thinking.

The first argument for God's existence, both because it is the most basic and because it is probably the oldest, dating at least as far back as the Greek philosopher Plato, is the *cosmological argument* (Gr., **kosmos** = world, universe). There are several variations on this argument, but its essence lies in a sense of wonder about the fact that there is anything—anything at all! Where did the universe come from? Modern scientists may speculate about what they call a "big bang" aeons in the past, but the cosmological question is this: if indeed our universe began with a big bang, why was there a big bang? Where did it come from? What was behind or before it? If this "bang" originated with a mass of hydrogen so dense as to defy our wildest imaginations, where did this stuff we call "hydrogen" *come from?* Why was it around? Is it satisfactory simply to reply, "It was just there"? The human mind expects and looks for *causes* for every effect, and the effect under consideration here is not simply this planet or its creatures, or even that original ball of hydrogen, but the basic "isness" of the universe itself. The cosmological argument is founded in a wonder about *being.*

The early-20th-century German philosopher Martin Heidegger posed the question this way: "Why is there anything at all, rather than nothing?" His colleague in the theology department at the University of Marburg, Paul Tillich, believed that this age-old question of the philosophers was the most basic, most deeply probing of all. In a sense, it underlies every other question. It may be next to impossible to imagine absolute emptiness, *no thing at all,* but to the extent that we can, the cosmological argument presses us to wonder why such a void is not the case. It asks us to ask not simply, "Why am I here?" but "Why is there anything anywhere? Why planets and stars and neutrons and hippos and quasars and swamps and *any thing at all?"*

Recall that this is an argument for God's existence. Hence, the argument states that there must be a cause adequate to account for the being of the universe, and that cause we call "God." Why is there anything? Because there is a Creator of everything.

Some critics have turned the logic of the argument against its conclusion, saying that if everything else must have a cause, and that our minds constantly seek a final cause in which they can rest, then we must ask also about a cause for God. We may smile at the common children's question "Mommy, who made God?" but the cause-effect assumption of the cosmological argument might seem to press for an answer. Why stop the process at some convenient and perhaps arbitrary point called "God"?

The answer, simply, lies in understanding the logic of the word God. By definition, in the theistic traditions (Judaism, Christianity, Islam) we mean by the word the self-existent, uncreated, uncaused One. We cannot ask, "Who made God?" because then we would not be talking about God anymore. Again, critics see this as an arbitrary answer, but the point of the cosmological argument is not so much to prove anything—certainly not God's existence!—as to demonstrate what it is we mean by the word God in relation to the universe as we know it. Perhaps at this level of the argument, we could say that God is the name for whatever it is that is the primary reality, the first and primal cause of being, the most fundamental reason for the being of *being*.

The second argument for God's existence, a relative of the first, is the *teleological argument* (Gr., **telos** = goal, aim). While the cosmological argument finds its sense of wonder in the fact that there is anything at all, the teleological argument points to the evidence of order, harmony, complexity, and beauty in that which is. This could include everything from a breathtaking sunset to a mother nursing her child, from the symbiotic oxygen-carbon dioxide relationship between plants and animals to the complexities of the human brain, from the earth's seemingly perfect spatial relationship to the sun to the ant colony in my garden.

In contemporary physics, this argument has been rejuvenated in the form of the "anthropic principle" (Gr., **anthrōpos**, human). This principle is derived from a long and impressive list of characteristics of our universe that together make life like ours possible. For example, astronomers tell us that the initial conditions of our universe were precisely tuned to produce galaxies and stars; had there been the slightest variation in those conditions, the universe would have collapsed back in upon itself or else exploded too fast for stars to form. Stars, in turn, are the carbon-producing factories of the universe, and carbon is one of the elements necessary to life. On the subatomic level, the charge of the proton and electron match exactly, which is surprising, since these particles are remarkedly different in virtually every other way—but it is also a very good thing, since their match is necessary to existence! Meanwhile, the neutron is but a fraction of a percent heavier than the proton; but if the proton were at all heavier than the neutron, nuclear fusion would run rampant and destroy the universe as we know it.[1] These and many other factors have led otherwise nonreligious scientists to speculate on the presence of a purposive Mind at work in the cosmos.

---

1. I am thankful to Karl Giberson, associate professor of physics at Eastern Nazarene College, for his helpful insights into the anthropic principle. For further reading, see Paul Davies, *God and the New Physics* (New York: Simon and Schuster, 1983).

In its more traditional form, this argument was stated most forcefully by Thomas Aquinas (1225-74), who argued (without the benefit of modern astronomy and physics) that the order and design observable in our world bespeak an Orderer and Designer, a Mind sufficiently complex to formulate purposes and ends and to carry them out. For what, in fact, would be the alternative? That the order we perceive has arisen by accident and chance, which would finally leave the order unaccounted for.

This last point, rooted as it is in the human desire to understand and explain the world around us, is itself a particular variation of the teleological argument. The human being is a creature of wonder who constantly asks questions of purpose: "Where did I come from? Why am I here? Where am I going?" Those questions reveal a mind that continually probes for *reasons,* and reasons suggest reasonableness, order, design. To recognize the wondering capacities of the human brain is again to confront a pair of alternatives: we humans, complex questioners that we are, have arisen either by blind accident and happy circumstance or as the result of a cosmic Mind that is at least as complex and creative as we (and presumably much more so). And if the first alternative is the correct one, then in fact it is not really a happy circumstance but a profoundly absurd tragedy—for then we are animals who have developed an intelligence that surpasses its own origins in a mindless swirl of accidents. Our own search for meaning, for purpose, for primal *answers,* would be tragically frustrated and unfulfilled. If there is no Creative Mind who directs the universe in meaningful ways, then the stream of human consciousness and intelligence has risen much higher than its source in dead matter and mindless chance. If indeed this is so, we human beings are the victims of a most cruel (but purely accidental) joke. To be sure, it is not impossible that this is the case—but it seems to those convinced by the teleological argument that it is far more likely that the order and design that the human mind both seeks and discovers is present because there is an Orderer and a Designer who is also the Cause of all.

This first pair of traditional arguments for God's existence, the cosmological and teleological, tend to focus on the world of nature around us. The second pair that follow, on the other hand, tend to arise out of specifically human thought and experience. They are, nonetheless, further examples of natural theology.

The next argument we shall explore is the one that has probably inspired the most fascination over the centuries, even in those who finally reject it. The *ontological argument* (Gr., **ontos** = being) is most readily associated with Anselm (1033-1109), one of the great theologians of the medieval church, though the argument in a similar form had been offered much earlier by Augustine (354-430). Let us attempt to follow its subtle path.

Anselm's meditation on God's existence begins with a quotation from the Psalms: "The fool says in his heart, 'There is no God'" (14:1; 53:1, NIV). There is, for Anselm, a simple and obvious reason why the atheist is a fool; it is all wrapped up in what we mean by the word God. God is "a being that than which none greater can be thought."[2] Even the atheist, who denies the existence of God, agrees that, by definition, the word God refers to this greatest conceivable being. But which is greater, asks Anselm, a being who exists only in my mind, or a being who exists in reality? Which is greater, a perfect being that I imagine to exist, or a perfect being who *actually does exist in reality?* And for that matter, would not a *perfect being,* in order actually to be perfect, have to *be?* In Anselm's words, "But clearly that than which a greater cannot be thought cannot exist in the understanding alone. For if it is actually in the understanding alone, it can be thought of as existing also in reality, and this is greater."[3]

This, then, is why the atheist is a fool, according to Anselm: he or she denies the existence of the being who, *by definition, must be*—for God is Perfect Being. The very idea of God demands the existence of God.

I remember well the sophomore theology class in which we were attempting to grab hold of this simple, yet sophisticated and slippery, demonstration of God's reality as the Perfect Being. Rachelle's right arm shot up defiantly, a glint in her eye. When I called on her, she abruptly challenged, "I can imagine the perfect guy, too, but that doesn't mean he actually exists!" It was a delightful response, if for no other reason than that it was essentially that of the monk Gaunilo, a contemporary of Anselm. To be sure, Gaunilo did not raise his objection with the example of a "perfect guy," but he did use the idea of a "perfect island." Simply to have the idea of a perfect island in one's understanding, said Gaunilo (perhaps he was in dire need of a vacation), did not necessitate the existence of such an island.

Of course, both Rachelle and Gaunilo were correct as far as their examples were concerned, but Anselm's answer covers both objections well: the topic of conversation in this case is not about finite things like guys, islands, cars (can you imagine the perfect car?), mountains, or ice cream flavors; these are all objects that can be grouped within larger classes. They are contingent objects; that is, they need not be.

---

2. Anselm, "Proslogion," in *A Scholastic Miscellany: Anselm to Ockham,* ed. and trans. Eugene R. Fairweather (Philadelphia: Westminster Press, 1956), 73.
3. Ibid., 74.

Finite objects like islands or cars are not what this argument is about. It is not about one "perfect island" among a bunch of other islands, it is about *perfect being;* and while an island that one imagines to be perfect may or may not exist, perfect being *must be,* or it is not perfect.

Anselm betrays a hint of comic sense in his reply:

> You claim . . . that [the logic of my argument] is as though someone asserted that it cannot be doubted that a certain island in the ocean (which is more fertile than all other lands and which, because of the difficulty or even the impossibility of discovering what does not exist, is called the "Lost Island") truly exists in reality since anyone easily understands it when it is described in words. Now, I truly promise that if anyone should discover for me something existing either in reality or in the mind alone—except "that-than-which-a-greater-cannot-be-thought" to which the logic of my argument would apply, then I shall find that Lost Island and give it, never more to be lost, to that person.[4]

God, then, is an absolutely unique case, precisely because by the word God we mean that which must necessarily be. It may sound like a circular argument, and to an extent it probably is, and yet its power lies not in being a rationalistic syllogism so much as in being a profound meditation on what the word God entails.

The fourth and final argument we encounter is that of the German philosopher Immanuel Kant (1724-1804). Kant, whose primary interests were in ethics and morality, rejected the three previous arguments as the imaginations of speculative reason. The cosmological and teleological arguments, he argued, reach well beyond the evidence; a finite world such as ours can never really provide evidence of that which necessarily transcends (rests entirely beyond) it. As for the ontological argument, Kant simply asked whether it could be demonstrated that there actually is anything that answers to Anselm's description, "that than which a greater cannot be thought." Kant thought not, but he had his own unique argument for God's existence based in what he called "practical reason," or thought rooted in human moral experience.

True to his deepest interests in human morality, Kant began his argument on the observation of the universality of human conscience. He did not believe that everyone's conscience dictated the same acts as right or wrong for everyone, but only that everyone *has a concept of right and of wrong.* Further, he argued that our conscience applauds us when we act according to its dictates, but it condemns us when we act otherwise.

---

4. Anselm, "A Reply to Gaunilo," in *Philosophy in the Middle Ages,* ed. Arthur Hyman and James J. Walsh (Indianapolis: Hackett Publishing Co., 1987), 157.

From this relatively simple foundation, Kant suggested his "three postulates of practical reason." *First,* there must be *freedom* for the human will, or else the conscience is a charade; we cannot be condemned when we act wrongly unless we could have done otherwise. Likewise, when we act according to conscience, it would be the worst self-deception to feel good about such an act if in reality we were not free to do something else. *Second,* there must be human *immortality.* Our conscience demands justice in the sense of reward for the good and punishment for the evil, but in this life we often find those demands terribly frustrated. Who, for example, would not feel that death by his own hands in a bunker beneath Berlin is simply too good an end for Adolf Hitler? And what of all the innocent and good people who suffered unimaginably because of him? Do they not deserve better? Thus, the practical reason postulates another world beyond our own in which moral virtue and happiness embrace. *Third,* there must be *God,* said Kant, for only such a being as the one we call "God" could provide the guarantee of both our immortality and perfect justice. God is the Moral Orderer and Guarantor.

None of the above four arguments, of course, actually proves the reality of God. And thank God! For any God who could be "proved," any God who lived at the conclusion of a logical syllogism, would be an unimpressive God indeed. Further, if God's reality could be proved to anyone beyond a doubt, like the indisputable evidence in a laboratory experiment, there would be no room for doubt, and thus no room for faith—and no room for ourselves or real relationship to God. As it is, we live by faith, and not by sight (2 Cor. 5:7). And if it is the case that God respects and encourages our sense of moral agency and autonomy, then living by faith is highly preferable.

In the biblical story, belief that God exists—or better, faith in God—is not a matter only of intellect and reasoning, though they are not to be disparaged. But "knowledge of God," as the Bible speaks of it, involves a claim upon our entire lives, a motivation of our whole existence in every dimension. Coming to know God is a matter of response to the God encountered in the Story, and of risking our lives to become a part of that story. Such a response cannot be generated by theoretical proofs; it must be risked and rewarded in the toil and sweat of everyday human existence. Remember what Jesus said to those who doubted His mission: "My teaching is not Mine, but His who sent Me. If any man is willing to do His will, he shall know of the teaching, whether it is of God, or whether I speak from Myself" (John 7:16-17). Or, in the words of theologian Heinrich Ott, "When someone is certain of God's existence and reality, this is not a theoretical certainty which could be proved by demonstration. It is a practical certainty involving personal *engagement*. The *certainty of a proof* consists in being able to regard some matter as more or less settled, and to be once and for all convinced about it. By contrast, the *certainty of faith* means a renewed and confident waiting upon God, and involves understanding, orienting and adjusting one's life accordingly."[5]

Nonetheless, the arguments outlined in this chapter have historically provided a sense of support or justification to people who already believe in God. Again, none of the arguments exactly proves anything, but taken together they possess a cumulative strength for the theist (believer in God; Gr., **theos** = God) who is concerned to marshal rational arguments either to buttress his or her own belief or to offer evidence to the doubter. Finally, though, no piece of rational evidence can remove the risk of belief in the God whose story the Scriptures tell.

5. Heinrich Ott, *God* (Atlanta: John Knox Press, 1975), 37.

4

Experience: Making the Story Your Own

We have spoken of the Bible as the Story of God, the primary Resource for theology, the Book of Faith witnessing to God's saving activities in history in behalf of humanity. But the Bible offers a particular overall interpretation of history (as God's arena) that can be, and indeed often *has* been, disputed; furthermore, the Bible itself can be, and regularly is, interpreted in various ways. This points to the reality and necessity of tradition, as historically accumulated bodies of interpretation of the Scriptures, passed on from one generation to the next. But it is the very nature of traditions that they exist in contradiction to, or at the very least in tension with, one another; there are, for example, very specific differences in belief and practice between the typical Protestant and the typical Roman Catholic. And reason, which we employ in the interpreting of God's Story and attempting to make that Story somehow fit our everyday human existence, also yields ambiguous results; the same human thought processes that can help establish good reasons for a Protestant interpretation can do the same for a Catholic. A great deal depends upon the presuppositions with which one begins, and those presuppositions often are inherited from those very traditions that nurture us! For that matter, as we have seen, the same human reasoning abilities that may provide good reasons for faith can also raise profound doubts about faith. It is no wonder that many Christians have sought a way out of this cul-de-sac of ambiguity with an appeal to personal *experience*.

It is, to be sure, one of the hallmarks of the Wesleyan theological tradition to make this very appeal. In John Wesley's era, most Anglican theologians spoke of the Scriptures as the primary and authoritative Source for Christian faith and practice, recognizing the important supporting roles of tradition and reason. But it was Wesley who, among his contemporaries, recovered a place for personal experience in con-

firming religious truth. It is in fact popular today among Wesleyan theologians to refer to the "Wesleyan quadrilateral" of Scripture, tradition,
reason, and experience, and to recognize the importance of each in the
hearing and telling of the story of God.

Wesley's recognition of the role of experience arose, I believe, out
of both his own story and the biblical story. As a young theology student and Anglican priest, he wrestled with the intensely personal questions of religious authority and certainty. How could he know that he
was saved? For that matter, how could he know that the God and salvation of Christian faith were real? He was haunted by the deathbed
words his father, Samuel, had spoken to him: "The inward witness—
that is . . . the strongest proof of Christianity." Soon thereafter the
young Wesley was challenged by the pointed questions of a Moravian
Christian named Augustus Spangenberg: "Have you the witness within
yourself? Does the Spirit of God bear witness with your spirit, that you
are a child of God? . . . Do you know Jesus Christ? . . . Do you know
yourself?"[1]

Such questions only succeeded in making John Wesley miserable.
And his situation worsened when his venture into missionary work,
on the foreign field of Savannah, Ga., failed miserably. During the return trip to England, he wrote in his journal that he, the unconverted,
had dared to go to America to convert the Indians. "Who, what, is he
that will deliver me from this evil heart of unbelief?" he wrote. "I
think, verily, if the gospel be true, I am safe. . . . But in a storm I think,
'What if the gospel be not true?'"[2]

Much of Wesley's unrest lay in his having no certainty, no unques-
tionable authority, upon which to base his Christian commitment. He
felt himself "tossed . . . with every wind of doctrine" (Eph. 4:14, KJV),
bouncing first from a Catholic emphasis upon good works, to a
Lutheran emphasis upon faith alone, to the "union with God" of mys-
tical writers, to just plain doubt. He had the resources of Scripture,
church tradition, and reason, but to him one element was missing—a
sure experience. "I had no heart, no vigour, no zeal in obeying; continually doubting whether I was right or wrong and never out of perplex-
ities and entanglements."[3] He could not rest in such uncertainty. On
the same day that he saw English shores once more, he wrote in his
journal, "The faith I want is 'a sure trust and confidence in God, that,
through the merits of Christ, my sins are forgiven and I am reconciled
to the favour of God' . . . which none can have without knowing that

---

1. John Wesley, *The Works of John Wesley*, 3rd ed., 14 vols. (Reprint of 1872 ed., Kansas
City: Beacon Hill Press of Kansas City, 1978-79), 1:23. (Hereinafter *Works*.)
2. Outler, *John Wesley*, 44.
3. Ibid., 47.

he hath it (though many *imagine* they have it, who have it not), for whosoever hath it, is freed from sin, . . . freed from fear, . . . and freed from doubt."[4]

It is a popular supposition that Wesley did gain this faith in his famous "Aldersgate experience" of May 24, 1738. He describes what happened to him in his journal: "In the evening, I went very unwillingly to a society in Aldersgate Street, where one was reading Luther's Preface to the Epistle to the Romans. About a quarter before nine, while he was describing the change which God works in the heart through faith in Christ, I felt my heart strangely warmed. I felt I did trust in Christ, Christ alone for salvation; and an assurance was given me that he had taken away *my* sins, even *mine,* and saved *me* from the law of sin and death."[5] Although this dramatic experience did not, in fact, put a complete end to Wesley's spiritual upheavals and occasional frustrations, there is no doubt that it was a pivotal chapter in his story and a formative moment in the development of his doctrine of *assurance.*

But why did Wesley believe that such an experience was possible? Why did he expect this assurance, this certainty? Primarily because he read of it in the New Testament. When he later described his Aldersgate moment and similar experiences, he framed it in biblical terms: "The Spirit itself bore witness to my spirit that I was a child of God, gave me an evidence hereof, and I immediately cried, 'Abba, Father!'"[6] This description of his experience directs us specifically to two passages in the writings of the apostle Paul:

> For all who are being led by the Spirit of God, these are sons of God. For you have not received a spirit of slavery leading to fear again, but you have received a spirit of adoption as sons by which we cry out, "Abba! Father!" The Spirit Himself bears witness with our spirit that we are children of God, and if children, heirs also, heirs of God and fellow heirs with Christ, if indeed we suffer with Him in order that we may also be glorified with Him *(Rom. 8:14-17).*

> But when the fulness of the time came, God sent forth His Son, . . . in order that He might redeem those who were under the Law, that we might receive the adoption as sons. And because you are sons, God has sent forth the Spirit of His Son into our hearts, crying, "Abba! Father!" *(Gal. 4:4-6).*

The fascinating point here is that this phrase, "Abba! Father!" occurs only three times in New Testament writings: the two times here in

---

4. Ibid., 50.
5. Ibid., 66.
6. Wesley, *Works* 5:127.

Paul's writings, and once in the Gospel of Mark. And because the Gospel of Mark is often thought to have been the earliest Gospel written, we could assume that Paul was familiar with its material, even if only through oral tradition. It appears likely that when Paul penned the phrase "Abba! Father!" using the Aramaic word "Abba" (father) in letters to audiences who would not particularly have known that language, he was evoking in his readers' minds a Gospel narrative with which they too would have been familiar:

> And they came to a place named Gethsemane; and He said to His disciples, "Sit here until I have prayed." And He took with Him Peter and James and John, and began to be very distressed and troubled. And He said to them, "My soul is deeply grieved to the point of death; remain here and keep watch." And He went a little beyond them, and fell to the ground, and began to pray that if it were possible, the hour might pass Him by. And He was saying, "Abba! Father! All things are possible for Thee; remove this cup from Me; yet not what I will, but what Thou wilt" (Mark 14:32-36).

If indeed Paul was intentionally pulling his readers' minds back to Gethsemane as the paradigm for what it means to receive the powerful witness of God's Spirit in the depths of our lives, *what dynamite!* It would mean that we find in those two Pauline passages a narrative theology of the Holy Spirit. (And even if Paul did not have Gethsemane specifically in mind, there is no reason why *we* cannot. Or, in words commonly attributed to the American theologian Bernard Meland, "If Paul didn't say it, he should have!") So understood, the Pauline doctrine of the Spirit's witness to God's adoption of us as children is not the promise of a bed of roses, but perhaps sometimes a crown of thorns on a sweaty brow. Certainly it would make sense of Paul's words about our coming glorification as Christ's fellow heirs, *"if indeed we suffer with Him"* (Rom. 8:17, italics added). The "Abba! Father!" experience of God's Spirit, then, thrusts us back to viewing Jesus in the garden, sprawled out upon the ground, crying out to God, "If it is possible, . . . Nevertheless not my will, but thine be done," and making His prayer our own (Matt. 26:39; Luke 22:42, KJV).

Perhaps this helps to set the notion of religious experience in a new context, a narrative context. Undergoing a religious experience may not be so much a matter of feeling happy and exhilarated, as William James suggested in his classic *The Varieties of Religious Experience.* Instead, it might often involve a deep yet conscious offering of ourselves to the divine will. The same divine Spirit who worked mightily in Jesus of Nazareth (see chap. 17) may also bring about in us a conscious awareness of God and a desire to accomplish His will. In the words of the Book of Hebrews, He who "offered up both prayers and supplications with loud crying and tears to the One able to save Him from death" was also He "who *through the eternal Spirit offered Himself* without blemish to God" (5:7; 9:14, italics added). The Spirit who witnesses to our hearts that we are God's children is the Spirit of Gethsemane.

This approach to the doctrine of the Spirit's witness, or assurance—from John Wesley to the apostle Paul, and from the apostle Paul to Jesus in Gethsemane—may indeed shed new light on the significance of *experience* in the Christian life. It would mean that the same Spirit who acted in Israel's history, and especially in the life and ministry of Jesus, is the Spirit who, as we encounter the story of those saving acts through the Scriptures (whether in sermons, Sunday School lessons, or in private reading), may make that Story so vital and living in our hearts as to draw us into it. We become participants, actors in the ongoing Story of God. No wonder the apostle Paul, by the same divine Spirit, could say, "I have been crucified with Christ; and it is no longer I who live, but Christ lives in me; and the life which I now live in the flesh I live by faith in the Son of God, who loved me, and delivered Himself up for me" (Gal. 2:20). The story of Jesus' own self-giving on the Cross had become the very centerpoint of Paul's own life and self-understanding.

In truth, the wisdom of Christian tradition generally has made a similar point: any so-called experience of God must always be judged in the light and the context of Scripture, because the Spirit who is working in our hearts and lives will not work contrarily to what is revealed in the Bible. Both our expectation and our experience of God's presence in our lives are, and ought to be, forged and formed by the the biblical narratives of God's saving acts.

To this point, our reflections upon the category of experience have had specifically *Christian* experience in view. That is, they have dealt with the Christian believer's consciousness of the presence and activity of God's Spirit in his or her life. But that very consideration raises important (and more daring) questions about (1) how to interpret religious experience in general, including that of people in religious traditions other than Christian; and (2) how to gain a broader understanding of human experience, such that the broader dimension of simply being human in the world becomes a recognizable factor in the task of hearing and telling God's story. We can make some headway on both of these questions by taking into account what Wesley, following the late-16th-century Dutch theologian James Arminius (1560-1609), whom we will meet later, called *prevenient grace* (Lat., **pre** = before; **vene** = come).

This "grace that comes (or goes) before us" simply means that

God is lovingly and graciously *present* and *active* in every human life, from fervent Christian to adamant atheist to mindful Buddhist. This is the Holy Spirit, God's own presence, that "light" of which John's Gospel speaks, "a light that enlightens every person" (1:9). It is this light, this gracious presence of God in human life, taught Wesley, that encounters us, calls us, and woos us from sin and self-centeredness back toward God. Prevenient grace is God never giving up on anyone. It is this gracious presence of God in human life and societies that makes and keeps us human and humane. The doctrine of prevenient grace affirms that no living human being is without at least some light, some glimmering, flickering awareness of the Holy. Certainly it can provide a basis in Wesleyan thought for the pursuit of natural theology, grounded in God's general revelation, as explored in the last chapter.

Often Wesley spoke of this universal yet particular presence of God's Spirit as being experienced in human life as *conscience*. We might be tempted to make a connection between Wesley on this point and Kant's treatment of conscience as treated briefly in the previous chapter, but there is an important distinction. While Kant believed that conscience was the one truly free and autonomous (Gr., **autos** = self; **nomos** = law, rule) sphere in human existence, as the capacity that distinctively inheres within human beings, Wesley saw conscience in specifically theological terms as the experience of human beings as they are encountered by God—though, most assuredly, they may not recognize His presence in their experiences at all. In Wesley's words, "There is no man that is in a state of mere nature; there is no man, unless he has quenched the Spirit, that is wholly void of the grace of God. No man living is entirely destitute of what is vulgarly called *natural conscience*. But this is not natural: It is more properly termed, *preventing* [=prevenient] *grace*. Every man has a greater or less measure of this, which waiteth not for the call of man. . . . Every one has some measure of that light, some faint glimmering ray, which, sooner or later, more or less, enlightens every man that cometh into the world."[7]

Like Kant, Wesley recognized that conscience does not dictate the same set of rights and wrongs for every person, and that in fact there are considerable differences among individuals and across cultures. This is an important recognition, for it underscores a critical aspect of Wesleyan theology: the Spirit who enlightens every person necessarily does so with respect to (and for) that person's own distinctive culture, ethics, and even religious beliefs. Again in Wesley's words, "Conscience . . . is that faculty whereby we are at once conscious of our

---

7. Ibid. 6:512.

own thoughts, words, and actions; and of their merit or demerit," with the necessary proviso that, far from speaking with one universal voice, the judgment of conscience "varies exceedingly, according to education and a thousand other circumstances."[8] This is an expression of what is called *synergism* (Gr., **syn** = together with; **erg** = work), the idea that God is pleased to cooperate with human beings *where they are*—in all their humanity, in all their social and historical particularity—as He begins to move them to *where they ought to be.*

If we apply Wesley's reflections upon conscience as the synergistic work of God's Spirit impinging upon the human consciousness within its own social, historical, and religious context (its "thousand other circumstances"), we can see the possibilities for affirming the relative authenticity of religious experience in religious traditions other than Christian. Though the Hindu, Buddhist, or Jew, for example, will hardly interpret and describe his or her religious experience in recognizably Christian terms, a Wesleyan estimation would be that such people truly do (or at least *may*) experience and respond to God according to their capacities and understanding, or "light." Wesley, in fact, typified such a relationship to God as the "faith of a servant," while authentic Christian faith is the "faith of a son" (Rom. 8:15; Gal. 4:1-7). This understanding of prevenient grace would not give an automatic stamp of approval to every claim to spiritual experience, for we should all be aware of the human capacity for self-deception, error, and distortion—it happens, after all, in Christian faith too. But it does provide a significant beginning point for a Wesleyan theological approach to religiously "experienced" peoples in non-Christian traditions and to understanding and appraising those traditions.

One can indeed argue that this approach to religious experience outside the Christian tradition is, in fact, a theological development of three passages in the Book of Acts, all of which involve theologically learned Jews preaching to Gentiles who stand largely outside the sphere of special revelation.

> And opening his mouth, Peter said, "I most certainly understand now that God is not one to show partiality, but in every nation the man who fears Him and does what is right, is welcome to Him" (10:34-35).

> "And in the generations gone by [God] permitted all the nations to go their own ways; and yet He did not leave Himself without witness, in that He did good and gave you rains from heaven and fruitful seasons, satisfying your hearts with food and gladness" (14:16-17).

---

8. Ibid. 7:187.

"And [God] made from one, every nation of mankind to live on all the face of the earth, having determined their appointed times, and the boundaries of their habitation, that they should seek God, if perhaps they might grope for Him and find Him, though He is not far from each one of us; for in Him we live and move and exist, as even some of your own poets have said, 'For we also are His offspring'" (17:26-28).

I would hasten to add that in each of these three sermons, Peter (in the first) and Paul (in the other two) moved from a recognition of God's gracious presence among all human beings and cultures to the proclamation of Jesus Christ as the decisive Revelation of that same God. So also a Wesleyan estimation of other religions ("faith of a servant"), while it need not belittle their adherents' experiences of the divine, also will "lift up Christ" as the One through whom all religious beliefs, practices, and experiences are to be sifted and judged ("faith of a son").

With what we have said about prevenient grace in mind, we may profitably shift to the second question, which concerns the role of human experience in general, of the human being in the world, in the task of theology. Very often the role of experience is reduced to our earlier considerations about specifically Christian experience of the Holy Spirit, in terms of the Spirit's witness or testimony to our hearts concerning our adoption into God's family. But if we recall that Wesley saw in the Scriptures the affirmation of a "going before" grace or presence of God's Holy Spirit in human existence generally, then suddenly the idea of experience as religious gets a lot bigger. Indeed, we find that Wesley, significantly influenced by the English empiricist philosopher John Locke (1632-1704), was constantly trying to be closely attentive to all of experience. It is fascinating to read Wesley's work and discover just how carefully he observed life and people, including, and perhaps especially, himself. But because he also believed so profoundly in the universal presence of God's Spirit to human lives and societies, his attentiveness to lived experience took on a religious depth. To quote from a contemporary Wesleyan, Thomas Langford, "A major characteristic of Wesley's theology is that importance is placed on empirical data as well as on direct immediate experience. . . . [Wesley] was . . . acutely aware of personal appropriation of God's grace and was careful in his observations, especially since he believed the Holy Spirit to be directly influential in human experience."[9]

In the Wesleyan tradition, then, there is a confidence in God's gra-

---

9. Thomas A. Langford, *Practical Divinity: Theology in the Wesleyan Tradition* (Nashville: Abingdon Press, 1983), 26.

cious presence to all life in its every dimension, and a certain attentiveness to lived experience, an authentic openness to learning in and from the world around us. In short, the concept of *experience* as understood here is that there is no aspect or avenue of our lives, no observation or experience, that need be ignored or unappreciated as we attempt to hear, interpret, and tell the story of God. For it is a story that involves the whole of our lives, in their all-embracing social, historical, educational, and religious contexts. Your particular humanity, with all of its quirks and quandaries, is welcome here.

The fact is, of course, that none of us could block out our own fund of experience, whether religious or in general, from the task of theology. We cannot negate who we are, or say that our own stories "don't count" as we grapple with God's story. In the words of Bernard Lee, a Roman Catholic theologian, "God's Spirit is where God's deep story is. Our spirit is where our deep story is. Through the immanence [Lat., **im** = in, **manere** = stay; nearness, presence] of God's Spirit in the human spirit, the deep story that is intended for history is transmitted."[10]

Let the transmission begin!

---

10. Bernard Lee, "An 'Other' Trinity" (Paper presented at Hebrew Union College, New York, April 13, 1986), 4.

PART II

THE BEGINNING OF GOD'S STORY: THE DOCTRINE OF CREATION

In the previous four chapters, which together comprise an introduction to the story of God, we have attempted to appreciate the various contributions of Scripture, tradition, reason, and experience to the task of theology. It should be mentioned, though, that while we can separate these four elements on paper and devote a chapter to each, in our actual experience the four interpenetrate and bleed into one another. For example, we necessarily utilize our reason in reading and interpreting the Bible, doing so through the "lens" of tradition and within the context (**con** = with; a text alongside of) of our vast array of experience in the world. Each of the four elements draws from the other three and also sheds a new light back on the other three.

As was briefly mentioned in chapter 4, this intradynamic of Scripture, tradition, reason, and experience is often called the "Wesleyan quadrilateral." While John Wesley did not go around talking about quadrilaterals (though he was better than average in geometry), it is clear that all four of these elements were important in his understanding of how we come to an adequate grasp of Christian faith and practice. Since a quadrilateral is a four-sided object, we might take the liberty to offer a diagram of Wesley's:

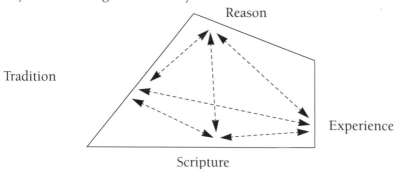

The Scripture base is the widest and provides the foundation for all the rest; Wesley is known, after all, for having called himself a "man of one book." More important, in his writings it is always clear that the Bible was to be the final Arbiter in theological matters.

Tradition is represented by a smaller line, yet larger than the other two, because while it is necessarily dependent upon Scripture, it also offers the wealth of the historic church's attempts to interpret and apply the biblical writings. Reason is necessary to reading, interpreting, and applying both Scripture and tradition, but it operates in a dependent relationship to both, because its presuppositions are derived from them. And experience, while not unimportant, has traditionally been considered to have a largely confirmatory rather than originative function in the matter of the formulation of Christian doctrine. We should also keep in mind that, even if it is Wesleyans who are most likely to talk about the quadrilateral's four elements, it is inevitable that anyone who attempts to think about Christian theology will necessarily incorporate Scripture, tradition, reason, and experience.

All of these introductory considerations are usually called *foundational* or *methodological* issues, for the question of method asks how one goes about a particular task. Thus far, we have attempted to lay a foundation in considering how a person in the Wesleyan tradition goes about the task of thinking about God, and about God's relationship to creation, including and especially human beings. Though certainly much more could be said about such methodological issues, the foundation has, I think, been laid for us. In Part II of God's story, about to get under way, we shall move to the more obviously substantive doctrines and issues of the Christian faith. And what better place to start than with God the Creator?

5

The God Who Creates

"Then God said, 'Let there be . . .'" (Gen. 1:3 ff.)

It is a fundamental assumption of the biblical story that God is the Creator of all things, the "Maker of heaven and earth" (Apostles' Creed). It is also commonly observed that, according to Scripture, God is Creator by virtue of His spoken word. The word of "let there be" in the beginning of God's Story receives amplification later in the prologue of John's Gospel, "In the beginning was the Word, and the Word was with God, and the Word was God" (1:1). Throughout the Bible, the creative and redemptive power of God's word is celebrated. When God speaks, things *happen!* And the New Testament Book of Hebrews insists that this creative power of the divine word continues to sustain creation, to call it into being, for God, in Christ, "upholds all things by the word of His power" (1:3). Hence, the Story of God has its foundation and continuation in the God who *speaks,* the God whose *Word* provides the possibility of the *words* that compose this ongoing Story in which we participate.

How appropriate it is for a narrative approach to theology that God is a God who speaks, and whose speaking initiates the very universe. For narrative is the meaningful arranging of words to tell a story, to pull the story's listeners in, to involve those listeners in the very telling and hearing of the story. And in Genesis, it is the speaking of God, the meaningful arranging of divine words, that begins the story our universe is.

It is critical, though, that we hear the nature of the creative word that God speaks. Repeatedly in the opening chapter of Genesis we find this phrase, "Let there be . . ." The word of God has the nature of *letting be,* of allowing things—zebras and zygotes, lizards and lions, rocks and rivers, microbes and mountains, plankton and people, *ad finitum*—to become. There is something about this word of "letting be" that bespeaks God's generosity in the giving of being out of the riches of His own being, a divine fascination with and love for beings of all

51

sorts, a wondrous stepping back by God in allowing creation truly to *be.*

Mainstream Jewish and Christian traditions have also insisted that this universe, called into being by God's word, truly does come into being purely by virtue of His word. That is to say, there is no other power, no other source, no other material out of which we and our world come, than that which God creates. Such a claim means that He did not have to begin with some preexistent "slush" or matter (or even energy) and somehow shape it into being; to think otherwise, after all, would be to give to this presumably preexistent, eternal stuff equal standing with God. The traditional language for this belief is *creatio ex nihilo* (creation out of nothing), and it underscores the biblical affirmation that God is God alone and that He is sovereign. Some modern theologians have suggested, however, that *creatio ex nihilo* has a rather barren ring to it, as though God simply conjured up beings from nothing out of sheer caprice. Perhaps the suggestion of one contemporary theologian, Paul van Buren, that it is more appropriate to speak of *creatio ex amore*—creation out of love—comes closer to the nature of the biblical narrative. It certainly resonates with the Wesleyan tradition's focus on God as holy Love. For in the phrase *creatio ex amore* it becomes evident that the God who speaks the word of "letting be" does so out of a *love for the other,* and a nurturing desire for the other to be.

In any event, the conviction that God creates the universe by the power of His loving word is an important affirmation of *monotheism* (belief in one God). According to the Story line, God has no competitor, no higher-up to answer to, and no preexisting material out of which He must create, all of which notions are examples of *dualism.* Any dualism, by definition, compromises the doctrine of God's *sovereignty,* of God's real *Godness,* throughout the universe.

This is, incidentally, one of the critical points at which mainstream Latter-day Saints (Mormon) theology seems to fall short, for it claims that there is an infinite begetting of "Gods" (including the God who created this world and fathered us all) and that the material universe, like the progression and proliferation of deities, is eternal. There is in such a theology no place or person at which the buck stops, and so the word God has a function different from its traditional implications of religious ultimacy. Unlike the monotheistic traditions of the world (most notably Judaism, Christianity, and Islam), for Mormon theology the word God does not name the universe's ultimate Source and Creator; it simply names a man who, like many others within the universe, has achieved the status of godhood. It just so happens that we are most closely related to this particular God.

Traditional monotheism, on the other hand, affirms that the word

God refers to the Creator of the universe and of all other possible universes or dimensions—God is Creator! Certainly it is permissible to speculate on the relative possibility of other created universes that preceded our own, or that will follow our own, or that are even operating in another set of dimensions alongside our own—for the main point that Christian faith affirms is that, wherever creation occurs, it is the doing of one Creator.

Christian tradition has developed in such a way as to safeguard the sovereignty of God over and throughout creation. It has done this primarily by speaking of God's *omnipotence, omniscience,* and *omnipresence.*

The barest definition of omnipotence is that all potency or power is inherently God's. There is no other power against whom God must compete, no other source of being or energy. God is, in the little phrase of the Jewish theologian Emil Fackenheim, *Sole Power.* Taken to a simplistic extreme, the doctrine of omnipotence could suggest that anything and everything that happens does so because God, who after all is omnipotent, causes, wills, or directly makes it happen. To be sure, there have been Christians, most notably those of a strict Calvinist tradition, who have indeed held such a doctrine of divine omnipotence.

Similarly, omniscience means that God, the sovereign Mind, knows all things. There is no event, no detail so tiny or insignificant as to elude His omniscience. More often than not, this belief in omniscience is assumed to include the future in all of its details *(foreknowledge),* so that God the omniscient One can never be surprised. All is known, and in fact is foreknown. Philosophers and theologians down through the centuries have wrestled with the question of whether such divine foreknowledge cancels any possibility of human freedom, and they have arrived at various answers. Calvinist theologians, for example, generally have not been particularly concerned to protect the idea of human freedom, since divine sovereignty is their highest concern anyway; the Dutch theologian James Arminius, on the other hand, affirmed divine foreknowledge but believed that this did not mitigate a person's freedom of response to grace. We will have occasion later to pursue the fine details of omniscience as it relates to divine foreknowledge.

Finally, omnipresence means that God is present to every point in the entire universe at every moment. There is no place where God is not. Down to the most infinitesimal subatomic particle, the doctrine of omnipresence affirms that God is truly and fully *present*—and that, thinking in the other direction, God is more than and larger than the immensity of the universe in its entirety, embracing and sustaining it.

Certainly theologians through the centuries have found biblical proof texts for each of these affirmations, but there is a relatively recent suspicion floating around among some thinkers that the *omni* doctrines owe their existence more to abstract analysis and deductive logic about what God "must be in order to be God," and less to attentiveness to the way in which God is encountered and described in the biblical story. The omni-God is metaphysically unimpeachable, but is such a God a philosophical construction, the idealistic invention of human minds, rather than the living God of Abraham, Isaac, and Jacob?

Undoubtedly one of the primary reasons for this suspicion about the *omni* doctrines, at least as they are often conceived, is a concern for *theodicy* (Gr., **theo** = God, **dikē** = justification), or for justifying God's ways in the world. Theodicy has to do most specifically with the theological task of defending belief in God in the face of extreme human suffering. While belief in the one sovereign, personal Creator satisfies the religious longing for one ultimate Cause of being, it also paves the path to this most troubling problem for people of faith: How can a good and loving God (*creatio ex amore*) allow a world with so much senseless suffering? After the Holocaust, after Hiroshima and Nagasaki, after Cambodia and Uganda and all the other horridly graphic scenes of dehumanizing torture, suffering, and violent bloodshed we have witnessed in our century alone, is it possible yet to believe in a good, powerful, and caring God? Many people, persuaded by the existentialist protest of authors such as Albert Camus in his classic *The Plague,* have answered this question with what might be called an "atheism of protest." There is probably no reason modern people offer more for their unbelief than this *problem of evil.*

The problem might be set up this way:

- An *omnipresent* God would certainly be aware of the presence of evil;
- An *omniscient* God would certainly know how to overcome that evil;
- An *omnipotent* God would certainly be able to enforce victory over evil; *and*
- A God of *love* presumably would desire to be rid of evil.
- *Yet evil does not disappear!*

By evil we might here include wars, murder, oppression, torture, abuse of all kinds (particularly when afflicted upon powerless children), hunger and starvation, homelessness, fatal accidents and illnesses, birth defects; and, of course, the list could go on. Elie Wiesel, in his gripping little book *Night,* tells of seeing cartloads of Jewish children being dumped into huge, fiery pits, literally a hell on earth. It has been suggested that any theology we do must be done at the edge of that pit, in the presence of those burning children. Such a demand should deeply chasten any theodicy we offer with a profound sense of inadequacy, humility, and pain. No attempt to justify God's ways in the world should lessen the seriousness of such sufferings or compromise our commitment to put an end to such evils. Nonetheless, an honest and self-searching faith in God demands that we do our best also to *do our theology in the ugly face of human suffering in all its depth and breadth.*

We may find a beginning in the distinction that Christian tradition has made between *moral evil* and *natural evil.* Moral evil includes all suffering that is a result of human decision, or more exactly, of the misuse of human freedom. The *freewill defense* of God is most effective in dealing with moral evil, since essentially it argues that evil is in the world because of human sin, not because of divine will or doing. In this case, God cannot be directly faulted for occasions in which one person suffers or dies at the hands of another, for God does not will that human beings so treat one another. Of course, God still is finally responsible for having created moral agents who can and often do resist His will, but at least then He is only indirectly responsible for evil. God, in creating free agents, has also created the *potential* for evil in creation.

This simple freewill defense, it seems to me, begins to open the door to a more adequate way of understanding divine omnipotence. In creating such a world as ours, and especially in "letting there be" human beings with the power of contrary choosing, God has in a sense divested himself of omnipotence in the act of sharing power with us. God manifests His creative power by "letting there be" that which is truly *other* to Him, that which can shake its fist and say "No!" to Him. There is a mystery in divine power, the mystery of sharing, of giving, of allowing others to live and to act. Perhaps it is possible that divine power is best understood as *empowerment* of the other, so that in the very breath we say "omnipotence" we also envision a kind of all-power that is, *by very nature,* shared. This is the intertwined mystery of divine power and human freedom.

But there is another dimension to the problem of evil, usually called natural evil. In this case, we deal not with obvious results of misdirected human freedom but with occasions such as hurricanes, volcanoes, deadly diseases, and drought. The fact is, of course, that human freedom wisely invested can and does reduce much of the suffering inflicted by natural evil: victims of drought, famine, or other disasters of nature can be sent food and water to relieve their need; cures can be discovered or developed for diseases. For that matter, such phenomena as hurricanes, volcanoes, and earthquakes are usually considered evil only when human lives or societies are destroyed thereby. (This may suggest a criticism of traditional theodicy as being too shortsighted, being concerned usually only for human, as opposed to animal, pain.) In many cases, then, one could extend the freewill defense by pointing out that people might have chosen to live elsewhere than where disaster struck. This does not mean, for example, that it was "their own fault" when people lost material goods or loved ones because they were living too close to Mount St. Helens when it blew in 1980. It simply means that, through what is normally a long series of complex decisions, we sometimes end up in the wrong place at the wrong time. This response to natural evil, then, involves a variation on the freewill defense.

Perhaps we can concede that many of our world's natural phenomena that wreak destruction are not evil per se but neutral. (Better yet, perhaps they are actually often good; earthquakes and volcanoes, for example, help the planet release pressures that, were they not "blown off," would eventually destroy us all.) But that does not help us deal with the problem of evil on the level where it really hits us: on the personal, existential level, where so often we feel at the mercy of destructive forces beyond our control.

It is at this level of theodicy that the Book of Job operates. It may seem at first glance that Job gives us the easiest of answers, since it tells of a kind of "gentleman's bet" between Satan and God, with poor Job as the prize (1:6-12; 2:1-7). It would be inviting to blame this satanic figure for all the bad things that happen, and save the good things for God! But, in fact, after the preface passage Satan never again appears in Job's story. And the preface makes it clear that Satan is answerable to God anyway, and able to go only as far as God will allow. This reminds us of an important implication of the doctrine of God's sovereignty as Creator and Sustainer of all: Satan, too, is created and sustained by God. Like every other component of creation, Satan's existence is immediately dependent upon the upholding power of God's word. Thus, to blame our experiences of evil and destruction upon Satan only pushes the problem back one step, for God remains the sovereign Source of all things—including the devil.

Further, when Job's pleas for an audience with God finally are answered, God shows no hesitation whatsoever about taking responsibility for the world in all of its joys and pains. His thunderous address to Job out of the whirlwind (chaps. 38—41) reaches its zenith in chapter 41, where He boasts of His handiwork evidenced in "Leviathan" or, of all things, the crocodile. Generally, we may experience more repulsion than admiration when it comes to crocodiles. But apparently God does not share our sentiments:

"Lay your hand on him; remember the battle; you will not do it
   again! . . .
No one is so fierce that he dares to arouse him; who then is he that
   can stand before Me? . . .
Who can open the doors of his face? Around his teeth there is ter-
   ror. . . .
His breath kindles coals, and a flame goes forth from his mouth. . . .
When he raises himself up, the mighty fear; because of the crash-
   ing they are bewildered. . . .
Nothing on earth is like him, one made without fear."

(vv. 8, 10, 14, 21, 25, 33)

To hear God's lengthy musings on the merits of the crocodile is to
begin to develop an appreciation for God as Creator and Lord of
"tooth and claw." The teleological argument for God's existence in
chapter 3 can certainly be conducive to romanticizing about the beauty and harmony of the world of nature. But there is an underside to
nature, too—where the big fish eats the little fish, and where blood is
spilled in the savage struggle. The Book of Job challenges us to appreciate this underside of nature, also, as God's handiwork. The harmony
remains, yes; but it is often a ferocious, tooth-and-claw harmony that
may suggest an almost brute power at work in creation.

Surely it is no accident that God speaks out of the whirlwind,
suggesting unleashed, uncontrollable energy; and it may be instructive
to remember that it is "a great wind . . . from across the wilderness"
that brings death to members of Job's family (1:19). And out of that
whirlwind comes a word of the divine delight in the incalculable diversity of creation. God speaks of the immensity of the oceans, light
and darkness, snow and hail, floods and thunderbolts; God calls to
Job's mind dew and ice, constellations and clouds, and even clods of
dirt. Also God speaks of lions and ravens and mountain goats, of deer
and donkeys. The ox is God's, as well as the ostrich, and the horse and
hawk and hippo. This majestic address from the whirlwind might in-
spire in us, as it did in Job, an awe in the presence of God's creative
imagination, for the created order is so multifarious and brimming
with life and vitality that God alone can contain, sustain, and integrate
its immense variety and precarious harmony. It seems, in fact, at times
to totter on the brink of chaos.

This brings us back to that crocodile. Why, after all, would a long
reflection on the crocodile be the punch line of God's oration, the evidence that finally drives Job to a profound sense of finitude and humility? Biblical scholars are quick to point out that the crocodile, or
Leviathan, was a creature of importance in Canaanite mythology. For
the Canaanites, whose religious imagery is often reflected (and harshly

judged) in the Hebrew Bible, the Leviathan-crocodile represented Lotan, a seven-headed monster of the swirling seas, a personification of the chaotic elements that are conquered in the act of creation. Psalm 74 reflects this mythic imagery of God's conquering and controlling of chaos:

> Yet God is my king from of old, who works deeds of deliverance in the midst of the earth.
> Thou didst divide the sea by Thy strength; Thou didst break the heads of the sea monsters in the waters.
> Thou didst crush the heads of Leviathan; Thou didst give him as food for the creatures of the wilderness.
> Thou didst break open springs and torrents; Thou didst dry up ever-flowing streams.
> Thine is the day, Thine is the night; Thou hast prepared the light and the sun.
> Thou hast established all the boundaries of the earth; Thou hast made summer and winter.
>
> (vv. 12-17)

It is a tantalizing possibility, then, that the crocodile that God so prizes in Job 41 is not simply the beast in the swamp, though it is certainly that; on a deeper, symbolic (and narrative) level, the crocodile evokes the image of the chaotic Leviathan, the swirling powers of the deep waters that threaten the order and well-being necessary to human existence. God has the monster under control—and is in fact its Creator!

Such reflections push us back to Genesis 1, where God's act of creation involves the divine Spirit-wind-breath (**ruach**) blowing over the chaotic, dark waters, and finally separating with the heavens "the waters which were below the expanse from the waters which were above the expanse," and then gathering "the waters below the heavens . . . into one place" so that dry land might appear (vv. 7, 9). This compelling picture of creation, in brief, involves God's act of "holding back chaos" or nothingness, symbolized by the formless, swirling void of deep, dark waters, so that order and structure ("dry land") may emerge. Creation is no less God's when it is characterized by swirling, threatening chaos, but creation as an ordered arena for living creatures, and especially human beings—giving them "a place to stand"— is that which God's life-giving Spirit, breathing and blowing upon the waters, brings into being.

Sometimes it is suggested that the creation account of Genesis is told in the light of the Jewish Exodus out of Egypt. If we keep in mind that the Exodus was, in fact, the central revelatory event in Jewish experience and memory, such a suggestion has merit. The psalm just quoted above, in fact, seems to bring images of creation and Exodus into convergence, like a double-exposure photo; creation is extolled as one of God's "deeds of deliverance" in which He did "divide the sea" (74:12, 13). The logic of such an approach to creation would be, "The God who delivered us out of Egypt's bondage is also Creator of heaven and earth." In both events there is the powerful Spirit-breath of God "dividing" the waters, blowing back chaos, so that a new creation might occur. In Exodus, it is the creation of a people before God, a people of identity and dignity; in Genesis, it is the creation of a world. In both cases, God's word is the word of "Let there be"—let there be a real creation, a real people, a true "other" that is other than God, that is not "under God's thumb" or at the end of puppet strings.

On the human level, that experience of otherness is found in human freedom, in our capacity to refuse God's love and will for us, which results in moral evil; on the level of the rest of the created order, perhaps that experience of otherness is found precisely in this notion of chaos (which, while profoundly biblical, also fascinates modern physicists), which lends a certain indeterminacy, even stubbornness, to God's own creation! Might our experiences of what we call "natural evil" be interpreted as the occasional intrusions of "chaos" into the predictable, structured order of our lives? Remember, after all, that it is his suffering that inspires Job's questions of God, and that it is God's whirlwind address on the Leviathan, the monster of the chaotic deep, that finally silences those questions. This "monster" (on both the literal and symbolic levels) is indeed God's creation, but that does not stop it from threatening or injuring us from time to time.

Of course, if the Jewish understanding of creation is framed by their collective memory of the Exodus, we might expect to see Christians, too, interpreting the creation of the world through their "deliverance narrative," the gospel of Jesus Christ. And that, in fact, is the case: John's Gospel, for example, tells us that the creative word (**logos**) that God spoke in creation is the same Word that became flesh in Jesus of Nazareth (1:1, 14). Similarly, Paul insists that "for us there is but one God, the Father, from whom are all things, and we exist for Him; and one Lord, Jesus Christ, by whom are all things, and we exist through Him" (1 Cor. 8:6). The point is that the early Christian community, living in the light of Christ's powerful redemption, now saw even God's deed of creation in that light. "He is the image of the invisible God, the first-born of all creation. . . . And He is before all things, and in Him all things hold together" (Col. 1:15, 17).

This has rich and profound implications for our understanding of God, of creation, and of the problem of evil. For understanding God, it means that our Christian confession is that the very heart of God in the moment of creation is a Christlike heart. The bold statement of 1 John, "God is love" (4:8, 16), while not the result of theological speculation but of Christ's self-giving on the Cross, is nonetheless telling us that *God is eternally and unchangingly love.* In some way, if Christ is at the center of the Christian doctrine of creation, it will mean that God's act of creation reflects the very self-giving, self-surrendering love embodied in the Crucifixion. It is the word of "Let there be," the word of a Love who shares being with the *other* that creation is—it is this Word of Love who became flesh and dwelt among us, who gave himself up for us. There is a cross in creation!

If indeed Christ on the Cross is the decisive revelation of God the Creator—the great historic parable of God's own suffering and vulnerability in relationship to the otherness of creation—then *the Creator truly is love,* and divine power is not a ruling fist but an open, bleeding hand. This only confirms our earlier hints about the need for a more adequate understanding of divine omnipotence. The very fact that Christ, the Word become flesh, was nailed to a cross by other men reveals a vulnerability on God's part, a willingness to suffer our abuses of freedom. God the omnipotent One does not hoard power but shares power. In the very act of creation, the God who is self-giving Love has shared His power, shared the quality of *being* that He alone possesses by nature. Anglican theologian John Macquarrie has written, "His creation was also a self-emptying. . . . His love and generosity led him to share existence with his creatures. [This is not simply] a limitation of power but also God's making himself vulnerable, for there cannot be this love and sharing and conferring of freedom without the possibility of suffering on the part of him who loves and shares and confers".[1] The God we call omnipotent does not exercise all power, if indeed power has been shared with us. But this is far more than a matter of quantity, of divvying up power; rather, it may be more accurate to say that the very nature of divine power is *empowerment of the other.*

The doctrine of divine omniscience, too, undergoes a significant shift when interpreted through the lens of Christ's cross as the decisive revelation of God as love. It points us now toward the deeply significant rendering of knowledge in the Hebrew tradition (**yada**, e.g., "Adam *knew* Eve"). Here to know another is active involvement, participation, transforming engagement with the other—intercourse with the other in the most profound sense. This moves omniscience away from a kind of disinterested, passive, computer-like knowledge of every detail of the universe, and instead toward the omniscience of love that probes deeply into our lives. God actively loves us, and thus

---

1. John Macquarrie, *The Humility of God* (Philadelphia: Westminster Press, 1978), 4.

God knows us. This seems far more in harmony with the Psalmist's declaration,

> O Lord, Thou hast searched me and known me.
> Thou dost know when I sit down and when I rise up; Thou dost understand my thought from afar.
> Thou dost scrutinize my path and my lying down, and art intimately acquainted with all my ways.
> Even before there is a word on my tongue, behold, O Lord, Thou dost know it all.
>
> *(139:1-4)*

Similarly, interpreting omnipresence in the light of the love revealed in the Cross unveils new shades of meaning. Yes, God is present everywhere, because His love impels Him to be *with* and *for* all creation. "God is love" means that He was in Auschwitz's fiery pits of burning children, in the eye-melting heat of the Hiroshima blast—and most particularly hanging on the cross of Jesus. But there is also a sense in which, because He is love, God in silence and pain awaits our response, our recognition of His presence. God does not *force* himself to be everywhere, in the sense of forcing our recognition and adoration. A story comes to mind of a Jewish rabbi who asked his students, "Where is God?" One bright and eager learner responded, "Everywhere, of course!" To which the rabbi answered, "God is wherever we let Him in." The omnipresence of God is an omnipresence of love, which quietly, even humbly, awaits our answering love.

This rather extended meditation on the character of the Creator as revealed in the Cross is important because it offers a different approach to theodicy, or the problem of evil. If, as the Wesleyan tradition has tended to say, divine sovereignty is in fact primarily a *sovereignty of love,* then the first thing to say about human suffering is that God, who is love, shares in it. When the Christian tradition pays heed to the cross of Jesus, it lays to rest any notion of an impassive, omnipotent deity on a distant heavenly throne, untouched and unaffected by the pains of creation. The God revealed in Jesus' suffering with and for us is a God who is vulnerable, who shares in the pain. The philosopher Alfred North Whitehead reflected his deep immersion in the Christian vision when he called God "the fellow-sufferer who understands."

Important as that is in a Christian theodicy, it is not enough; it is good if God suffers with us and understands our sorrows, but finally we seek a deliverance from evil. And this is what the resurrection of Jesus from death promises us. If the Cross bespeaks God's willingness to suffer at the hands of creation, to feel with us the pangs of chaos as it threatens and sometimes harms us, then the Resurrection reminds us that God is the victorious Power. He has created with a purpose, a *telos,* which the Hebrew prophets most often called *shalom.* This is an all-embracing sense of well-being that will permeate all creation, a vision of peace that sustains God's own struggle against the destructive effects of our freedom. Whether or not God will at some point in the future overrule our freedom in the interests of universal *shalom* is virtually impossible to say; but the indications of Scripture are that He would prefer our cooperation, our working together with Him, to accomplish a fulfilled creation. And as we offer ourselves as partners of God in His world, we are sustained by the conviction that "God is love"—that the love embodied in Christ is the Creative Power of the universe. This is the confidence in divine sovereignty the apostle Paul celebrated in the following passage: not the idea that God determines every event in our lives like some master solitary chess player, but that God's love for us is the one indestructible power in the universe.

> For we know that the whole creation groans and suffers the pains of childbirth together until now. And not only this, but also we ourselves, having the first fruits of the Spirit, even we ourselves groan within ourselves, waiting eagerly for our adoption as sons, the redemption of our body. . . . But in all these things we overwhelmingly conquer through Him who loved us. For I am convinced that neither death, nor life, nor angels, nor principalities, nor things present, nor things to come, nor powers, nor height, nor depth, nor any other created thing, shall be able to separate us from the love of God, which is in Christ Jesus our Lord (*Rom.* 8:22-23, 37-39).

6

The Universe as Creation

"And God saw all that He had made, and behold, it was very good" (Gen. 1:31).

The setting for this story of God that Scripture tells is the created order. Genesis tells us that it was "very good" in the eyes of the One who called it into being, meaning that creation is capable of fulfilling God's purposes. This world and this life, as God's own creation, are profoundly and deeply affirmed in the Scriptures.

Thinking carefully about the universe we inhabit as God's creation, and, in fact, as a "very good" creation, yields some important theological themes. In this chapter we will explore two of those themes.

First, to say that the universe is God's creation is to recognize its radical dependency upon Him. Its being is grounded not in itself but in the Creative Power who wills it and calls it to be. It is therefore finite, contingent, and utterly dependent. Meanwhile, God remains God with or without creation; God is *transcendent* (Lat., **trans** = beyond; **scandere** = climb; to be beyond, superior) Creator of all things.

This proclamation that God is Creator of everything is, in fact, the fundamental message of Genesis 1. In other words, the creation account is making a *theological* point. Those who attempt to reconcile the creation account with pet scientific theories, or who use it as a weapon against evolutionary theory, are missing that theological point. The weight of theological opinion is that Genesis 1 is not a scientific statement; it is, rather, a theological polemic against the idolatry of Israel's neighboring cultures. It cannot today be used as a scientific polemic against any particular cosmology (theory of origins) per se, whether ancient or modern. For most ancient peoples, all the various elements of nature were divine: sun, moon, and stars; gods of light and darkness; rivers and vegetation; animals; and the reproductive processes. The world was populated, even overpopulated, with nature deities, and in cultures such as Egypt's and Assyria's, the political rulers also

[handwritten note: THE Point is Who Created, not How.]

were worshiped as gods. What Genesis 1 is about, first and foremost, is the denial that any thing, creature, or person in the created order should be worshiped—for there is but one God who creates all things, the God of Israel, the God of the Exodus. Genesis 1 is a narrative sermon against idolatry.

This iconoclastic (lit., "to break or smash idols") impulse in Genesis 1 is illustrated by the author's use of the phrases "greater light" and "lesser light" in verse 16 in place of "sun" and "moon," words that had specifically idolatrous connotations. Sun and moon are not gods to be worshiped, but elements of God's creation. And last chapter we met "the great sea monsters" (v. 21), who played such a critical role in Canaanite creation mythology, but in Genesis 1 are radically *creaturized*—they are good creations of the one God. Such allusions to the religious ideas of neighboring peoples abound in the opening chapters of Genesis and make it clear that the intent of the opening chapter of the Bible is not actually to give a literal description of the events of creation but to affirm Israel's conviction that there is one God, the God of Israel, who is Creator of all.

People who attempt to use Genesis as a scientific textbook, then, as well as those who simply reject it as ancient guesses at cosmology that have been rendered obsolete by modern scientific advance, both equally miss the point of the narrative. It is not science, and to read it as such is to do violence to its intentions; it is, rather, poetic theology, a "hymn of creation" (H. Orton Wiley) that points us to God as our Creator. It is concerned with who creates, and why—not particularly with when or how.

Christians, then, can (indeed *must*) believe that God is Creator and Upholder of all things, and at the same time may (and *should*) allow natural scientists to do their best to discover how the processes of creation occur and when they began. Granted, every scientist will be selective about his or her data and will also have to interpret the data selected. Naturalistic evolutionists do that, and so do creation scientists, and so do theistic evolutionists. The problem with a scientific-literalist approach to Genesis 1 is that it often seems to assume that the Bible gives us scientific descriptions that render null and void the scientific quest for understanding the processes of life's origins. Though I am not a scientist, I think that trying to understand those processes would be something like asking, "If I had been there, however long ago this planet was formed and however long ago life appeared and in whatever way, what would I have seen?"

The Bible does not answer that question, and we should not try to make it do so. If we had been there on the "third day" of creation, what would we have seen? Trees popping full-grown into existence, already rooted in the ground, bearing ripe, red apples? Was the process of creation a matter of objects and living things simply appearing, in an instant, out of nowhere? Certainly this is not impossible with God, but neither should anybody assume that to be a Christian one must assume that this is what the primeval act of creation "looked like."

Evolutionary theory may be entirely wrong, or it may be partially correct; certainly many scientists themselves are raising questions about the theory's viability. The point is, the validity of the theory is a scientific issue, to be settled as surely as possible by appeal to the observable data our world offers (most specifically the fossil record), and not to the Bible, as though that were Scripture's function. For the most part, Wesleyan denominations have tended to view the Bible not as an inerrant science or history text, but as a witness to the possibilities of relationship to God through Christ, "inerrantly revealing the will of God concerning us in all things necessary to our salvation."[1] (See Appendix.)

Thus, the only thing a Christian, by definition, must say is that evolutionary theory can never be completely adequate if it leaves out God. Evolutionary theory, in and of itself, is religiously neutral; the scientist who mistakenly believes that such a theory decisively does away with God has moved from science into philosophy. Granted, most evolutionists have been *naturalistic* evolutionists, believing that the world is best explained entirely on the basis of nature's own capabilities. The universe they argue for is built purely on chance and natural selection. But if one believes that there is a Creative Mind who directs the processes of creation, one also is rejecting the notion of naturalistic evolution. That, however, does not automatically exclude the possibility of *theistic* evolution, i.e., that God's way of creating and sustaining the universe is through the processes that human beings have called evolutionary.

But remember: Genesis 1 cannot be used to support either evolution or any other scientific theory of origins; to read it for science is like reading Jesus' parable of the compassionate Samaritan as if it were a newspaper account. The Bible affirms that the God of Israel, who would later reveal himself decisively in Jesus Christ, is Creator and Sustainer of the universe. It is concerned with the *who* of creation. How God creates is His business; how we attempt to discover and understand God's deed of creating is ours.

A second important theme in the doctrine of creation is that, regardless of the processes whereby God creates, all that He creates is *good.* The created order, as it proceeds from God's creative hand, is to be affirmed and celebrated. There is an eminently proper biblical sen-

---

1. *Manual of the Church of the Nazarene* (Kansas City: Nazarene Publishing House, 1989), 30.

suality that invites us to enjoy this world: its delicious foods; its physical beauties, whether a star-filled sky, an ocean beach, or the human face or body; its good music; its delights of touch, whether stroking the cat's fur or lying down in the grass or touching another human being; its fragrant aromas, from that of the rose to that of freshly-mown hay. The world of senses is a world of delight, a world that is "very good" in the Creator's eyes. "For everything created by God is good, and nothing is to be rejected, if it is received with gratitude; . . . [for] God . . . richly supplies us with all things to enjoy" (1 Tim. 4:4; 6:17).

All of this is important in light of the recurring religious impulse to deny the flesh, the senses, and the joys of life in order somehow to reach God, or at least a more spiritual stage. Much of the popular fascination with leaving this world to go to heaven, for that matter, shares in a less-than-scriptural estimation of creation. The biblical doctrine of creation—not to mention the Christian doctrine of the Incarnation—historically has helped to guard against a world-denying asceticism such as that. In the moving words of the modern Jewish philosopher Martin Buber, "Exclusive love to God is, *because he is God,* inclusive love, ready to accept and include all love. . . . God limits himself in all his limitlessness, he makes room for the creatures, and so, in love to him, he makes room for love to the creatures. . . . Creation is not a hurdle on the road to God, it is the road itself. We are created along with one another and directed to a life with one another."[2]

Similarly, John Wesley wrote, "Love the creature as it leads to the Creator,"[3] implying that the created order truly is capable of fulfilling God's purpose for it as the place where relationship between God and human beings takes place. This points us toward the specific way in which creation is "very good": because it is the sphere in which real relationship is possible with the Creator, because its real otherness is upheld, indeed cherished, by God. Philosophers have argued for centuries over whether this is the best possible world, and the only suitable answer is, "That all depends." If you think the best possible world would be one without pain, without threat or hurt or risk, where "a good time is had by all," then this is not it. If you consider the possibility that the best possible world would be the one that best suits God's purposes of establishing real, covenantal relationship with humans, complete with freedom and the risks that entails, with the realities of struggle and pain and the growth those enable, then perhaps this world comes awfully close.

2. Martin Buber, *Between Man and Man* (New York: Macmillan Co., 1965), 51-52.

3. John Wesley, *A Plain Account of Christian Perfection* (Kansas City: Beacon Hill Press of Kansas City, 1966), 13.

7

Humanity: The Creature in the Creator's Image

"In the day when God created man, He made him in the likeness of God. He created them male and female, and He blessed them and named them Man [adam] in the day when they were created" (Gen. 5:1-2).

"When I consider Thy heavens, the work of Thy fingers, the moon and the stars, which Thou hast ordained; what is man, that Thou dost take thought of him? And the son of man, that Thou dost care for him?" (Ps. 8:3-4).

What *is* man? What does it mean to be human? These may be the most intriguing and mysterious questions human beings ask, for they are the questions that turn the questioner in upon himself or herself. Already, then, we find the first glimmers of an answer to the questions humanity presents to itself: human beings are those creatures who can *ask after themselves*. The human appears to be unique among God's living beings as the one who can and does ask, "Who—or what—am I?"

The answer that the Scriptures offer to that question is a complex one, but several characteristics can be identified in a biblical narrative foundation for theological *anthropology*. If we turn to the ancient narratives of the Hebrew Scriptures and read them intentionally for their theological point—that point being the story of God—then these characteristics become evident.

We have already been alerted to the distinct probability that to think that Genesis gives its readers a strict scientific account of human beginnings is asking more than the text intends. For example, in Genesis 1 we read simply that God created humanity, as male and female, in God's image (1:26-27). The method whereby God accomplished this is not part of the narrative—except for these two possibly significant observations: (1) the creation narrative clearly suggests a progression or development in the creative processes of God, moving ever to more complex forms, from one "day" to the next; and (2) the creation of the human beings occurs on the same "day" as other land creatures. On this second point, it is worth noting that human beings do not have their own special "day" of creation, a "day" to themselves; they are, after all, fellow creatures among and within all of God's created works.

And yet this creature we call the human does have a unique place before God. The creation narrative takes a radical turn when, quite suddenly, God speaks to this creature. He *addresses* the male and female and gives them dominion over, and responsibility for, the earth. The words of Psalm 8 provide the Psalmist's own answer to the question he posed, "What is man?"

> Yet Thou hast made him a little lower than God,
> And dost crown him with glory and majesty!
> Thou dost make him to rule over the works of Thy hands;
> Thou hast put all things under his feet.
>
> (vv. 5-6)

Here I believe we uncover the root meaning of what it means for humanity to be created in God's image. This is the creature to whom God speaks, and by His speaking the creature is called to relationship, to accountability, to response-ability before the Creator. This allows human beings an opportunity to *speak back* to God, to answer, to offer their own meaningful words to this great Story of God. For Him to create human beings in the divine image and likeness is, according to the creation narrative, God's great venture into the risk of relationship. For here He creates a living being in whom He intends to "see himself" as in a mirror, a being who will correspond ("co-respond") to Him, who will answer to Him.

Several theologians, including the 20th-century giant Karl Barth, have suggested that this capacity for relationship to God as an essential component of being created in His image extends also to relationships with fellow humans. Such scholars point out that, while nearly all of the created order shares in the male/female distinction, "man as male and female"[1] assumes a larger importance in the creation narrative. "And God created man in His own image, in the image of God He created *him*; male and female He created *them*" (Gen. 1:27, italics added). Here the interesting parallel in tension between "him" and "them" is paired with "image of God" and "male and female." The point would not be that God is actually a pair of beings, a male deity with a heavenly consort, nor even that God is both "male and female" within the divine self. The point would be, primarily, that human beings, precisely as and because they are created in God's image, are created for relationship with one another. This does not mean only, or even primarily, sex-

---

1. A fascinating discussion of these ideas can be found in Paul K. Jewett's *Man as Male and Female* (Grand Rapids: Wm. B. Eerdmans Publishing Co., 1975), esp. 23-43.

ual relationship, though that is not to be excluded; rather, the intimate bond between woman and man stands as a symbol of the quality of human relationship for which we are created in the divine image.

It is interesting that John Wesley anticipated a good deal of this understanding of theological anthropology when he wrote that God created human beings "to exist and to love." To *exist* means, literally, to "stand forth," implying a sense of separate and independent being. Wesley was suggesting that God creates us not to be puppets on a string; the paradox of being human is that while we are entirely dependent upon Him in each moment for our very being, God sustains us in each moment precisely to "stand forth," to be able to make choices and to be answerable for them. In fact, without the first half of Wesley's formula, "to exist," it is impossible to have the second half, "to love." For to commit ourselves in love, whether the object of love be God or neighbor, it is necessary that we stand forth as individuals who are other than, distinct from, the loved one. Authentic relationship ("to love") cannot occur without a strong sense of selfhood ("to exist").

This suggests, in turn, that the same sort of answerability or responsibility before God, for which we are created in His image, belongs also to our relationships with one another. It may be suggested, in fact, that our capacity to *ask after or about ourselves,* with which we began this chapter, may derive from the Creator's asking after us, and our asking after each other. In all, the human being, this mysterious being created in the "image and likeness" of God, is that being who is questioned, who is addressed, who is called to account—but who can do his or her own questioning, addressing, and calling to account, whether of God, of neighbor, or of self.

We find much of this theological anthropology beautifully woven into the fabric of the Genesis narrative in its early chapters. In chapter 2, for example, we find a story of the creation of the human that portrays God, somewhat like a potter, shaping a man out of the dust of the earth, and then perhaps "down on his knees," breathing into him the breath, the **ruach**, of life. The text announces that, with this, the man became a **nefesh**, a "living being" (v. 7). The King James Version's translation, "And man became a living soul," has exercised considerable influence upon the way Christians have thought about what it means to be human. But it is permissible to translate the Hebrew word **nefesh** into the English term "soul" only if we are prepared to see that Genesis uses this word to refer to other animals, so that all creatures are "souls"; the word **nefesh** means "living thing." Genesis 2, accordingly, states simply that the human creature became alive, animated by the breath of God. The Greek philosophical notion of the soul as an imperishable, eternal substance unique to human beings tends to mislead us in our attempt to piece together a theological anthropology rooted in the Story of God.

It is not necessary, by the way, to take the Genesis 2 narrative literally in order to hear its profound theological contribution to the human story within God's story: that human beings share in the materiality of the earth, that our bodies come from the elements of this world and will soon enough return to earth; *and* that our life, our livingness, depends upon the life-bestowing presence of God's spirit-breath. We are, biblically speaking, simply "dust in the wind"—the wind of His living Spirit. So in one of the earliest passages of Scripture we encounter the foundation of theological anthropology, grounded in narrative about God: human beings are finite creatures, yet among all these creatures He is well pleased to draw near to this one, to bend near this one, to *in-spire* this one. He breathes upon this creature in a unique and intimate way, forging a relationship that other creatures do not share, at least not nearly to the same extent. We are finite creatures of dust, yet also creatures with whom God desires to maintain covenantal relationship. We are those of His creatures who are most clearly able to respond to Him, to answer His questions. Is it coincidental that, early in the Story of God, it seems that whenever God speaks to a human being, this speaking takes the form of a question? The first one is that most profound query, "Where are you?" (3:9). Not long thereafter is the closely related "Where is Abel your brother?" (4:9). But there are many others within those chapters, all of which demonstrate God's desire to evoke a response, an answer, from us.

By the same token, God's questions intended to invoke our response also open the real possibility of our asking questions of Him too. The Scriptures, particularly in the writings of the prophets and Psalmists, abound with questions. For example,

> Why dost Thou stand afar off, O Lord?
> Why dost Thou hide Thyself in times of trouble?
>
> *(Ps. 10:1)*

> How long, O Lord? Wilt Thou forget me forever?
> How long wilt Thou hide Thy face from me?
>
> *(Ps. 13:1)*

And of course, there is the Psalmist's plaintive cry uttered by Jesus himself on the Cross:

> My God, my God, why hast Thou forsaken me?
> Far from my deliverance are the words of my groaning.
> O my God, I cry by day, but Thou dost not answer;
> And by night, but I have no rest.
>
> *(Ps. 22:1-2)*

The Scriptures teach us, then, that God creates us for conversation, for an ongoing dialogue within the rough-and-tumble of historical existence. God calls out to us, but just as surely He invites us to call out to Him. God asks after us but also allows and even encourages us the freedom to ask after Him—to cry out to Him with the Psalmist, to wrestle with Him like Jacob, even to challenge Him with Abraham, "Wilt Thou indeed sweep away the righteous with the wicked? . . . Far be it from Thee to do such a thing . . . Shall not the Judge of all the earth deal justly?" (Gen. 18:23, 25). To be created in God's image means to be addressed by Him, and thereby to be invited to address Him back, even occasionally to question Him. God is not so insecure as to deny us our capacity to ask questions of Him. The Jewish religious tradition has tended to take more seriously and to encourage this human role of wrestling with God—"wrestler with God" is, after all, what the word Israel essentially means—but Christians certainly can find a striking example of this in Jesus' struggling prayer in Gethsemane. Asking tough questions, in fact, is a vital aspect of growing in intimate relationship, whether with other persons or with God.

In the Scriptures, nonetheless, it is most definitely God who is the primary Asker of questions, and we who are the answerers. But for what are we answerable to God? The Genesis narrative suggests that we are answerable for our relationship to Him ("Where are you?"), for our relationship to one another ("Where is . . . your brother?"), and for our relationship to the rest of the created order. Perhaps this third dimension of our answerability deserves a bit more mention. For it is clear that, along with the capacity for relationship to God and to one another, an important element in being created in God's image is His commission upon humanity to "fill the earth, and subdue it; and rule over [it]" (Gen. 1:28). It has become popular among some thinkers to accuse biblical faith, largely on the basis of this passage, of having encouraged a view of humanity's role to be the despotic and greedy *user* of the earth's resources. Hence, they argue, the present ecological crisis can be laid at the feet of a Western scientific mentality shaped historically by Christian faith. This argument has received telling criticism in recent years, but to whatever extent it is legitimate, what it most reveals is the typical human abuse of biblical texts. Genesis does not encourage of us a rapacious and consumptive attitude toward earth; we are to tend it, to care for it, to be God's representatives within it, representing the loving character of the Creator to the creation. And we are all the while answerable to the Creator for how we tend to it.

At the same time, God has given to us a wonderful and terrible freedom within the realm of creation. There is a profound sense in which, as His responsible creatures who exercise rule over the creation, He has entrusted humanity with a role in *creating!* As mentioned earlier, we too have the power of speaking, which is a creative (and potentially destructive) capacity. And that power is, again, graphically portrayed in the Genesis 2 narrative of the man's naming of the animals. If we recall the significance that a name, and the process of naming, had for the ancient Hebrews, the richness of that narrative emerges. God gives the man the power of naming, of giving meaning, order, and structure to the creation. Humanity has the capacity—derived from the goodness and generosity of God, to be sure—to join in the conquering of chaos, of continuing to bring order to God's good creation. And as far as the text is concerned, God flashed the human no "cue cards" during this task; the creatures were his in his freedom to name, "and whatever the man called a living creature, that was its name" (v. 19). Such is the humble, empowering, "let there be" power of the One in whose image we are created!

And even as you read these words, there are scientists who are discovering and naming new species in God's grand, vast created order. There are others who dream of someday seeking, and perhaps finding, other forms of life in altogether different worlds. Human beings have an insatiable thirst to discover, to learn, to understand more about themselves and the vast universe they inhabit, to overcome the chaos of ignorance and fear with the order of knowledge and understanding. And that drive, Genesis tells us, derives from our divine calling as those who are created in God's image.

PART III

THE TRAGEDY OF GOD'S STORY: THE DOCTRINE OF SIN

As we shift our attention from the doctrines of creation and anthropology to the doctrine of sin, or *hamartiology* (Gr., **hamartia**, missing the mark), we shall find that we have already anticipated some of the problematics of this area of Christian thought in chapter 5. There, in grappling with the problem of evil, it was suggested that the so-called freewill defense goes a long way toward a solution. Essentially, the freewill defense states that most, if not all, of the world's ills are due to the human misuse of freedom. The implication of this line of defense is that God is willing to take the risks inherent in bestowing freedom upon us, because our moral agency, necessary to authentic relationships, is of sufficiently great value to Him.

Whatever value the freewill defense might have in the task of theodicy, or defending God's goodness, it does not do much for the human ego! It insists that it is we human beings who are at fault, not God, for the world's ills. True as that might be, it does not plumb the depths of the mystery of human sinfulness. *Why is sin in the world?*

Indeed, there are some modern philosophers who claim to be unimpressed by the freewill defense for maintaining belief in a good God. Such philosophers ask, "If the evil in the world is due to God-given freedom, could not God have created human beings who would always freely choose to do the loving thing, who would consistently choose the good?" The question, however, seems to become inextricably bogged down in self-contradiction; what sort of freedom would it be whose options would be so severely limited? Even if we say that there would still be choices among good and loving options, how could limits be placed on freedom in such a way that other less loving, and even destructive, options might not be pursued? Does not the experience of choice of any kind open up into a vast ocean of possibilities? Could God truly create personal beings for relationship and *not* run the risk of sinful, destructive rebellion?

Such questions as these, probably finally impenetrable, suggest to us the depth of the mystery of human sin. It is ironic that God, who is holy love, should be so committed to the project of authentic relationship grounded in freedom and responsibility that He would be willing to create the possibility of sin—and thereby call into being the possibility of hatred, envy, and suspicion; rape, murder, and torture; warfare and blood-spilling instruments from sharp-edged rocks all the way to nuclear bombs. Yet such is the mystery of divine-ordained freedom, and the costs that both God and humanity have paid for such a gift.

On the other hand, would we really *want* it any other way?

8

Human "Response-ability" and Sin

The great Story of God, which begins with the bright promise of a good creation by a good Creator, all too quickly gets interrupted by human sin. And truly this is an interrupture, a splitting and breaking apart of the serene simplicity and wholeness of the created order symbolized in the Garden of Eden. Sin is an intruder, an interrupter, an interferer in God's good purposes.

The Bible is clear that human disobedience truly is a tragedy, for it brings destructive consequences upon not only the individual who sins but upon the entire created order. While the possibility of disobedience must be real in order for authentic responsibility ("response-ability") to thrive, Scripture never accepts sin as an unavoidable consequence of human freedom. Sin is a misuse, a perversion, of God's intentions and God's creation.

To read the story of humanity's fall in Genesis 3 is to encounter far more than a simple account of long-ago events. That saga of human sin rings a bell that is all too clear in our own experience; we too know good and evil, living through them in the struggle against temptation, in disobedience against the divine will, in rationalization and projection. We are the sinners in the garden; we do well to remember that the name Adam means, literally, "humanity." Thus, to read of Adam's fall is indeed to read of our own. Truly the narrative of the Fall in Genesis 3 is "Your Story and Mine."[1] In fact, to make it the story only of our first parents is to foist the problem of sin, *our* sin, onto others as though we had no responsibility and they had it all. Such projection may itself, in fact, be a manifestation of sin, since sin often involves the abdication of one's own responsibility, one's own answerability, for

---

1. This "title" for Genesis 3 was suggested by Dr. Rob Staples during a 1977 lecture at Nazarene Theological Seminary, Kansas City.

one's actions. We often have told the Story as though it were all "Adam's fault," without recognizing that, even had our first parents not sinned, it seems certain that somebody *else* would have! "It's me, it's me, O Lord . . ." Sin as disobedience to the divine will is an always-lively possibility for us humans, who are constantly exercising choice. Surely we cannot imagine that, had our first parents not sinned, none of the rest of us would have either! Sin is simply too accessible to creatures of choice—and once sin's domino effect gets started, it is not easily stopped.

If it is the case that Genesis 3 does represent us all—if we are all, in some sense, Adam or Eve, "because all sinned" (Rom. 5:12)—then the simple yet profound story of the Fall sheds some critical light upon the doctrine of human sin and its effects. Let us consider some of the important truths about the nature of sin as they arise in this, "your story and mine."

First, sin is rooted in a shifting of attentiveness from the Creator to the creature. It is important to notice what the Genesis narrative says: the serpent, "more crafty than any beast of the field which the Lord God had made," approached Eve (lit., "living" or "life") with a question about what God had commanded. We owe it largely to Christian tradition that we immediately read Satan into the narrative, when the text throughout treats the serpent as nothing more than a creature (3:1, 14), indeed as one of God's creatures. If all of creation was "very good" (1:31), where did this crafty tempter come from?

It is clear that the narrative is offering us a critical observation concerning the nature of temptation and sin. The serpent is a creature of God, and yet it seems to represent the recurring human possibility of deifying some aspect of the created order; Eve pays heed to the serpent, rather than to the serpent's Maker. In the beauty, sensuality, and attractiveness of the created order (3:6), there is always the danger of idolatry, of focusing our hearts upon the legitimate joys and blessings of creation apart from the Source of those goods. "Love the creature, as it leads to the Creator,"[2] wrote John Wesley, and for the dedicated Christian life, all of creation ought to inspire us to love God. But we are also all to be aware of the temptation to consume creation's goods in a lustful, egocentric, godless way. When the apostle Paul writes about the fall of humanity into sin, it is precisely in these categories: we humans "exchanged the glory of the incorruptible God for an image in the form of corruptible man and of birds and four-footed animals and crawling creatures. . . . For they . . . worshiped and served the creature rather than the Creator" (Rom. 1:23, 25). We will miss the

---

2. Wesley, *Plain Account*, 13.

profound point of both Genesis and Paul if we think simplistically about heathen idolatry as worship of animal images, for idolatry occurs any time we "bow down and worship" some aspect of God's good creation with driving, self-gratifying obsessions (e.g., sexuality, food, money, pleasure, etc.).

It is probably not incidental to the Genesis narrative that the serpent was an important deity for many of the Israelites' neighboring peoples. Israel's neighbors did not worship the serpent because they were particularly attracted to snakes, but because it was for many pagan religions a symbol of sexuality and fertility. If we understand the serpent along these lines, then the narrative works on several levels: it warns against being drawn into pagan idolatry; it reminds us that God's good creation itself has tempting allurements; it points out the destructive consequences of allowing those whispering allurements to usurp the place of God's command; and it serves as an indirect reminder that the human responsibility is to exercise dominion over creation (Gen. 1:26), not to be sucked into worshiping it. In the words of theologian Harvey Cox, "[Eve's] 'original' misdeed was not eating the forbidden fruit at all. Before she reached for the fruit she had already surrendered her position of power and responsibility over one of the animals, the serpent, and let it tell her what to do. Thus self-doubt, hesitant anxiety, and dependency actually preceded that fatal nibble that has fascinated us for so long and made us fuse sin with pride. Adam and Eve are the biblical Everyman and Everywoman. Their sin is our sin. . . . We fritter away our destiny by letting some snake tell us what to do."[3]

Second, sin is a matter of pitting self-sovereignty against the divine. God is the Creator and Sustainer of the universe, while we are but creatures. But the lure of idolatry is that we pursue the goods of creation as though we ourselves were the very center of the universe. Idolatry, the worshiping of the creature, is founded in the drive to take everything into oneself, to absorb all pleasures, goods, and peoples into one's own experience and agenda. Sin, in the picturesque phrase of the Reformer Martin Luther, is "the self curved in upon itself," and what an apt description of Eve as she takes the fruit forbidden by God. If God is our loving Creator who has our highest good in mind, surely His sovereign will is trustworthy. However, we all have experienced Eve's moment of temptation, in which we are attracted to the possibility of denying God's sovereignty for the sake of our own, of usurping His place, of becoming "like God" (3:5).

Third, sin quickly weaves its web throughout the social-corporate di-

---

3. Harvey Cox, *On Not Leaving It to the Snake* (New York: Macmillan Co., 1964), xiv.

mension of humanity. We are not alone. Like the ripples created by the stone tossed into a pond, the things we think, say, and do proceed out from us and influence (lit., "flow into") those around us. And this happens because human beings truly are interrelated; we truly are Adam and Eve to one another.

The narrative at this point warns us not to underestimate the power of our influence with each other. Though unfortunately Augustine's occasional speculations about sin being passed on through the sexual act have exercised too much influence in Christian tradition (any amount was too much!), it is clear in this narrative that sin gets "passed on" in the influence of relationships between the human beings, quite apart from sexuality: "and she gave also to her husband with her, and he ate" (3:6). And surely we have our relational and intergenerational ways in which we, too, inherit and pass on the alienating power of sin against God and neighbor.

Fourth, sin involves the breaking of relationship and the attempt to hide. When the eyes of Adam and Eve are opened, they not only perceive their nakedness but are shamed by it; prior to sin's intrusion, they "were both naked and were not ashamed" (2:25). Their unabashed nakedness before one another suggests the openness and vulnerability of relationship unencumbered by deception and dishonesty. Before sin, theirs is a relationship of transparency; after sin, it is marred by shame's need to cover itself, to delude itself and the other (3:7).

But, of course, sin involves not simply our hiding from one another. Even more profoundly, it is our hiding from a loving and seeking God. Yet the gospel rings out already in Genesis, for God "called to the man"—and continues to call to each of us—"and said to him, 'Where are you?'" (3:9). But it is difficult for us to answer God's probing question, because to do so is to allow our sins and shame to come out of hiding and into His scrutiny. No wonder John wrote of the rejection of God's search for us through Jesus, "For everyone who does evil hates the light, and does not come to the light, lest his deeds should be exposed" (John 3:20).

Fifth, sin includes often the denial of responsibility. Even when Adam does slink out from behind his tree, he tends to embody all too well our attempts to find someone else to blame for our sin. It is easy to read between the lines: "The woman [it's *her* fault!] whom Thou gavest to be with me [well, it may even be *Your* fault!], she gave me from the tree, and I ate" (3:12). But of course the abdication of responsibility does not end with the man; the woman, too, when confronted by God, finds a scapegoat. "The serpent deceived me [it's not my fault; I was just an innocent victim], and I ate" (v. 13).

This is not to suggest that there are never times when human be-ings are indeed the innocent victims of the sins of others; such victim-ization is, in fact, an all too common experience. Some certainly have been victimized more than others, but there is a sense in which the doctrine of *original sin* suggests that we are all victims, that we have all been victimized by the sins and violence of our forebears. And yet, sig-nificantly, the Bible never relieves human beings of their responsibility for themselves and their actions. To every one of us is addressed the Edenic question, "What is this you have done?" (v. 13). And it is a profound aspect of sin's deceitfulness that would allow us to shift our responsibility onto someone or something else, whether it be parents, environment, trauma, tragedy, or the devil.

Finally, sin becomes a destructive factor in all our relationships. It is not simply our relationship to the Creator that is distorted and per-verted by our disobedience. We have seen already that it plants the seeds of alienation in our relationships to fellow human beings (Adam and Eve's hiding from one another, Adam's blaming of Eve, Cain's sub-sequent envy and even murder of his brother Abel). But God's judg-ment upon this rebellion seems to include also a recognition of the alienating and destructive effects of sin upon the broader environment in which humanity dwells. The hatred between the serpent and the woman, alluded to in verse 15, may well point to the adversarial rela-tionship with their environment into which human beings appear of-ten to have cast themselves by their self-seeking. The earth itself seems to harden itself against this hardened man and woman (vv. 17-19), and even their relationship to one another takes on a sense of hierarchical rule and antagonism (v. 16) that belies the side-by-sidedness of their creation by God (1:27; 2:22-25). No relationship, whether to God, to one another, or to the natural environment, goes unaffected by human sin.

Hopefully, this way of reading Genesis 3 suggests some of the rich theological implications of this ancient Hebrew narrative. To be sure, these observations are far from exhaustive, but they should nonethe-less help us see how story and theology are often woven together in the Bible to reveal profound truths about ourselves, our temptations and sins, and the probing presence and grace of God, who never lets us go.

9

Sin and Human Solidarity

One of the profound observations about human life and relationship that arises out of the opening narratives of the Bible is, quite simply, that we are *interconnected* with one another. "No man is an island," wrote the poet John Donne, and surely that truth comes to life for us in Genesis. It is the Creator who says, "It is not good for the man to be alone" (2:18), underscoring the profoundly social dimension of human life. We truly do influence one another by what we say, think, and do, and simply by being who we are. It is this interconnectedness, this *solidarity* with one another, that underlies the Christian doctrine of *original sin*.

We saw already in the previous chapter that the power of sin lies in its capacity to pervert or even destroy our relationships with God, neighbor, and the created order. Ironically, it is precisely because we are relational and social beings—precisely because God created us for relationship to himself and others—that sin can exercise such power. Sin is the distortion of our very being, for it describes the situation in which the human self rejects authentic relationship to God and others and turns in upon itself, thus poisoning the very relationships without which we cannot truly live. And to poison our relationships is to poison those with whom we exist in relationship. No wonder Paul could write, "Therefore, just as through one man sin entered into the world, and death through sin, and so death spread to all men, *because all sinned*," and that "through the one man's disobedience the many were made sinners" (Rom. 5:12, 19, italics added)—because no human deed, word, thought, or even attitude occurs in isolation.

Surely it is this relational situation of sin that is described further in the narrative of Cain and Abel (Genesis 4). In this story we find the rawest of human emotions laid bare: sibling rivalry giving way to jealousy, jealousy to hatred, hatred to violence and murder, and all followed by a casual and cavalier denial of the whole thing. Cain and Abel are brothers; they are kindred—but this kinship does not prevent sin's growing. It may, in fact, encourage its spread.

80

I remember well hearing a Jewish scholar named Pinchas Peli, lecturing in Jerusalem, use this story to provide a biblical basis for understanding how such atrocities as the Holocaust could occur. "Cain exercised his God-given freewill," said Peli, "and obliterated one-fourth of the human race . . . while God stood by and did nothing."

Peli, in fact, proceeded to suggest that God arrived at the murder scene like some Johnny-come-lately, provoking Cain with the question, "Where is Abel your brother?" after it was too late to do anything about it (4:9). If God could ask such a question after the death of Abel, could not God have said or done something to restrain Cain from the act in the first place? Peli's thinking reflected a rabbinic tradition of commentary on the passage that, in effect, put words like these into Cain's mouth: "You, God, are the Almighty! You come here and ask me where Abel is, when You know full well You could have stopped me before I did this horrible thing! *Where were You* when I killed my own brother? You could have stopped me, but You didn't lift a finger! *Maybe it's Your fault* that Abel is dead!"

That line of thinking may have a familiar ring to us. There is something frightening, something all too threatening about the freedom we exercise. It would be preferable, in some ways, to be able to forfeit our freedom in favor of God's overruling dictatorship. We would like to be able to blame someone other than ourselves when our choices go bad, or even sour. Surely a horror like the Holocaust would have been a perfect spot for God to do what He did not do in Cain's case: step in and prevent the meaningless bloodshed.

The rabbinic tradition tended to overlook the earlier portion of the narrative, however, where in fact God does step into the situation. But God's intervention is not an intrusion upon Cain's moral agency nor a negation of his freedom; God simply is portrayed as gently but persistently probing Cain with a series of questions: "Why are you angry? And why has your countenance fallen? If you do well, will not your countenance be lifted up? And if you do not do well, sin is crouching at the door; and its desire is for you, but you must master it" (4:6-7). God, the Bestower and Encourager of freedom, will not overrule Cain's murderous intentions. God simply speaks to Cain, attempting to lure him to exercise his freedom in a different, less destructive fashion. God is with Cain, whispering to him, questioning him, attempting to draw him away from hatred and murder. But God will not coerce Cain—and therefore allows human bloodshed to break loose.

In the violence committed by brother against brother, we get another angle on the picture of what Christian tradition has meant by *original sin.* It is the refusal to trust in God, to listen to His voice, and instead to enthrone ourselves as the center and lord of our world. Cain had his moment during which God appealed to him not to surrender to the hateful impulse, but instead to "do well" (4:7) and so avoid the sin crouching at the door. Could Cain have chosen otherwise than he did? Christian tradition affirms that Cain could indeed have chosen otherwise, or else Cain cannot be held responsible for his murderous act. On the other hand, Christian tradition recognizes that once sin (as the fundamental turning of oneself from God) had entered the world, a certain momentum in human attitude and behavior got rolling. Cain was still responsible, but his act is more understandable in a world in which rivalries, jealousies, mistrust, and animosity are already woven into the complex of human relationships. And while God's holy presence confronted Cain with the possibility of choosing against his developing animosity toward Abel, God could do nothing to prevent it while maintaining a world in which human freedom, necessary as it is to authentic relationships to himself and others, is so highly valued.

Most understandings of the doctrine of original sin, in fact, state that it is only God's holy, loving presence in human life (or *prevenient grace*) that enables us to choose against the chains of sin. God may not have nullifed Cain's freedom, but at least He attempted to sway him to exercise his freedom in a positive and constructive direction. In Rabbi Peli's reflections upon Cain's abuse of freedom, I recall that he asked us, his students, "Where was God when one-fourth of the human population was destroyed in one blow?" Only one answer is possible: God was right there with Cain every moment, attempting to persuade him to choose life rather than death.

Scripture and tradition affirm, in fact, that God has been "right there" in every moment of all persons' lives everywhere, wooing them and luring them toward himself, toward righteousness and life. But we have made it difficult to hear God's voice or sense His presence, precisely by the accumulated tendency in human history to reject Him just as Cain did. That historical tendency, as it has snowballed down through the centuries and crept into our collective consciousness, is the original sin. The fact that we all are affected by this original sin is a sign of human *solidarity*. Whether we like it or not, our lives are intertwined in such a way that the sin of one person exercises destructive effects throughout the human race, like the ripples of a pebble thrown into a pond.

Sin is, accordingly, an abuse of our God-bestowed freedom; He calls us to freedom, as Paul writes in Galatians, but not freedom to do whatever we please ("an opportunity for the flesh") rather freedom to love ("through love serve one another") (5:1, 13). Thus sin can first of all be described as a fundamental turning away from God's love, and from the dynamic of a life committed to loving; as Paul continues, "For the whole Law is fulfilled in one word, in the statement, 'You shall love your neighbor as yourself'" (v. 14). Sin, then, is a word-concept that describes, in Luther's words, "the self curved in upon itself" rather than turned outward in servanthood toward God and neighbor. This is the essential sinful orientation, the original sin out of which sinful actions arise.

But if God creates us for, and toward, a life of self-giving love, it becomes clear that sin is not essentially an aspect of human nature as created and willed by Him. Sin is an intruder. Sin is not to be identified with natural human limitations, finitude, or shortcomings; rather, it is essentially the fundamental act of rebellion against the God who is Love. And that act of rejection is the basis of *estrangement* (of being a stranger) from God. This does not mean that God sees human beings as strangers, but that we can, through our rejection of His love, estrange ourselves from Him and turn Him into a stranger to ourselves. But if God creates human beings for fellowship with himself and with one another, then to make ourselves strangers to His love is to "miss the mark," the New Testament's primary metaphor for sin. It is to "fall short of the glory of God" (Rom. 3:23): to fall short of God's likeness and image in our lives, to miss the mark of God's ideal calling for us in Christ Jesus.

But our recognition of human solidarity in this chapter pushes us another step. None of us make this kind of decision in isolation. The Bible does not teach that we are each our own Adam or Eve. Essentially, it was this point that marked the famous debate between Augustine (354-430) and the British monk Pelagius. Emphasizing the biblical idea of human solidarity, Augustine argued that Adam's sin has resulted in humanity's universal bondage to sin. In Augustine's interpretation, human beings are incapable of choosing anything but sin, and only divine grace can save us. Augustine veered toward *predestination* as a result, claiming that certain human beings are divinely favored and chosen by God, since it cannot have been the human beings' choice to believe and repent.

Pelagius, on the other hand, feared that people influenced by such teaching tend to dismiss any responsibility for their own actions. Their sins became, in this view, "Adam's fault." Pelagius countered by insisting that Adam's sin does not negatively affect human freedom, except in giving us a poor example of how to behave. Pelagius, then, taught that human freedom is not essentially hindered by Adam's sin, and that God's grace is manifested quite naturally in our God-given freedom. Indeed we are our own Adam and Eve, argued Pelagius.

As debates generally do, the nature of this debate tended to push the contestants' ideas to extremes. Augustine's ideas on original sin and predestination tended to make human beings into little more than enslaved pawns on a cosmic chessboard. Pelagius' ideas on unmitigated human freedom tended to make human beings into isolated units of individual freedom. We do not have to take Augustine's extreme position in order to recognize that Pelagius did not do justice to the reality of our solidarity; he did not see clearly that what each of us says, does, and thinks profoundly impacts and influences those around us, and they deeply influence those around them, ad infinitum. And the reality of this influence, of course, continues beyond our deaths. Pelagius did not recognize that no one comes into this world with a clean slate, precisely because the world into which we come is already a history filled with sin, manifested in war, bloodshed, slavery, abuse, torture, fear, and a thousand other nightmares. There are, to be sure, good things we inherit, too; but when dealing with *hamartiology,* the emphasis correctly falls upon a world in which rejection of God's love and God's way of love is a pronounced reality, already out there before us, waiting for us in the very moment of our conception. We are born into a world dominated by the "me-first," self-centered orientation; we are members of one another, and thus the sin of our ancestors continues profoundly to affect, even to infect, us all. It is this reality, already there before us and into which we are thrown at birth, that Pelagius apparently failed to appreciate.

Augustine's doctrines of original sin and divine predestination, on the other hand, led to an extreme understanding of God that would later show up in Calvinism: God decrees certain individuals for salvation, since human beings, enslaved to sin, can have no real choice in the matter. Both for Augustine and the Calvinism that arose over a thousand years later, God is merciful to save *anybody,* since all of humanity is a "damned mass" (**massa perditionis**). If Pelagius seems to have missed the biblical and experiential reality of human solidarity, Augustine seems to have missed the biblical narrative's emphasis upon human responsibility and the biblical call to human beings to cooperate willfully with God's intentions for human life. For indeed the Bible does hold us answerable, so that no matter what we might say about the reality of "original sin" that surrounds and infests us even before our birth, it may not be allowed to lessen our sense of response-ability before God. This tension between solidarity/sin and individuality/responsibility would eventually be resolved, at least for Christians of the Wesleyan tradition, by a recognition of *prevenient grace* much like the narrative of Cain with which we began this chapter: that God is ever-present in our lives, enabling us, if we will, to desire and even choose His will for us. His gracious presence and Word can be resisted, but if yielded to, we can be liberated to the true freedom of loving servant-hood toward God and neighbor. While in a certain sense a fuller explication of the doctrine of prevenient grace must await a later chapter in the story of God, in another profoundly biblical sense it is the very basis for what is sooner to follow in Part IV: a theology of divine-human *covenants.*

10

Human Sin and Divine Persistence

"And the Lord was sorry that He had made man on the earth, and He was grieved in His heart" (Gen. 6:6).

The opening chapter of Genesis resounds with the goodness of God's creation, punctuated by the divine pronouncement that it was all "very good" (v. 31). The enthusiasm of this biblical view of creation reveals a sense of divine joy in the very act of creating. But for all the satisfaction that God apparently derives from this created order, we now meet the opposite response of profound disappointment. Sin, by which we mean the human rejection of God's sovereign love, has spread like a dreaded virus throughout humanity and all its relationships: from Eve to Adam, to their offspring Cain and Abel, down to the Tower of Babel. And the Scriptures say that God was sorry even to have created the human—the same creature He had delighted over as "very good"—and turned away in grief. What a vision of God the biblical narrative offers: a God who can grieve, a Creator who cries!

But Genesis, after all, is correct. Creation has not turned out particularly well, and this pains the Creator. Such a portrait of God may trouble some people, but usually this is because they approach the Story of God with their own preconceived ideas about how He should behave. I can hear it now: "If God knows everything, surely God knew before the creation of the world that human beings would sin, right?" But if we take seriously the story of Noah, introduced as this chapter's epigram, then a legitimate reply would be, "No." At least Genesis 6 suggests that things had gotten much worse than even God had anticipated. Theologians throughout history have attempted to sidestep passages such as these, calling them *anthropomorphic* (Gr., **anthrōpos** = humanity; **morphē** = shape or form), or thinking about God in human terms. Anthropomorphism might be permissible for ancient peoples, but it is hardly worthy of sophisticated theists! Or so the argument goes. Even while we grant the anthropomorphism of a passage such as this, it does not necessarily follow that the passage cannot or does not tell us anything about God! Let us take the narrative seriously: since the Creator was grieved over the results of human sin, it might be argued that He was not entirely certain about the outcome of this experiment in freedom.

How can this be? The simplest answer seems to be that, because God created a world in which freedom and contingency play roles, unpredictability and perhaps even chance are factors with which He, too, deals. Remember: what God creates is *truly other* to Him, even while sustained by Him in every moment. God is free and apparently treasures freedom sufficiently that He desires its growth in us. The human being, made in God's image, surely is created to reflect the very freedom He enjoys. And He does in fact profoundly limit himself simply by extending to every human being the real possibilities of choosing.

A further illustration of God's willingness to yield to human freedom in the process of moving into an open, undetermined future occurs not much later in Genesis. In chapter 22 we read the story of Abraham's obedience to God, even to the point of nearly offering his son Isaac as a sacrifice. But why did God make this demand? Some have suggested that, like any test, this excruciating experience was intended to strengthen Abraham, to show to Abraham himself the depth of his commitment. This probably was a side effect, yet when the narrative reaches its dramatic zenith, God speaks: "Do not stretch out your hand against the lad, and do nothing to him; for now I know that you fear God, since you have not withheld your son, your only son, from Me" (v. 12). Yet we have already argued that God's omniscience, His profound and thorough *knowing* of us in love, lays our hearts and lives bare in the Divine Presence (cf. Heb. 4:13). Did not God truly know Abraham's heart without subjecting him to such emotional torture?

To ask this question, though, is to miss the very truth that this story of God can teach us: human faith in God is a living *relationship* that must find expression in this world through human decisions and actions. Promises of commitment, pledges of allegiance, are insufficient. Faith in God is a faith tested, tried, and stretched in the crucible of everyday existence in this world, in the realm of real sacrifice, rather than simply in some inner sanctum of the heart. Relationship to God is measured in concrete actions, in our actual response to His will. The New Testament Book of James, in fact, draws upon this Genesis story to emphasize the place of human works within faith. "Was not Abraham our father justified by works, when he offered up Isaac his son on the altar? You see that faith was working with his works, and as a result of the works, faith was perfected; . . . and he was called the friend of God" (2:21-23). These stories of Noah and Abraham, in short, tell us that God is the God of history—of everyday history, day-to-day decisions, of the here and now.

Repeatedly, then, Genesis suggests to us a God who says, *"Let there be,"* One who has ventured out into the risk of creating free beings, who has called life into being, and thereby has effected a real change not only in what composes reality but in His own self. Having taken the risk of creating and sustaining free beings, and having called us humans to be His partners in creation, God could never be the same. While Christian tradition states that God does not change, Genesis on the other hand tells us that God does not simply stay God— God *creates,* and God bestows the precious gift of *being* to this other-than-God we call the universe. The doctrine of divine *immutability* or changelessness, in fact, should not suggest to us that God is flat and static Sameness, but that God is immutably and eternally *love.* But this, in turn, implies that God, the Cosmic Lover, is eternally ready and willing to love and to be loved, to be engaged and involved and at risk in the creation and for the creatures. God's decision to share freedom with human beings (and perhaps analogously with all of creation), to create beings who can and quite often do act against His purposes, is actually a decision to limit himself. God has emptied himself into the creation in a grand "experiment," which, tragically, has tended to go sour. As Genesis 6 tells it, God is sorry and grieved, and in response to the sinful depths into which humanity has fallen, He prepares to let all chaos break loose again.

Yet even as God decides to cleanse the world with a flood and begin again, it is striking that He does not junk the project entirely. God is still determined to work with His partners, these human beings created in the divine image. And in Noah God finds someone He can work with. Certainly this should tell us something about God's deep commitment, a *covenantal* commitment, to making this creation succeed. God persists, and this persistence we call *grace,* for grace refers, in part, to His unwillingness ever to give up on us. Perhaps God has thrown himself so enthusiastically (**en theos** = in God) into the task of creating that to quit on it would be to deny His own character as Creator.

But it is still natural to find oneself squirming with the notion of God as the great Taker of Risks. Perhaps it is because we face so many uncertainties in our lives, take so many risks, and make such questionable choices, we want to feel that *somebody* must have everything under control! Or perhaps it is because we feel that the divine attributes of omniscience and omnipotence would demand that God exercise this kind of rule in the universe. However, it is easy to overlook the real power of God if we imagine Him to be a transcendent chess player who moves His pawns where He will in what finally amounts to a game of solitaire. Such a deity would only be revealing weakness and insecurity, fearing that if He did not hold the reins tightly enough, the universe might get out of hand. But if God is sufficiently certain about His power to share that power and freedom with His creation and not be threatened, then certainly He has no fear of losing control. God can hold creation lovingly yet loosely, allowing us room to be people, room to be free, and He is not threatened. In the words of philosopher Frederick Sontag, "If God prizes freedom, . . . a world which did not reflect this could not be his creation. . . . Since God's self-confidence is high, he can afford to take risks. He feels no need to force us into a system of strict personal control just to secure his own protection. Actually, we are the ones who plead for a fixed future, not God. His power is fully adequate to sustain himself against uncertainty."[1]

If Sontag is right, then we would do well to reconsider our ideas about God and the future. If God enjoys running the risk of creating free beings—which, by all indications, He does—then perhaps God prefers *not* to know the future, at least in detail. What joy is there in reading the last page of a mystery novel first? God certainly has sufficient power to write the last page of the "mystery" that God's Story is, just as He wrote the first page. In the meantime, Genesis 6 suggests that God's Story is, in a sense, an "open book"; even for God, the future is not a series of preprogrammed inevitabilities, but a wide-open horizon in which each of us plays a role. It also suggests that God is persistent and that God graciously and vulnerably sustains the created order and its freedoms. The God who is free creates an open future in which, because of the freedom He has shared with us, His own heart can be broken.

---

1. Frederick Sontag, *What Can God Do?* (Nashville: Abingdon Press, 1979), 88, 89.

PART IV

THE JEWISH PEOPLE IN GOD'S STORY: THE DOCTRINE OF COVENANTS

The story the Bible tells is one of human rebellion and divine redemption. Already this dual theme has surfaced in the Eden narrative, for there we encounter One who patiently and lovingly haunts the human creatures, a redeeming God who seeks sinners with the poignant question, *"Where are you?"*

Again, the question might seem almost ludicrous, coming from an omnipotent and omniscient God—but perhaps that is just the point. The *omni* doctrines pay all kinds of metaphysical compliments to God but seem to miss the central biblical affirmation that He is a God of relationship. The God of this Story calls into being a created order that is other than himself and intimately sustains it precisely in its otherness. The apex of this otherness in creation, as far as we can tell, is the human race. In human beings we find creatures who can both seek God and flee God, who can cooperate with God or rebel against God, who can reflect upon God or categorically deny God. In human beings we find those creatures who exercise the power of conscious choice, which is the greatest evidence of our *otherness* from God.

And this, says the Story line, is as God wills it. He calls the other into being as *the other*, for this sense of human agency grounded in distance from Him is essential to relationship. I cannot be in true relationship to that which is not other than myself; to borrow from the Jewish philosopher Martin Buber, in an authentic I-Thou encounter the Thou must truly be *Thou* to me. "I become through my relation to the *Thou*; as I become *I*, I say *Thou*. All real living is meeting."[1] Buber

---

1. Martin Buber, *I and Thou*, trans. Ronald Gregor Smith (New York: Charles Scribner's Sons, 1958), 11.

is not speaking here only or even primarily of relationship to God, but of the possibility of relationship at all; it is only in our otherness, in relation to God, other people, and the world, that we can either give or receive the grace of relationship. So also it is with God: God the Sole Power, the omnipotent Creator, empties himself of the prerogatives of Absolute Being in order to enter into relationship with beings of His own making. This self-emptying, in turn, makes it possible for Him to ask of human beings the question, "Where are you?" and mean it. God does not control us—He calls us; God does not manipulate us—He beckons to us. Before God is anything else, God is *love*—the Love who creates us, sustains us, and longingly seeks us out, all for the sake of relationship.

These ideas about relationship are no better demonstrated than in the Bible's stories of the *covenants* (Lat., **co** = together; **vene** = come) that God initiates. This idea that God is the God of covenants, of pacts or agreements, is much too often ignored in theology to its own detriment. To say that God is a covenantal God is to suggest a divine interest in our cooperation, a divine commitment to partnership, a divine power that is empowering and affirming of the other. A biblical theology of covenant relationships would suggest that God is not interested in performing solos. Instead, He invites our participation, our cooperation, in the tasks of creation and redemption. Of course, God's very act of creating the universe as other, and of creating us as *others* from himself, is what makes covenant relationship possible.

In Part II we dealt with God as Creator and the world as His creation. In Part III we saw this risky process of creation unfold with the painful reality of human rebellion. In this, Part IV, we shall attempt to tell the story of God's grace—that is, His desire yet to love and redeem His fallen creatures—in the history of the covenants. The fact that these covenants are established by the divine will reminds us that they are all grounded in grace. The Wesleyan tradition has tended to call this grace *prevenient* (Lat., **pre** = prior to; **vene** = come) to emphasize that it is always God who makes the first move toward us in covenantal relationship. Of course, all grace is by definition prevenient, but it never hurts to be reminded of this!

All of God's covenants originate and are sustained in His gracious love for His creation. But the fact that these are *covenants* also reminds us that God chooses not to redeem us apart from our willing cooperation. For this reason, Wesley delighted to quote the little line from Augustine, "He who made us without ourselves will not save us without ourselves." Just as surely as covenants are grounded in God's prevenient grace, so also this grace encourages, enables, and empowers us to be "fellow laborers with God" (1 Cor. 3:9). The theological term describing this labor of God to enlist our labor is *synergism* (Gr., **syn** = together; **ergon** = work). One of the great mysteries of the Bible is that God Almighty bends low into creation to covenant with human beings, to work together with them toward the divine vision of *shalom*. In the next few chapters we shall trace the outlines of this truly wondrous work of God.

11

Noah: God's Commitment to Creation

Amy raised her hand in class and asked a question that very likely has crossed the mind of anyone who has thoughtfully read the story of Noah and the Flood. "How could a loving, caring God destroy everything in a flood, including all those innocent children?"

This is a good and difficult question—the kind of question that both enlivens and challenges theological discussion. Perhaps we could define a good question as one that is better than any answer that can be given to it! If so, then the good question Amy asked is representative of many good questions the Noah narrative raises. This, in turn, means that the Flood story provides fertile ground for theological reflection.

The first step in answering Amy's question involves taking a cue from the New Testament Book of 1 Peter, which includes a mysterious and most controversial passage:

> For Christ also died for sins once for all, the just for the unjust, in order that He might bring us to God, having been put to death in the flesh, but made alive in the spirit; in which also He went and made proclamation to the spirits now in prison, who once were disobedient, when the patience of God kept waiting in the days of Noah, during the construction of the ark . . . And corresponding to that, baptism now saves you . . . through the resurrection of Jesus Christ, who is at the right hand of God (3:18-22).

Few commentators agree on the particular meaning of the details of this passage, but one general truth stands out: the Early Church interpreted the story of Noah, and all of the Old Testament Scriptures for that matter, within the context and through the prism of the story of Jesus Christ. For the Christian, whatever is said about God on the basis of the Flood narrative, or any other biblical text, must be consonant with what we believe to be the case about God on the basis of Jesus' words and works. Christian tradition has throughout its history strongly endorsed this *Christocentric* or *Christonormative* approach to understanding the nature and character of God. And while the revelation in Jesus Christ may not give us clear and simple answers to the question Amy raised, it at least provides a context for adequate Christian thinking about such problems.

The next step in dealing with this difficult question of theodicy (see chap. 5) is to recognize that the Flood is presented in Genesis as an act of divine wrath and judgment against human sin (6:5-7). It would be erroneous, though, to assume simply that the God of the Old Testament is a God of wrath, while the God in the New Testament is a God of love. A significant part of the problem, in fact, occurs when we contrast wrath over against love as though they were opposites. On the contrary, a better term of opposition to love is apathy. If God did not respond in wrath to human sin and perversion, then one could justifiably ask whether He cares about human beings. God's love, on the other hand, means that God is intimately involved in our lives and has invested himself in our redemption. The term *wrath,* then, denotes God's deep, heartfelt love for us—a love that burns hot and will not let us go.

But there is a second New Testament text that may shed light on the Flood narrative. Paul, in his letter to the Romans, develops a fascinating "theology of wrath" whereby God *does,* in a sense, *let us go.* Paul first states that there is evidence aplenty in the created order for all people to recognize God's "invisible attributes, His eternal power and divine nature, . . . being understood through what has been made" (1:20). Even knowing so much about God, however, humanity has fallen into idolatrous sin (vv. 21-23). Paul then explains how "the wrath of God is revealed from heaven against all ungodliness and unrighteousness of men" (v. 18): God *allows* people freely to pursue their lusts and idolatry. Paul states three times that "God gave them over" (vv. 24, 26, 28), suggesting that God, *precisely because He loves us,* allows us our freedom even when our actions are destructive of ourselves and others. God's wrath consists precisely in His willingness to allow human freedom to wallow in the depths of "impurity" (v. 24), "degrading passions" (v. 26), and "a depraved mind" (v. 28). While God in His infinite love will not let us go in the sense of giving up on us, God does indeed let us go in the sense of giving us over to pursue self-destructive practices and addictions. God is love, and therefore He allows us freedom that we too may love; the freedom necessary to love, on the other hand, can also be employed in wrongful directions, and freedom's misuse (sin) inevitably issues in death (Rom. 1:32; 6:23).

Granted, the Flood narrative represents divine wrath in decidedly more active and aggressive terms than God simply allowing human sin to take its destructive course. God, after all, sends the Flood! But there is more than this going on in the text of Genesis. What God does is not so much an active sending of a flood; rather, it is an allowing of the chaotic dark waters, which were separated in creation so that dry land might appear (Gen. 1:6-7), to engulf the earth's order once more. Just as divine wrath, out of love, allows human beings to go their own destructive way, so in the Flood story divine wrath allows chaos "back in" to inundate the dry land. Old Testament scholar and commentator Gerhard von Rad writes,

> *Mabbul* does not mean "flood," "inundation," or even "destruction," but it is a technical term for a part of the world structure, namely, the heavenly ocean. . . . Here we have the same realistic and cosmological ideas as in Gen. ch. 1. . . . We must understand the Flood, therefore, as a catastrophe involving the entire cosmos. When the heavenly ocean breaks forth upon the earth below, and the primeval sea beneath the earth, which is restrained by God, now freed from its bonds, gushes up through yawning chasms onto the earth, then there is a destruction of the entire cosmic system.[1]

In other words, for the ancient Hebrew people this was far more than a story about waters covering the earth; it was about God's freedom and power to allow primeval chaos and formlessness to return and undo the entire universe as they knew it! God let loose chaos upon the creation because of all the human corruption and violence (6:12-13), which in fact generate their own chaos in human existence. The story thereby narrates the ultimate significance God places upon human action and responsibility. Divine judgment upon human sin takes on a cosmic dimension in a way that foreshadows Christian eschatological expectations. The God of the universe is indeed the Judge of our lives.

Yet out of the depths of the watery chaos arises the triumphant gospel note of God's continuing care for His creation. Re-creation takes place, as God's **ruach**-wind again broods over the earth to allow dry land to emerge. Noah and his family, as well as the creatures harbored on the ark, also emerge as the beginning of a new chapter in God's Story. And for the first time in the Scriptures, the word-concept *covenant* appears.

The terms of this covenant provide insight into the cosmic, universal nature of God's loving care. It is a covenant not simply with Noah and his kin as the new Adam, but indeed "with every living creature . . . [even] every beast of the earth" (Gen. 9:10). God makes

---

1. Gerhard von Rad, *Genesis: A Commentary* (Philadelphia: Westminster Press, 1961), 124.

covenant with each individual creature! An adequate recognition of this truth should move us away from an exaggerated *anthropocentrism* (lit., "human-centeredness") in our understanding of God and of His relationship to the world. To be sure, the Scriptures teach that we human beings are created in the image of God, an idea that is in fact reiterated in the aftermath of the Flood (vv. 6-7). But this truth should never obscure the biblical conviction that all of creation is cherished by God and is in fact His covenant partner!

At the root of this covenant is God's recognition of human weakness and frailty, even evil, with which God must deal patiently. "I will never again curse the ground on account of man, for the intent of man's heart is evil from his youth; and I will never again destroy every living thing, as I have done" (8:21). The portrait of God this narrative paints is of One who is coming to understand more profoundly, and more sympathetically, these creatures of freedom that He himself has created. The reflections of a contemporary Jewish philosopher-theologian, David Hartman, are pertinent:

> Prior to the Flood, all of nature was doomed to destruction because God "regretted that He had made man on earth"; human corruption was sufficient reason to justify the destruction of all living things. After the Flood, however, God proclaims His awareness that although human beings are created in His image, they do not automatically embody all that God wishes them to be. God's reflections on them are, as it were, similar to a parent's realization that his child is not his mirror image but is a separate being with limitations, weaknesses, and an independent will. The child may come from the parent, but it is nevertheless separate and independent.[2]

Human beings are created in God's image, to be sure, but they are also dust (Gen. 2:7)—poor, finite, threatened creatures striving to survive and thrive in an often savage world. It is in recognition of this, in fact, that God concedes to human beings that "every moving thing that is alive shall be food for you," when prior to this point the only divinely ordained food was "the green plant" (9:3). Again, this should be seen as a divine concession to the violent drives underlying much of human behavior, or what the rabbis would later call the "evil inclination" (**yetzer hara**). In this context, we can understand covenanting as evidence of God's gracious willingness to love and sustain us in all our weakness and frailty, to accept us for what we are even as He nurtures us toward what we can become. "For He Himself knows our frame; He is mindful that we are but dust" (Ps. 103:14).

---

2. David Hartman, *A Living Covenant: The Innovative Spirit in Traditional Judaism* (New York: The Free Press, a division of Macmillan, Inc., © 1985), 28. Used with permission.

There is an unavoidable implication in the story of the Flood, however, and it is that God was *learning through experience* about the human beings of His own making. In His decision never again to destroy the earth on account of human sin, and instead to uphold the regularity of nature (8:22), there may even be a hint of remorse. This does not square with traditional notions of divine omniscience, but this need not be overly bothersome. The point is, the Scripture narrative suggests that the mystery of human freedom has opened up new possibilities of experience even for God! In allowing us freedom and responsibility, God manifests a willingness to call into being that which is truly "other" to himself, and thus to enter into the give-and-take of authentically mutual relationship.

Given these reflections, the answer to Amy's question about the Flood might finally lie in a recognition that God, too, had second thoughts about His response to human sin. But perhaps such an answer creates a new batch of problems: can we really think of God as learning, perhaps in some sense growing in and through relationship with the "other," just as we do? At what point does such anthropomorphism (see chap. 10) become misleading and even dangerous? These are difficult questions, but it is arguable on the basis of biblical narratives like the Flood that God truly *interacts* with His creation in such a way that the interaction makes a difference in the divine life and experience. This is, after all, part of what the prophets mean when they call Yahweh *the living God.*

But if on the one hand we say that God truly interacts with us, and so perhaps even grows and learns through relationship to the "other," there is a basic and fundamental dimension of His eternal being wherein He does not change. God's character as holy love, God's commitment to the well-being of His creation, God's intimate care for human beings and desire for relationship with them—these things do not change. God is faithful—and, of course that is one of the fundamental truths underlying His covenanting with us. God's love, God's desire for our wholeness and salvation, God's goal of leading creation to shalom—these are the constants of the human relationship to God. This utter reliability of the covenantal God finds beautiful expression in words of assurance spoken to the people of Israel in exile, words which in fact allude back to Noah:

> "For a brief moment I forsook you,
> But with great compassion I will gather you.
> In an outburst of anger
> I hid My face from you for a moment;
> But with everlasting lovingkindness I will have compassion on you,"
> Says the Lord your Redeemer.

"For this is like the days of Noah to Me;
When I swore that the waters of Noah
Should not flood the earth again,
So I have sworn that I will not be angry with you,
Nor will I rebuke you.
For the mountains may be removed and the hills may shake,
But My lovingkindness will not be removed from you,
And My covenant of peace [**shalom**] will not be shaken,"
Says the Lord who has compassion on you.

(Isa. 54:7-10)

12

Abraham: God's Calling of a People

My daughters occasionally sing a silly little song with accompanying motions (i.e., aerobics) that are virtually impossible for old theologians to keep up with. "Father Abraham had many sons, / Many sons had Father Abraham. . . ." They do not know the half of it.

It is fascinating, indeed almost unbelievable, that a remote figure shrouded in mystery has been the personal source of three great living streams of monotheistic (lit., "belief in one God") faith. Father Abraham indeed had many sons and daughters, and what a sibling rivalry flourishes among them! Jews, Christians, and Muslims all vie for the honor of being Abraham's favorites, his true heirs. It is the narrative of Abraham, and the various interpretations thereof, that provide the foundations for each of these faiths. They are all grounded in the ancient root story of this wandering Semite. They all tell, and relate to, his story in different and often contradictory ways; yet Abraham is understood by all to be their "father." If nothing else, this figure of the ancient Abraham is a unifying figure for all three of these great monotheistic faiths.

In Judaism, Abraham is seen as the ancestor of the Hebrew slaves who escaped from Egypt, the people Israel. For Jews, to call Abraham "father" is to affirm biblical assertions that God, in seeking to carry out the divine will for the world, called Abraham out of a pagan and idolatrous culture and covenanted with him, vowing that his descendants would be great and be a blessing in the world, flourishing in the land of promise. Roughly two millennia after Abraham, another Jew, Paul by name, forged a connection between the figure of Abraham and faith in Jesus, writing that Abraham was a model of faith because he believed in God's promise to make the old man the father of many nations (Rom. 4:18-25). For Christians, to call Abraham "father" is an affirmation not "according to the flesh" but "according to the spirit":

99

Abraham is the father of faith, so that God's promise of descendants to Abraham is fulfilled in the lives of those who exercise faith in Jesus of Nazareth. In turn, Islam, which arose six centuries after Christianity's beginnings, holds that the residents of Mecca, the holy city, are physical descendants of Abraham through the "real" child of promise, Ishmael. To Muslims, Abraham is one of their own, a true Muslim in his submission to Allah and his hatred for idols. How many wars have been fought, how much blood has been shed, over this argument about who are Abraham's legitimate children, and who are pretenders!

It is ironic that such violence in the name of faith in God begins in a story of *laughter.* For that is what we discover in Abraham's story, and surely such a discovery could make an important contribution to the theological task. Theologians all too often take themselves too seriously, and perhaps the same could be said for many Christians. The atheistic philosopher Friedrich Nietzsche once observed that he might be more inclined to believe that Christians were redeemed if they *looked* a little more redeemed. These followers of Christ, he said, seemed always to wear such long faces. Nietzsche revolted against what he perceived to be a stuffy, somber pietism that apparently regarded with suspicion even the simplest pleasures of this life. To him, their humorless faces bespoke a humorless God.

Perhaps all too often Nietzsche has been correct. Perhaps Christianity tends to foster an image of God as an old, stern, gray-bearded hermit who has forgotten how to smile, let alone to laugh. On the one hand, there can be no doubt that God is serious about the creation and is deeply committed to redeeming this risky venture into freedom. We have already seen in the Noah story how God's heart may be broken by our refusal to cooperate with Him. But on the other hand, the story of Abraham allows theology a peek at the God who is free to laugh as well as to cry.

There is probably only one way a narrative theology could ever do justice to the theme of divine laughter as explored in the story of Abraham: in the form of drama, complete with five scenes.

Scene One

It all begins with God's promise of a son to Abram. But Abram, getting up there in years, suggests that a more logical course of action would be to appoint Eliezer, his head servant, to become heir of the household (Gen. 15:1-2). This was a common practice among the surrounding peoples and certainly was the expected thing to do. But a good sense of humor delights in the unexpected, and with tongue in cheek God replies, "No, you'll have an heir of your own." God obviously has something up His divine sleeve.

Scene Two

Time passes, and by all appearances, God has forgotten about that laughable promise to Abraham. He and his wife, Sarai, are not getting any younger; he's in his mid-80s, she's in her 70s. She is old, wrinkled, and humorless, embittered against her stingy God. "Now behold," she laments, "the Lord has prevented me from bearing children" (Gen. 16:2). The curse of childlessness, especially horrid in such cultures, has stifled her smile and muted her laughter. Sadly realistic, bereft of imagination, Sarai suggests that Abram have children through her handmaiden Hagar. In that sociohistorical setting, there is nothing unusual about the suggestion; and after all, God had said nothing about Sarai being the mother.

The plan seems reasonable to Abram, and the child Ishmael is given birth by the surrogate mother, Hagar. Now, at last, Abram has that child of promise, that boy through whom God would bless all peoples! End of story. Or is it?

Scene Three

Thirteen whole years later and Abram's pushing 100. God, apparently in no hurry, appears and repeats the promise. It's like a running joke that Abram simply does not catch: "I will make you exceedingly fruitful, and I will make nations of you, and kings shall come forth from you" (Gen. 17:6).

As the divine promises are issued, we might visualize Abram nodding his head and smiling ever so slightly, thinking he gets the joke. "Yes, Lord, I know. I'm really looking forward to the great family You're giving me through my son Ishmael. Boy, am I proud of him! He's 13 years old now, You know, so pretty soon he'll be marriage material. Isn't it great?"

"Oh, and by the way, Abraham," the Lord God, Creator of heaven and earth, a twinkle in His eye, unexpectedly continues, "as for your old wife, Sarah, I'm going to give you that child of promise through *her.*"

Abraham does a double take. What God has just delivered is one of the great one-liners in all history. It is so hilarious that Abraham falls flat on his face and laughs (Gen. 17:17). We cannot discern from the text whether he falls out of reverence and worship, prostrating himself, or out of laughing unbelief, pounding his fist on the ground in uncontrollable guffaws. Is he worshiping, or rolling in the aisles? Or is it a strange combination of the two, "an almost horrible laugh, deadly earnest, not in fun, bringing belief and unbelief close together"?[1] Only God and Abraham know for sure.

---

1. Von Rad, *Genesis*, 198.

"Come on now, Lord! You really don't have to go to all that trouble! I mean, let's be reasonable. Sarah's 89, and I'm no spring chicken. Why don't You just work Your plan through Ishmael?"

But God is determined to use His own material. "No, old Sarah is going to have a boy next year, and you'll name him Laughter *(Isaac)*. Get it?"

Scene Four

Soon thereafter, God—disguised as a wandering vagabond in cahoots with a couple of friends—drops by to visit with Abraham and Sarah. That crazy promise gets repeated, and this time it is an eavesdropping Sarah who's caught laughing. Certainly laughter would be the normal reaction of any 89-year-old woman who is told she's on the verge of motherhood for the first time. It is God's totally unexpected, completely surprising revelation that shatters Sarah's old, dry bitterness. God speaks, and she laughs! And though she tries to deny her spinsterly tittering, God knows better: "No, but you did laugh" (Gen. 18:15). Yet God does not condemn Sarah, for He also knows that His actions sometimes seem laughable from the purely human, all-too-often flat, humorless, unimaginative point of view. The divine humor bursts through her adult "realism" with the chuckling promise of a child named Laughter.

Scene Five

A year later (Genesis 21) we find Sarah laughing once more, this time *with* God rather than *at* God. She laughs with joy in the fulfillment of God's promise to make Laughter for her—and laughs at the thought of what the neighbors must be saying (v. 6). That which was laughable from the human perspective is not too hard for the Creator and Sustainer of all life. The promise that had evoked laughter, now fulfilled, produces another sort of Laughter. God's laughter becomes incarnate in Isaac, and for all the chuckling Abraham and Sarah do in this narrative, it is obvious who really has the sense of humor. It is humorous enough that God produced the child of promise, the child of laughter, through such old folks. But to have the good humor to put up with human beings' grave attempts to fulfill God's promise in their own feeble ways, and still to work His purposes through them, is a rare and divine quality indeed. It is one of the characteristics that marks God as *the God of covenants,* faithful to the promises He makes to His people. As any married couple will testify, it takes a good sense of humor to make a covenantal relationship work!

We should recognize that to refer to God as laughing is an anthropomorphism, yet that should not hinder us from surmising that, according to this narrative, the same confidence that allows God to take risks in creation also frees Him to laugh. Though the Creator takes himself and the created order seriously, He knows that, in the end, His status as God is not in danger. "He who sits in the heavens laughs" (Ps. 2:4), and can well afford to, since He is certain that His imaginative, humorous creativity can redeem even the bleakest human tears and make them the seeds of joyful laughter. Such a conviction is in fact the ground of *eschatology,* or the doctrine of last things.

To entertain such an image of God liberates *us* to laugh, too. Certainly there is much in our world to cry about—and if we have been correct in earlier reflections, God cries with us and for us—but we have this hope that when all is said and done, God will create laughter out of tears and bitterness, just as He did for Sarah. The fact that God began to create a covenant people through the miraculous birth of Isaac underscores the biblical truth that it is *God* who initiates covenant, *God* who reaches out to humanity in mercy and faithfulness, and *God* who finally will accomplish His purposes through the covenants He has made. "Faithful is he who calls you, who will also bring it to pass" (1 Thess. 5:24), wrote the apostle Paul, and we are reminded that God shoulders the lion's share of the load in covenantal relationship. When we realize our own limitations, as God does—He remembers that "we are dust" (Ps. 103:14, KJV)—then we can laugh at ourselves, knowing full well that to take ourselves too seriously is to forget who is God, and who promises the last laugh.

13

Moses: God's Gift of a Way to Walk

We have already noted that the exodus of the people Israel out of Egyptian bondage is, as far as most religious Jews are concerned, the central revelatory event in Jewish history. This deliverance, which occurred roughly 1,400 years B.C., cast its light even upon Jewish creation theology: God's "creation" of a people of covenantal dignity out of the "nothingness" of dehumanizing slavery, delivering them by "separating" the threatening, chaotic waters of the sea, is a bit of *creatio ex nihilo* on a small scale. For Israel, God had revealed himself decisively as their Redeemer in this liberating act.

But this paradigmatic event was not an end in itself. Just as God called creation into being for the sake of relationship, so God delivered this multitude of Jewish slaves also for the sake of relationship. They were not simply liberated, for the flip side of the Exodus event is the covenant initiated on Mount Sinai through the leadership of Moses. The brief prelude to the Decalogue (Gr., **deca** = ten, **logos** = word), more popularly known as the Ten Commandments, reveals the inseparability of the Exodus and Sinai. "I am the Lord your God, who brought you out of the land of Egypt, out of the house of slavery. You shall have no other gods before Me" (Exod. 20:2-3). Simply put, and in more recognizably Christian categories, the "law" of Sinai arises out of the "grace" of Exodus. The important implication of this for the Story of God is that grace is joined with obligation, gift with task, and freedom with responsibility. The German theologian Dietrich Bonhoeffer said it well: there is no "cheap grace."

There is, however, an old tendency within Christian theology to understand the Sinai covenant not as grace at all, but only as harsh, unbending law meant to frustrate people into a sense of their own sinfulness and inability. But it is difficult to support such an interpretation on the basis of the biblical text. First, this Hebrew term **torah** is probably better translated "way," as in a way to walk, than as "law." For centuries of Judaism, Torah has not been seen or experienced as an excessive burden; it is, rather, God's gift to Israel as a way to live as God's people in the world. The divine revelation to Moses is not that of a harsh taskmaster, but of "the Lord [Yahweh], the Lord God, compassionate and gracious, slow to anger, and abounding in lovingkindness and truth; who keeps lovingkindness for thousands, who forgives iniquity, transgression and sin" (Exod. 34:6-7), but who is also just in His punishment of the guilty. The essential portrait of the God of Israel, then, is a God of love and mercy, whose Torah is a gift that leads to life: "See, I have set before you today life and prosperity, and death and adversity . . . So choose life in order that you may live, you and your descendants, by loving the Lord your God, by obeying His voice, and by holding fast to Him" (Deut. 30:15, 19-20).

Perhaps the utterly gracious nature of the Torah is best grasped in thinking about the fourth commandment in the Decalogue, observance of the Sabbath. The seventh day was to be set apart (or sanctified) as a day of rest for the Israelites, their children, their animals, and even the "sojourner," or resident alien (Exod. 20:10). One Jewish tradition links Sabbath observance with the Exodus, as a temporal sign that this people is God's own liberated people called to covenant. Certainly in this case the Sabbath is the celebration of grace, of God's loving redemption of this people dehumanized under Egyptian oppression. Another tradition connects Sabbath observance with the creation narrative, where God is said to have created the universe in six days and rested on the seventh day. (Perhaps this dual significance for Sabbath may help to demonstrate the close connection between Creation and Exodus in the Hebrew mind.)In tying Sabbath observance to God's activity of creation, we find that God's people are, ironically enough, *commanded to do nothing* every seventh day! The people of Israel, like God, were simply to rest, to recycle. This is the precise inverse of the notion that the Law created a works mentality; the Sabbath is for resting, for stopping, for simply being. This is a radical notion for modern Western society, in which the patron saint very often is the workaholic.

A Sabbath mentality, in fact, may shed light on our own society's fascination with busyness. Why this obsession with being busy? It has been suggested that at least a partial answer is our need to justify our existence. Often we feel the need to prove to others that we *are* important, that we *do* have a reason for being around. We do not want simply to be deadweight slowing down the technological machinations of society. New Testament scholar Robert Jewett writes, "There is an assumption . . . deeply grounded in the American mentality that status is grounded in quantitative achievement. For the effort to justify oneself by works has shifted from doing what is right or legal to simply doing much."[1]

This obsession with doing much spills over into the modern tendency to regard people more for what they do than for who they are. Martin Buber perceived this tendency well when he suggested that modern human beings tend to treat the other person as "it" rather than as "you." Buber asks with characteristic precision, "When we . . . consider the fashion of modern work and possession, don't we find that modern developments have erased almost every trace of a life in which human beings confront each other and have meaningful relationships?"[2] The mentality of Sabbath, written into the very heart of the Torah, is to resist such a reduction of human life and significance to the "itness" of function.

Echoing Genesis, the Decalogue indicates that God labored in creation for six days and then rested on the seventh (Exod. 20:11). The rabbis of Jewish tradition, carefully noting that every other day mentioned in Genesis 1 followed the pattern of "evening and morning," were struck by the absence of that phrase in regard to the seventh day. Apparently, they said, there is no end to the seventh day, this day set aside to be holy, because the day of divine rest is neverending! There may be a profound truth in that rabbinic interpretation.

Obviously this truth would not be that God has done nothing since creation. That is the belief of **deism** (Lat., **deus** = God), i.e., that God created the universe, set its laws and conditions into place, and has since retired from active duty. Mainstream biblical faith has never embraced this "absentee landlord" notion of Deity. The facts belie the notion of a static, completed creation; for example, astronomers tell us that new stars, perhaps some with accompanying planets, continue to be formed and will for some time, if present conditions persist. An example literally "closer to home" is the creation of new life, human and otherwise, which is an ongoing process in our world. God continues to call forth new beings into existence; hence, creation is a continuing process. More important, in the Scriptures we read of a God who is at work, taking an active role in upholding creation, directing history, and redeeming the world.

But what does all this mean if combined with the rabbinic idea that the seventh day of rest is also in effect? Perhaps it would suggest, simply, that God's "rest" means not that God discontinues His labors,

---

1. Robert Jewett, *Letter to Pilgrims: A Commentary on the Epistle to the Hebrews* (New York: Pilgrim Press, 1981), 68.
2. Buber, *Between Man and Man*, 37.

but that His creative labors are rooted in an enjoyment of, and a nurturing care for, the created order. God does not regard it as His "works," His output, or what He "does for a living." God does not treat His world as an "it," but as a "you" with whom He covenants (cf. Gen. 9:9-17). God regards the entire created order with tender love and care. If the rabbis' speculation can be woven into narrative theology, the conclusion would be that God's work certainly continues, but that all His labors are infused with the quality of Sabbath rest.

In John 5:17 we hear some fascinating words from Jesus along these lines. In response to criticism for having healed a man on the Sabbath, Jesus replies, "My Father is working until now, and I Myself am working." Perhaps we could draw on the rabbinic interpretation of the Sabbath in the creation account of Genesis to suggest that Jesus was saying, "You charge Me with breaking the Sabbath by working on it. But while God's sabbath began after the work of creating was finished, and is still going on, yet the Father continues to work—and therefore so do I." John proceeds to say that His critics were horrified, not only because Jesus broke the Sabbath, but also because by calling God "My Father," He was making himself equal with God. A third offense might be added: according to His critics' definition of the Sabbath, Jesus was calling God himself a Sabbath-breaker! But not so, if all of God's creative and sustaining activity is permeated with the tender and loving quality of care for creation, of Sabbath rest. One might say, in fact, that to the extent that Jesus' critics regarded rules as more important than persons, they had reduced persons to the status of "it"—which is to transgress God's Sabbath rest (cf. Isaiah 58). Certainly this was an unfortunate distortion of God's Torah graciously given to the people Israel, but that in no way lessens the gracious, loving intent of the Sinai covenant.

If this interpretation is valid, then to celebrate the Sabbath as God celebrates it is not a matter of doing absolutely nothing, at least not in the sense of legalistic "don'ts." It is, rather, to share in the divine care for creation in all our actions and relationships. To enter into Sabbath rest is to cease attempting to win divine favor through much doing. There is a time, a divinely ordained time, simply to take a deep breath and relax! To be simply ourselves before God brings a liberating rest from the "works" mentality, in which we are attempting to justify our existence by impressing either God or other people, or perhaps to soothe our guilt or feelings of inadequacy. The Sabbath is a sign of grace, an invitation simply to *be* in God's presence, and to be accepted and cherished by God simply for being.

Perhaps we have sufficiently established the utter graciousness that undergirds God's gift of Torah to the people Israel. Having said that, it is crucial to recognize that this grace also includes obligation. God, according to the Story, chose this people called Israel to be "a kingdom of priests," mediators between God and creation. This people, visibly marked by circumcision and Sabbath, is to be "a holy nation," set apart from all other nations (as the Sabbath is set apart from all other days) in order to be God's "treasured possession" (Exod. 19:5-6, NIV). In other words, God renews the call that human beings should represent (or *re-present*) God, in whose image they have been created—but it is a call that is now offered to a specific and particular people. It is offered to this people, though, for the sake of all creation and with the redemption of all peoples in mind; God calls and commands *this* people precisely because "all the earth is Mine" (v. 5). This has often been called the *scandal of particularity:* that the God of the entire created order, the universal Creator and Sustainer, works in very specific, particular, and historical ways in redeeming fallen humanity.

It is for this divine work of redemption, then, that the people Israel are graciously called into covenant at Sinai. In obedience to the conditions of this covenant, Israel "incarnates" God's love and concern for every detail of human existence. God calls this people to share in His holiness and love, to embody His holiness and love in their life together.

This helps to explain the intent of the second commandment of the Decalogue, regarding the prohibition of fashioning "an idol in the form of anything in heaven above or on the earth beneath or in the waters below" (Exod. 20:4, NIV). Part of the rationale, to be sure, is to guard Israel from the polytheism of their neighbors, who tended to divinize the various components of the created order. Part of it, too, is that God in His transcendence cannot be represented by figures of wood and stone. But an often overlooked aspect of this command is that, because God cannot be physically re-presented, He can be encountered only in the commanding Voice and re-presented in human obedience. He is not to be visualized or objectified, but to be heard and obeyed. All of this is so well wrapped up in Deuteronomy 4:

> Remember the day you stood before the Lord your God at Horeb [Sinai] . . . You came near and stood at the foot of the mountain while it blazed with fire to the very heavens, with black clouds and deep darkness. Then the Lord spoke to you out of the fire. *You heard the sound of words but saw no form; there was only a voice.* He declared to you his covenant, the Ten Commandments, which he commanded you to follow and then wrote them on two stone tablets. . . .You saw no form of any kind the day the Lord spoke to you at Horeb out of the fire. Therefore watch yourselves very carefully, so that you do not become corrupt and make for

yourselves an idol . . . But as for you, the Lord took you and brought you out of the iron-smelting furnace, out of Egypt, to be the people of his inheritance, as you now are (vv. 10-13, 15-16, 20, NIV, italics added).

The people Israel are denied physical images of God precisely so that, in their obedience to the Sinai covenant, *they themselves* represent the image of God—the image in which all people are created and to which God desires to restore all, beginning with the Israelites. This notion is presented powerfully in another Deuteronomy passage:

For the Lord your God is the God of gods and Lord of lords, the great, the mighty, and the awesome God who does not show partiality, nor take a bribe. He executes justice for the orphan and the widow, and shows His love for the alien [stranger] by giving him food and clothing. So show your love for the [stranger,] for you were [strangers] in Egypt (10:17-19).

Liberation theologians have rightly directed our attention to passages such as these, rooted in the Exodus and Sinai, for they remind us that God is not content that Israel (or we) should simply ascribe power and majesty to Him, or to laud Him as Creator and Sustainer of all things. True worship inevitably involves hearing God's voice and responding by becoming involved in His work. It is easy to become fixated on a mental image of God such as that of Deut. 10:17, lifted from its context: God is the almighty Ruler of the universe, the great, the mighty, the awesome God who is always just. But mental images of God can be just as idolatrous as metal images of God, if they do not move us to an **imitatio dei** (Lat., "imitation of God"). This is the obligation side of the Sinai covenant, grounded in grace, which God initiated with Israel through Moses.

This is one of those qualities that makes the God of Exodus and Sinai particularly unique: God is able to be the Awesome One, dwelling in holy habitation, and *at the same time* to be a lover of outcasts and a struggler for justice. Perhaps traditional Christian theology comes close with the categories of transcendence and immanence, stating that God is both transcendent to, and yet immanent within, His creation. But those categories are concerned with metaphysics and refer to the divine nature. The compelling factor in this chapter of the Story of God, though, is moral rather than metaphysical, for it refers to the divine *character:* the amazing skill with which God combines religion and ethics in His own dealings with the world.

God could very well be content with the praise due the Creator of all things, but He is not; this God of gods and Lord of lords gets off the throne and *does something* for those who suffer need. More important, God calls those of the Sinai covenant to join Him, to represent Him, in

His concern. God has raised this people Israel from slavery into a position of responsible partnership with himself, and He expects them to be just as humanitarian as He is. This may be the only adequate biblical response to the criticism of faith that Albert Camus put into the mouth of his character Dr. Rieux in the classic existentialist novel *The Plague:* "'After all,' the doctor repeated . . . 'it's something that a man of your sort can understand most likely, but, since the order of the world is shaped by death, mightn't it be better for God if we refuse to believe in Him and struggle with all our might against death, without raising our eyes toward heaven where He sits in silence?'"[3]

If God does sit in heavenly silence, then Camus' question must be answered affirmatively. But the Story does not describe its primary Character as a throne-sitter but as a justice-doer who leads human beings in the struggle, a "Prometheus [who] himself undertakes on the side of man and in the utter solidarity of love the restoration of man's right and power to be free in the world."[4]

Grace and obligation, gift and task—these are inseparably linked in the logic of Sinai. But there is no question that this grace is bestowed on Israel for the sake of all the nations. In this covenant at Sinai, God graciously elects a people who will re-present Him, who will be a kingdom of priests to the other nations, because all of creation is God's—and His intention is to redeem and restore what He has created.

---

3. Albert Camus, *The Plague* (New York: Modern Library, 1948), 117-18.

4. Jose Miguez Bonino, *Christians and Marxists* (Grand Rapids: Wm. B. Eerdmans Publishing Co., 1976), 108.

14

David:
The Quest for Kingship

It would be difficult to find a finer example of God's willingness to labor together with human beings in covenantal relationship than in the stories of David and his predecessor, Saul. Scripture bears witness to God's promise to David to establish his throne forever (2 Sam. 7:16). Ironically, though, the very idea of a human king over Israel was apparently not even God's intention for His people. It is interesting that the biblical narratives of Israel's quest for authentic kingship contain several such instances of God's power to compromise (lit., "to promise together with") with His people for the sake of His redemptive purposes.

First, we find that God concedes with regret to the Israelites' clamoring to the prophet Samuel for a king "to judge us like all the nations" (1 Sam. 8:5). God, in fact, is more open to the people's wishes than Samuel:

> Listen to the voice of the people in regard to all that they say to you, for they have not rejected you, but they have rejected Me from being king over them. Like all the deeds which they have done since the day that I brought them up from Egypt even to this day—in that they have forsaken Me and served other gods—so they are doing to you also. Now then, listen to their voice; however, you shall solemnly warn them and tell them of the procedure of the king who will reign over them (vv. 7-9).

Samuel does indeed proceed to paint a grim picture of the royal power to dominate, oppress, and tax common folks to death—and solemnly warns, "Then you will cry out in that day because of your king whom you have chosen for yourselves, but the Lord will not answer you in that day" (vv. 10-18). The Scriptures clearly recognize that power can indeed corrupt, and that too much political power in one pair of hands is always potentially destructive of human life and society. Nonetheless, God displays the humility of a king rejected and allows the people their wish: "Listen to their voice, and appoint them a king" (v. 22).

Perhaps God's readiness to cooperate with the people Israel reflects His seriousness about covenant. By initiating covenantal relationship with this people, God was manifesting His commitment to taking His human partners seriously. God wants to make the relationship work! Generally speaking, the Christian theological tradition has said very little (if anything) about the divine power of compromise as reflected in the kingship narratives. But it is undeniably one of the crucial truths about God that surfaces in these stories.

With Samuel's anointing of Saul as the covenant people's first king, the knotty problem of God and politics begins to impose itself upon our theological reflections. Theologians usually tend to prefer the rarefied air of heavenly speculation, but the God of Israel is the God of covenants—and for God to become involved in history covenantally is inevitably a dirty business. The covenantal God is One who enters into the creaturely realm of human existence in all its dimensions: individual, social, cultural, and political. This means that God truly is involved in the give-and-take of human decision and indecision, of human relationship and rationalization, of human loves and fears. The Creator and Sustainer of the universe deigns to make His dwelling among us whom He has dignified by creating us in His image, but who are nonetheless poor creatures of dust. As Solomon wondered aloud in his prayer of dedication of the Temple, though "heaven and the highest heaven cannot contain" the Holy One, yet God does "indeed dwell with mankind on the earth" (2 Chron. 6:18).

Later, after the anointing of Saul as king, the tragic story of his fall from divine favor provides a further illustration of the ways of God in history. "Then the word of the Lord came to Samuel, saying, 'I regret that I have made Saul king, for he has turned back from following Me, and has not carried out My commands'" (1 Sam. 15:10-11). The King James Version has it, "It repenteth me that I have set up Saul to be king," and yet in the same chapter Samuel subsequently says to Saul, "The Strength of Israel will not lie nor repent: for he is not a man, that he should repent" (v. 29). Many translations attempt to soften the apparent contradiction—God repenting and not repenting—but the fact remains that the same Hebrew verb is used in both places. While translating the verb in verse 11 as "regret" and in verse 29 as "repent" undoubtedly does help to shed light on the intent of the verses, we ought not to smooth over the paradox too readily. Perhaps the tension in the image of God as a "repentant nonrepenter" originates within God's own being as He works in His world for our redemption.

The thrust of what the prophet Samuel says to Saul is indeed a fundamental biblical truth: God does not lie. God is not fickle. The very trustworthiness of covenantal relationship rests in God's utter reliability. God has a plan and a purpose for His creation, a specific goal toward which He strives, and God does not relax His determination to achieve it. In this profound and important sense, God is a nonrepenter.

On the other hand, by becoming covenantally involved with human beings, God has committed himself to using fickle, often unreliable agents to accomplish His redemptive purposes. Thus, while God maintains His commitment to redeeming fallen humanity, God is not bound like a slave to some predetermined master plan, controlled down to the finest detail, according to which His work must be accomplished. God works with, in, and through women and men, and though God does not repent (lit., "turn away") from his overarching goal, He can repent or turn from one plan of action to another if the humanly created situation dictates it, as in Saul's case. Certainly, such a give-and-take relationship with the world requires a far deeper sense of creativity from God than would the inevitable unfolding of some predetermined, irresistible master plan.

God's will, then, is not eternal, changeless decree; rather, as God acts and reacts covenantally with the world (Gen. 9:9-17) and particularly with His people, His will becomes the best possible for each situation in the light of His goal of *shalom* for the created order. God's will is forged out of the stuff of human decision and response and is often thwarted and changed. It truly matters to God what we think and do and pray! Yet He is not threatened by adversity or defeated by disappointment. God is creatively flexible enough to alter His plans when He meets with human sin and rebellion.

This is essentially what contemporary theologian John Cobb intends when he writes, "God in every moment works with and upon the world that is given to him in that moment."[1] At first reading, the phrase "given to him" might raise a question: "given to him" by what, or by whom? The answer: the "given" with which God chooses to work, according to the Scriptures, is the real "otherness" of the world God creates and sustains, and particularly the otherness of human beings' decisions.

Admittedly, such an understanding of God's relationship to the world and history does not square with popular conceptions of prophecy, in which God has all future events already mapped out. The latter, though, is a narrow and generally warped understanding of biblical prophecy. The biblical prophets dealt far more with God's word to His people in their present historical situations or impending circum-

---

1. John B. Cobb, Jr., *God and the World* (Philadelphia: Westminster Press, 1969), 91.

stances (forthtelling) than with far-future events (foretelling). The truly prophetic words of Samuel, spoken when the Lord tore the kingdom from Saul's hands, provide a fitting example:

> Has the Lord as much delight in burnt offerings and sacrifices
> As in obeying the voice of the Lord?
> Behold, to obey is better than sacrifice,
> And to heed than the fat of rams.
>
> *(1 Sam. 15:22)*

If the considerably popular notion of God as the Predeterminer of all details were correct, then to sacrifice would indeed be better than to obey. Our obedience or disobedience would not matter in the least, since they would ultimately be illusory anyway. Obedience to God's will would not have any particular value; it would be better simply to offer sacrifices of worship, and watch what God does next. But obedience is better than sacrifice largely because God has chosen human beings to be His partners in shaping history. Obedience is the human dimension of cooperating with God's intentions for redemption, but our own desires and disobedience certainly can hinder His work. Hence, because Saul rejected the word of Yahweh, He in turn rejected Saul as king and sought a new course of action in David.

If indeed it was not God's first intention that Israel be ruled by a human king; and if, after having made that first adjustment, it was His new intention to make Saul His ruling agent over Israel; and if, having regretted His choice of Saul, He turned to David, we continue to discover in this new royal relationship yet more of God's amazingly humble willingness to work with and through human frailty. David's foibles and failures, as well as his indomitable passion for life, are well known and need not occupy us at present. It is his interest in building a temple for Yahweh that provides a telling focus for the concern of this chapter: God's flexibility in covenantal relationship as it is played out in the vagaries of history.

We read that King David, victorious over his enemies on all sides, said to the prophet Nathan, "See now, I dwell in a house of cedar, but the ark of God dwells within tent curtains" (2 Sam. 7:2). But the word of God given to Nathan betrays little interest in David's idea.

> Go and say to My servant David, "Thus says the Lord, 'Are you the one who should build Me a house to dwell in? For I have not dwelt in a house since the day I brought up the sons of Israel from Egypt, even to this day; but I have been moving about in a tent, even in a tabernacle. Wherever I have gone with all the sons of Israel, did I speak a word with one of the tribes of Israel, which I commanded to shepherd My people Israel saying, "Why have you not built Me a house of cedar?"'" (vv. 5-7).

The divine word proceeds to proclaim that, instead of David building a house for God, it is God who "will make a house for you [David]" (v. 11), "and your house and your kingdom shall endure before Me forever; your throne shall be established forever" (v. 16). Again, there is an explicit tension that arises in this coalition of political rule and divine sanction: God desires to bless and sustain the reign of David's line but is not particularly interested in his plan to build a visibly imposing monument that would tend to identify God's intentions with some stately status quo. God's word through Nathan suggests a divine preference for mobility: "I have been moving about in a tent"! Covenantal relationship to humans in history requires flexibility, not the generally inflexible and coercive power of political institutions that presume to have God's full blessing. The word given to Nathan suggests that the Creator and Sustainer of all things prefers a tent to a temple.

Yet, once again, God condescends to David's idea—for the Temple is David's idea, not God's command. But God, through His spokesman Nathan, indicates that it will be a son of David who will build a temple. "Your son Solomon is the one who shall build My house and My courts; for I have chosen him to be a son to Me, and I will be a father to him" (1 Chron. 28:6). But before he died, David was privileged to offer a prayer of dedication prior to the beginning of the Temple's construction. Certainly the poetic powers of Israel's greatest Psalmist are evident in that prayer:

> Blessed art Thou, O Lord God of Israel our father, forever and ever.
> Thine, O Lord, is the greatness and the power and the glory and the victory and the majesty, indeed everything that is in the heavens and the earth;
> Thine is the dominion, O Lord, and Thou dost exalt Thyself as head over all. . . .
> But who am I and who are my people that we should be able to offer as generously as this?
> For all things come from Thee, and from Thy hand we have given Thee.
> For we are sojourners before Thee, and tenants, as all our fathers were.
>
> *(1 Chron. 29:10-11, 14-15)*

David found a good deal of irony in the fact that finite, utterly dependent creatures would attempt to build for God a temple, since "all things come from Thee, and from Thy hand we have given Thee." Yet it reminds us again that God delights to accomplish His work through His finite, frail covenant partners. It is all of grace that God seeks us out for fellowship and service—we who are, in David's imagery, vagabonds, temporary tenants in a world on loan.

Even more remarkable is that God himself apparently enjoys identifying with us as sojourners and wanderers. This ancient Hebrew sense of God's preference for mobility, for being on the move, came into tension with the developing Israelite desire for a king, a throne, and a temple, all of which signified the institutionalization of religious faith as well as political entrenchment. Israel's quest for human kingship, even when divinely sanctioned, threatened to suppress the historical dynamics of covenantal relationship with God in history. Let us recall, for example, the story of Abraham.

Revealing a distinct spirit of adventure, God began His redemptive work in history by calling Abraham to "go forth" from all human securities, to break all bonds with his past, and to trust God to guide his every wandering step (Gen. 12:1). Our society tends much more toward mobility, but in Abraham's time one's clan, tribe, and village were inseparable from one's identity, and asking Abraham to sever those ties was asking the nearly impossible. God's call to adventure sliced through Abraham's earthly ties and securities: "Go forth!" In the words of New Testament scholar Robert Jewett, "To leave the certainties of the past and the familiar, to break away from the bonds of family and nation, and to move courageously into the unknown is the requirement for both maturity and creativity. . . . So the person of faith must necessarily be a pilgrim, breaking resolutely from the illusion of security and moving courageously toward the unknown."[2]

God himself moves courageously toward the future and calls Abraham to follow Him into the unknown. There is no map—only God's promise to lead him. Yet Abraham, on the strength of God's promise, "went out" from his comfortable existence into the life of a wanderer (Heb. 11:8, KJV). Stephen, the first Christian martyr, in the speech that prompted his stoning, said of Abraham that "God removed him . . . [a]nd . . . gave him no inheritance in [this country], not even a foot of ground" (Acts 7:4-5). God gave him only the lure of a promise, and Abraham, as well as Isaac and Jacob after him, lived on nothing but that promise. And they lived in tents, so that they could quickly pull up stakes and follow wherever their nomad God would lead.

This vision of God on the move was a crucial one for the fledgling faith of the Israelites. One of their earliest creeds begins, "My father was a wandering Aramean" (Deut. 26:5), referring to the nomadic Jacob. Thus, Israel's growing fascination for a king with a palace and power, and the king's own fascination with building a monument to God's (and his) reign, came at the expense of losing the dynamism of

---

2. Robert Jewett, *Letter to Pilgrims,* 200, 201.

God's calling to Israel to be "aliens and sojourners *with Me*" (Lev. 25:23, italics added).

If the idea of God as an alien and stranger in His own world seems strange, keep in mind that, for Christian faith, the renewal and fulfillment of the Davidic covenant occurred in Jesus of Nazareth, "the son of David" (Matt. 1:1). The closest this Son of David came to royal treatment was as the Grand Marshal of an impromptu donkey parade into Jerusalem (21:1-11). In fact, John's Gospel puts it in the most graphic and compelling imagery: this Son of David is the very Word of God, and the Word who is God has invaded this world largely unknown, unreceived, and unwelcomed (1:1, 10-11). Such a revelation of God poses an obvious threat to any institution that attempts to construct, in the words of the Epistle to the Hebrews, a "lasting city" (13:14). David's desire to build a temple for God exemplifies the typical human desire for an immobile deity, a God we can encapsule in our temples. Israel's quest for kingship, ironically, probably had more to do with trying to rule God than with seeking the rule of God. Jesus' own subsequent proclamation and embodiment of the kingdom of God, and the reception He received at the hands of the religious and political institutions of His day, tend strongly to unveil this stubborn human tendency to attempt to tame God with our temples.

Thus, the deepest irony of David's prayer lay in dedicating a temple at all for the God of Abraham, Isaac, and Jacob, the wanderers. For we human beings not only are sojourners *before* God, as David prayed, but also are called to be sojourners *with* God. The Creator of the universe neither needs nor desires any permanent place of abode. This truth, to be sure, was to become more evident later when the Temple was destroyed but God was not. God continues to move ahead, and we would not be far wrong to modify Israel's ancient creed to say, "Our Father is a wandering God . . ."

15

The Prophets:
The God of Partnership

The very heart of the relationship between God and Israel, throughout the ups and downs of the history of that relationship, was (and for most religious Jews, *is*) the Torah, the covenant of divine commands received by Moses at Mount Sinai. It was most obviously the basis for the priestly regulations concerning everyday morality and behavior, hygiene, ritual sacrifice, family and societal relationships, and virtually every other dimension of Israelite life. The centrality of the Torah came to be symbolized in the building of the great Temple of Jerusalem, the holy center of Israelite society insofar as it was personifed in the figure of Moses and revolved around the priestly traditions.

But the Torah was also central in the kingly tradition of Israel, personified in the figure of David. He who would properly fulfill the role of Israel's king, according to the Scriptures, must be obedient to God's will as embodied in the Sinai commands (Deut. 17:18-20). The law, in fact, was to have a humbling and equalizing effect upon the king; he was to "read it all the days of his life, that he may learn to fear the Lord his God, by carefully observing all the words of this law . . . that his heart may not be lifted up above his countrymen" (vv. 19-20). There were, in other words, conditions placed upon the divine covenant and promise to bless David's throne.

Though the priesthood and kingship both were rooted in the giving of the Torah, the Israelites dealt constantly with the temptation to think of these institutions as having authority in themselves, as though they were guarantees of divine favor. To be sure, it is a human tendency to identify with religious authority figures, and thereby to assume that sound relationship to God is assured. But the very purpose of the Torah—to be that divine instrument whereby God might draw near to all of His chosen people (Deut. 30:11-16)—could be seriously compromised by this tendency.

It is at the point of this recurring threat to Israel's religious understanding and practice that the prophets made their contribution to the Story of God. The Hebrew prophets, for all their differences in historical period and message, each lived and spoke out of a burning awareness of God's immediate presence. Their own sense of His vibrant nearness, in turn, ignited their conviction that every Jew stood in God's immediate presence: shoulder-to-shoulder with fellow members of His covenant community, yet each personally answerable to Him. The prophet Micah, for instance, raised a series of questions of the priestly tradition:

> With what shall I come to the Lord
> And bow myself before the God on high?
> Shall I come to Him with burnt offerings,
> With yearling calves?
> Does the Lord take delight in thousands of rams,
> In ten thousand rivers of oil?
> Shall I present my first-born for my rebellious acts,
> The fruit of my body for the sin of my soul?

Micah's reply to his own question is one of the classic passages in prophetic literature:

> He has told you, O man, what is good;
> And what does the Lord require of you
> But to do justice, to love kindness,
> And to walk humbly with your God?

(6:6-8)

Out of their profound awareness of God the prophets could preface so many of their statements with a thundering, "Thus says Yahweh!" Out of this awareness they could chastise Israel's kings (e.g., 1 Sam. 13:13-14) and challenge Israel's priests (e.g., Jer. 1:18). This awareness of God, usually characterized by the prophets as "the word of Yahweh" but also occasionally as "the Spirit of Yahweh," provided them the necessary inspiration to interpret His actions in the history of Israel.

More than any other figure in Israel's history, then, it was the figure of the prophet that constantly beckoned the Jewish people to faithfulness to the God revealed first in the Torah but also in the ongoing events of Israel's communal life. While the prophets were uniquely God's partners as those through whom He spoke to Israel, their message was also one of partnership in covenant: that God yearns for a faithful partnership with His people that would slice through the tendencies toward empty ritualism in the priestly and kingly traditions. One of the most powerful prophetic orations dealing with this issue is Isaiah 58, in which the prophet, speaking for God, first recognizes that the people seem to think that they "seek Me day by day, and delight to know My ways, as a nation that has done righteousness" (v. 2) The people, in fact, supposedly "delight in the nearness of God" (v. 2), and thus are frustrated by the apparent lack of divine blessing upon their lives and nation: "Why have we fasted and Thou dost not see? Why have we humbled ourselves and Thou dost not notice?" (v. 3). The answer the people receive from God through the prophet is earthshaking:

> Is it a fast like this which I choose, a day for a man to humble himself?
> Is it for bowing one's head like a reed,
> And for spreading out sackcloth and ashes as a bed?
> Will you call this a fast, even an acceptable day to the Lord?
> Is this not the fast which I choose,
> To loosen the bonds of wickedness,
> To undo the bands of the yoke,
> And to let the oppressed go free,
> And break every yoke?
> Is it not to divide your bread with the hungry,
> And bring the homeless poor into the house;
> When you see the naked, to cover him;
> And not to hide yourself from your own flesh? . . .
> Then you will call, and the Lord will answer;
> You will cry, and He will say, "Here I am."
> If you remove the yoke from your midst,
> The pointing of the finger, and speaking wickedness,
> And if you give yourself to the hungry,
> And satisfy the desire of the afflicted,
> Then your light will rise in darkness,
> And your gloom will become like midday.
>
> *(vv. 5-7, 9-10)*

God's concern for the oppressed and marginalized of Israelite society, as here revealed in Isaiah 58, is in fact a dominant theme throughout the prophetic literature. Amos' poetic cry to "let justice roll down like waters" (5:24) became a rallying cry two and one-half millennia later for Martin Luther King, Jr., and the civil rights movement in America—and continues to ring in the ears of all who take the message of the prophets seriously. Abraham Heschel, a 20th-century Jewish philosopher of religion who, arm in arm with King, led in many civil rights marches during the '60s, has characterized the prophets' power as a sharing in "the divine pathos," or the pain of God. Heschel argued that "this notion that God can be intimately affected, that He possesses not merely intelligence and will, but also pathos, basically defines the prophetic consciousness of God."[1] Heschel's powerful analysis would suggest that the prophets were enabled by God to share in His own compassion (lit., to "feel pain together with" another) for those who

---

1. Abraham Joshua Heschel, *The Prophets* (New York: Harper & Row, 1962), 233.

suffer. Thus, it is God's own compassion, rather than simple humanism, that fueled the prophets' deep concern for social and economic justice. It was also this sharing in the "pathos of God" that empowered the prophets to address Israel's religious, political, and social circumstances not simply from the divine perspective, but from *within the divine heart!* Contemporary German theologian Jurgen Moltmann, drawing upon Heschel's portrayal of the prophets, writes, "Prophecy, therefore, is in essence not a looking forward into the future to see what is appointed in unalterable destiny or a predestined divine plan of salvation, but insight into the present *pathos* of God, his suffering caused by Israel's disobedience and his passion for his right and his honour in the world. . . . At the heart of the prophetic proclamation there stands the certainty that God is interested in the world to the point of suffering."[2]

Surely the power of divine pathos comes to expression most graphically in the prophecy of Hosea, whose entire life and love for Gomer the prostitute became a parable enacting God's passion for His people (1:2; 3:1). Once again we find the typical prophetic call to justice (4:1-3) and condemnation of pagan religious practices, but these concerns are set within the context of God's deep and enduring, yet tender, love for his people.

> When Israel was a youth I loved him,
> And out of Egypt I called My son.
> The more [I] called them,
> The more they went from [Me] . . .
> Yet it is I who taught Ephraim to walk,
> I took them in My arms;
> But they did not know that I healed them.
> I led them with cords of a man, with bonds of love,
> And I became to them as one who lifts the yoke from their jaws;
> And I bent down and fed them. . . .

Perhaps it was because of Hosea's own tragic love for Gomer that he could share in God's pain:

> How can I give you up, O Ephraim?
> How can I surrender you, O Israel? . . .
> My heart is turned over within Me,
> All my compassions are kindled.
> I will not execute My fierce anger;
> I will not destroy Ephraim again.
> For I am God and not man, the Holy One in your midst,
> And I will not come in wrath.

(*11:1-4, 8-9*)

---

2. Jurgen Moltmann, *The Crucified God* (New York: Harper & Row, 1973), 271.

The prophecies of Hosea conclude with a divine wooing that verges on seduction: "O Ephraim, what more have I to do with idols? It is I who answer and look after you. I am like a luxuriant cypress; from Me comes your fruit" (14:8). Probably better than any other prophet, then, Hosea typifies both the prophet's partnership with God (as His spokesman) and God's passionate desire for partnership with His people Israel.

But the prophets all shared in a deep awareness, too, of Israel's past failures in the adventure of partnership with God. That was, in fact, the root experience of divine pathos, not only in Hosea but in all the prophets: Israel had not been a faithful marriage partner. And, of course, the prophets agreed in interpreting Israel's national-political woes as a divinely ordained consequence of its wandering heart. (The short Book of Habakkuk, for instance, is a wonderful example of inspired prophetic insight into Israel's historical circumstances.) And even with the promises given through Hosea, Jeremiah, and Isaiah that God would never abandon His people and would finally restore them to *shalom,* there was always the nagging possibility that they would fall into disobedience again, disrupting partnership with Him and inviting further destruction and exile. What would keep the people from falling again?

It was this haunting question that seems to have been rumbling in the hearts of the prophets Ezekiel and Jeremiah, and in their sharing in the divine pathos for faithful partnership, they found an answer: God in His wondrous, transforming grace would do a new thing! After gathering the exiled Jews back to the land of promise,

> Then I will sprinkle clean water on you, and you will be clean; I will cleanse you from all your filthiness and from all your idols. Moreover, I will give you a new heart and put a new spirit within you; and I will remove the heart of stone from your flesh and give you a heart of flesh. And I will put My Spirit within you and cause you to walk in My statutes, and you will be careful to observe My ordinances. And you will live in the land that I gave to your forefathers; so you will be My people, and I will be your God (*Ezek.* 36:25-28).

Similarly, Jeremiah envisioned "a new covenant with the house of Israel and with the house of Judah," written not on stone but "within them, and on their heart I will write it; and I will be their God, and they shall be My people" (31:31, 33). Both prophets reveal God's desire for authentic partnership by citing the prominent biblical formulation that Israel would be God's people and Yahweh would be their God. This partnership would become possible because of the empowerment of God's Spirit, creating a new heart of *flesh* (sensitivity? compassion?) in which the Torah would be inscribed by the very hand of God! In short, God's gift to the prophets in sharing in the "divine pathos" would become a gift available to every Israelite! Truly then, Israel could become a kingdom of priests, a light to the nations, as God intended in the initiation of the Sinai covenant. "And the nations will know that I am the Lord who sanctifies Israel, when My sanctuary is in their midst forever" (Ezek. 37:28).

There were glimmers and glimpses among the prophets, moreover, that God's gift of transforming and enabling grace would finally overrun Israel's boundaries and touch the non-Jewish world. Isaiah wrote of a divine servant, especially chosen by God and anointed by the Spirit, who would "bring forth justice to the nations" (Heb., **goyim**, non-Jewish peoples), who would indeed "establish . . . justice in the earth; and the coastlands will wait expectantly for His law" (42:1-4). Of this servant Isaiah later proclaims in the voice of God,

> It is too small a thing that You should be My Servant
> To raise up the tribes of Jacob, and to restore the preserved ones of Israel;
> I will also make You a light of the nations
> So that My salvation may reach to the end of the earth.

> (49:6)

The Isaiah prophecy reached most radically into an unimaginable future in God's relationship with non-Jewish peoples when it envisioned Israel's traditional enemies, deeply hated and feared, as fellow servants and siblings in the family of God: "In that day Israel will be the third party with Egypt and Assyria, a blessing in the midst of the earth, whom the Lord of hosts has blessed, saying, 'Blessed is Egypt My people, and Assyria the work of My hands, and Israel My inheritance'" (19:24-25). In short, the prophets recalled Israel to its role as God's representative *for the sake of the nations.* Indeed, this is a major theme in the theological narrative of Jonah the reluctant missionary.

Of course, Christian tradition finds at least the beginning of the fulfillment of such prophecies in the coming of God's holy anointed Servant Jesus (Matt. 12:18-21; Acts 4:24-30), "who," as Paul cites Isaiah, "arises to rule over the Gentiles," and in whom "the Gentiles . . . shall . . . hope" (Rom. 15:12). In Jesus Christ, faith in the God of Abraham, Isaac, and Jacob had indeed leapt beyond the borders of Israel in a thoroughly surprising and unprecedented way. Through Jesus and the new covenant sealed by His blood, we "Gentiles in the flesh," at one time "excluded from the commonwealth of Israel, and strangers to the covenants of promise, having no hope and without God in the world," have now "been brought near" to the God of partnership (Eph. 2:11-13)! The vision and goal of Sinai, that Israel should become a kingdom of priests and a light to the nations, has indeed been fulfilled in Christ. Through Christ the promised gift of God's Spirit, outpoured that Israel might, like its prophets, share in the pathos of God, has reached us. But we who are Gentiles ought not to take this gift for granted; rather, we ought to remember the surprising graciousness of God who desires to share himself with all people. It is noteworthy that when the Spirit was given to the non-Jew Cornelius and his household during Peter's first brief sermon addressed to Gentiles, "all the circumcised believers who had come with Peter were amazed, because the gift of the Holy Spirit had been poured out upon the Gentiles also" (Acts 10:45).

Even as we rejoice in the fulfillment of the prophetic visions by Christ's coming, and particularly Jeremiah's and Ezekiel's prophecies by the outpouring of God's Spirit, it may be worthwhile for us to remember that those prophecies had to do first of all with the people of Israel and their covenant partnership with God. Remember that the divine promise through Ezekiel had to do with observing the statutes and ordinances of the Torah, and with living in the land promised to Abraham, Isaac, and Jacob. Further, even as we rejoice in the new covenant in Christ whereby we enter into partnership with the God of the universe, let us recall that God's promise through Jeremiah had to do with a new covenant for the houses of Israel and Judah, and with a Torah not cast away but written on the people's hearts.

In fact, as we conclude our reflections of Part IV, having to do with the matter of the Jewish people in God's story, we do well to ponder the words of Jeremiah's prophecy as he continues beyond his musings about the new covenant:

> Thus says the Lord,
> Who gives the sun for light by day,
> And the fixed order of the moon and the stars for light by night,
> Who stirs up the sea so that its waves roar;
> The Lord of hosts is His name:
> "If this fixed order departs
> From before Me," declares the Lord,
> "Then the offspring of Israel also shall cease
> From being a nation before Me forever."
> Thus says the Lord,
> "If the heavens above can be measured,
> And the foundations of the earth searched out below,
> Then I will also cast off all the offspring of Israel
> For all that they have done," declares the Lord.

(31:35-37)

PART V

A NEW TWIST IN GOD'S STORY: THE DOCTRINE OF CHRIST

As we follow the plot of the Story of God as found in the Scriptures, it is obvious that we now reach a decisive turn, a new twist, in the telling. For we have heard again of the loving Creator who, out of love and an interest in relationship and partnership, calls the entire universe into being. We have witnessed the tragic rebellion of that creature most specifically and especially created for relationship and partnership, the human. And we have seen the Creator, in persistent love, initiate the gracious process of restoring the human to relationship through the establishment of covenants. And now, at this point, the Christian telling of this Story begins to diverge from the Jewish. For now, in the person of Jesus of Nazareth, Christians confess that a new and decisive covenant has been established.

But even as we begin to talk about a divergence from the Jewish telling of God's Story, and about a new covenant reaching beyond Noah, Abraham, Moses, and David, we must take care not to overstate this sense of Christianity's difference or distance from Judaism. Christians on the whole could profit by a deeper sense of appreciation for what the Jewish people and their history have meant for Christianity. Apart from Jewish faithfulness through the centuries before and leading up to Jesus, there would be no Story for us to tell. Paul said it well when he warned early Gentile Christians against a sense of pride or superiority toward Jews who had not responded to Jesus:

> If some of the branches have been broken off, and you, though a wild olive shoot, have been grafted in among the others and now share in the nourishing sap from the olive root, do not boast over those branches. If you do, consider this: You do not support the root, but the root supports you. . . . After all, if you were cut out of an olive tree that is wild by nature, and contrary to nature were grafted into a cultivated olive tree, how much more

readily will these, the natural branches, be grafted into their own olive tree! *(Rom. 11:17-18, 24, NIV)*.

The "olive tree" to which Paul referred is Israel, the Jewish people, to whom belong adoption, divine glory, the covenants, the Torah, divine promises, and the patriarchs Abraham, Isaac, and Jacob (Rom. 9:4-5). The Story we have been telling has been not only God's Story but also the Jews' story, both in the sense that it is *about* them and that it has *been told by* them. It is a story into which, through Christ, we non-Jews have been invited.

All of this is important precisely because the Church, throughout much of its history, has tried either to deny Jews their story or else deny the Jewishness of the story itself. For instance, in the Church's historical development of Christology it was recognized that Jesus was "truly God" and "truly human," but no one bothered with the obvious but important fact that He was, and is, "truly Jewish." This is but one example of a historical trend that has led not only to a severing of our own roots but also to repressive and often even violent attitudes and practices toward the Jewish people. One recent and obvious example of such treatment is that the Nazis' anti-Jewish programs were fueled by the propagandist use of one of Martin Luther's 16th-century tracts titled *Concerning the Jews and Their Lies*. The great Reformer had suggested such things as renewing the medieval Christian practice of herding the Jewish population into ghettos, outlawing Jewish commentaries, forbidding rabbis to teach, and even burning down synagogues. Unfortunately, in many cases the Nazis, about four centuries later, were able to enact Luther's items of advice almost to the letter.

Many historians of the Nazi Holocaust—which was directed at Jews first, but at other political undesirables as well—argue that without the long history of Christian anti-Judaism in the West, it is inconceivable that the Holocaust could have occurred. This does not mean that Christian faith *caused* the Holocaust, but that it was a necessary factor. Such an observation should give us pause. And it should serve as a warning as we begin the difficult but challenging work of Christology, of attempting to understand just who Jesus is for us, in our lives and destinies. We shall attempt to be careful about how we talk about Jesus, that it not at the same time involve castigation or belittlement of Judaism and the Jewish people. This would be far from the spirit of love espoused by Jesus of Nazareth, himself of course a Jew. May we, as we enter into consideration of the doctrine of Christ, be careful to represent His own concern for authentic love for God and neighbor. For every time Jesus highlighted that dual command of love, He was reaching back into the very heart of the Jewish covenant at Sinai—a covenant grounded in grace and fulfilled by love.

16

A Covenantal Context
for Christ

From early on in the Church's history, most of its theologians have been careful to emphasize the vital importance of the history of the people Israel for correctly understanding the mission of Jesus. Biblical faith, after all, is a thoroughly *historical* faith, in the sense that it is preeminently concerned with events—especially events that have been interpreted, under the inspiration of God's Spirit, as being the saving activities of God—and their consequences. In order to understand any event well, it is helpful and even necessary to attempt to understand its historical context. And certainly it is no exception when the event under consideration is the life and ministry of the first-century Galilean Jew, Jesus of Nazareth.

Thus, the Christian movement showed good judgment in the second century when it condemned as heretical the ideas of a popular teacher named Marcion, who believed that Christians should have nothing to do with the Hebrew Scriptures (what we now call "the Old Testament"). In putting together his own canon for his followers, Marcion got rid of most of the Gospels also (they were simply too Jewish!) and did a scissors-and-paste job on Paul's letters to make them sound as un-Jewish as possible. Even in its youth, however, the fledgling Church sensed the danger of this pseudogospel: Marcion was attempting to cut off Christian faith from its historical and religious roots in the Jewish people's covenantal life before God. In other words, Christians were convinced that the God of Abraham, Isaac, and Jacob, of Moses, Miriam, and Deborah, was indeed none other than the God and Father of our Lord Jesus Christ. Marcion did not last.

When the early Christian fathers rejected Marcion, they were putting into practice the (theo)logic of the New Testament, which everywhere assumes the importance of Israel's history with God as the proper context for understanding the significance of Jesus Christ. The creation of the universe, the making of humanity in God's image, the human fall into sin, the calling of Israel to covenant, the priests, prophets, and kings anointed by God—the whole of God's Story was now told with a new twist and in a new light, "the light of the knowledge of the glory of God in the face of Christ" (2 Cor. 4:6).

The critical point for our consideration, then, is that the Story we have heard so far—a Story of divine love expressed in God's *Let there be* of the otherness of creation, of divine humility expressed in the willingness to work in covenant partnership—now moves to a new depth of love and humility in this One called the Christ. But what God does in Christ is not essentially unlike what God was already doing in creation and in covenant—emptying himself, sharing His love, creating partnership. For when God comes in Christ, He comes not in overwhelming divine splendor that squelches or negates human freedom; in fact, God does precisely the opposite by coming to us in a man, a covenant partner, a faithful Son who constantly prays to the Father, "Not what I will, but what you will" (Mark 14:36, NIV; cf. John 8:29). In other words, just as we have already seen that God's power is primarily *an empowering love of the other* and that His activity *enlists and enables partnership*, so now, in the person of Jesus, we see God's power and activity most clearly revealed in the freely offered obedience of this faithful Son, this covenant Partner (Rom. 5:17-19).

Such considerations give us the necessary covenantal context for Christ, so that we understand Him in terms of God's prevenient activity in the history of the Jewish people. There was one Gospel writer who was most concerned that his readers understand Jesus in precisely this way, and that is Matthew. It is not difficult, in fact, to read Matthew's Gospel as a narrative theology (or narrative *Christology*) in which the underlying plot is the deep significance of Israel's history for appreciating who Jesus is and what He means.

Israel's history with God is so important to Matthew, in fact, that he begins with it when he tells Jesus' story. He does genealogy as his opener. No modern publisher would let him get away with beginning a story with a bunch of begats! But this is not simply genealogy—it is historical and theological narrative. This is clear when, in introducing this genealogy, Matthew identifies Jesus as "the son of David, the son of Abraham" (1:1). To be David's son was to be an heir in David's royal line, and as we have seen, for the Jewish people King David represented the height of Israel's glory. When they dreamed of a messiah, they often had someone like David in mind—someone who would restore that glory, someone who for all his faults and downfalls was a man after God's own heart. Hence, Matthew's genealogy does far more than simply show that Jesus' legal father, Joseph, counted David as an ancestor. Rather, Matthew proclaims Jesus as Israel's new David, as the fulfillment and zenith of God's history with His people Israel.

In order to demonstrate this, Matthew begins the genealogy with Abraham, the beginning and foundation of the people Israel, and moves down through the history of Israel to the point of Jesus, "who is called Christ" (1:16). In contrast, the other Gospel with a genealogy, Luke, begins with Jesus and traces backward all the way to Adam. (We shall have opportunity in the next chapter to look for the Christological significance of Luke's genealogy.) But Matthew also divides his genealogy in an interesting way: from Abraham, the beginning of Israel, to David, the height of Israel's glory, he counts 14 generations; from David to the time of the Babylonian Exile, the depths of Israel's despair, he counts another 14 generations; and from the time of the Exile to the coming of Jesus, he counts yet another 14 generations. To read this literally (i.e., mathematically) or to worry too much about whether or not Matthew got all the genealogical details right is to miss the narrative point, which is that Israel's history is fraught with theological significance. Matthew sees God's providential hand at work throughout the history of Israel: from that call upon Abram to leave the comforts of home for an unknown parcel of land, to the glorious reign of King David, to the suffering and despair of exile and homelessness, to the moment of fulfillment in Jesus Christ. From beginning to end, in the best of times and the worst of times, whether recognized or not, God was always there, always patiently laboring, always directing the history of His people toward fulfillment in the coming of Jesus.

But we must give attention, too, to the second half of Matthew's opening designation for Jesus: "son of Abraham" (1:1). For not only was Abraham the beginning point of what would become the people of Israel, but also he was the one who believed God's promise that, in his descendants, all the peoples of the earth would be blessed (Gen. 12:2-3). Thus, Abraham is important not only to the Jewish people (through Isaac) and the Arabic peoples (through Ishmael) but to all peoples (through Jesus), as Paul argues in Romans 4 and Galatians 3. And this is a theological point also driven home in the genealogy itself; in tracing Jesus' lineage, Matthew does the unusual by including women—and not good Jewish women, or even just any women, but those like the following.

Tamar (1:3), probably a Canaanite woman, disguised herself as a temple prostitute and seduced her own father-in-law, Judah, giving birth to twins through that union and thereby continuing the family line of Judah's son, who had died (Genesis 38).

Rahab (1:5), a Canaanite prostitute, sheltered Joshua's spies in Jericho.

Ruth (1:5), a Moabite woman, cunningly arranged her own marriage to Boaz. (Moabites, according to the Scriptures, had their origins in incest, so that their offspring were considered impure down to the 10th generation.)

Bathsheba (1:6), wife of Uriah the Hittite, was seduced by King David and later married him after David had Uriah placed on the front lines of battle, where he was killed.

Why did Matthew mention women in his genealogy, and why these women? All of them either were Gentile (non-Jewish) or had some kind of Gentile connections, and all of them were of questionable activity. In each case, their sexual unions can fairly be described as scandalous, and yet through them God worked to bring the Messiah into history! Matthew is proclaiming the grace of God, who chooses to work through the likes of Gentile prostitutes and adulterers!

And so we see Jesus: Son of David, King of Israel, God's holy anointed One, *and* Son of Abraham, Descendant of unsavory Gentiles, skeletons in the closet. Truly Jesus' genealogy is a proclamation of the grace of God, quietly but patiently redeeming human life in entirely unexpected ways.

Furthermore, Matthew is the only Gospel to tell the story of the pagan astrologers (Matt. 2:1-12), thereby expanding on this theme of Jesus as the Son of Abraham. Matthew makes no apologies for God, who so often prohibited His people from practicing astrology, but who now in inscrutable grace works through the paganism of Gentile astrologers to announce the birth of a Prince. In the words of the Roman Catholic biblical scholar Raymond Brown, "The magi . . . represent the best of pagan lore and religious perceptivity which has come to seek Jesus through revelation in nature."[1]

But these hints of a divine interest in redeeming the Gentiles is clearly a backdrop for the central theme of Matthew: that Jesus lives out of, and relives, the story of Israel in His own history. His life is a *recapitulation* of the history of Israel, for He restates the theme of what it is to be a covenantally faithful child of God. And in fact, in passages that are unique to Matthew's Gospel, Jesus is presented as having understood His earthly ministry to be directed toward regrouping and renewing the people of Israel (10:5-6; 15:21-28). But if in fact the final goal of the Torah, or God's covenant with the people of Israel, was to make them a nation of priests for the sake of all peoples, then Jesus' embodiment of Israel's story could not help but finally extend beyond Israel's borders. This, in fact, is what we discover in the Great Com-

---

1. Raymond E. Brown, *The Birth of the Messiah* (Garden City, N.Y.: Doubleday & Co., 1977), 168.

mission, which involves making disciples "of all nations" (28:19, NIV).

But first things first: let us appreciate a few of the ways in which Matthew's telling of Jesus' story roots Him firmly in Israel's soil. Matthew is the only Gospel that tells us of Herod's attempt to be rid of the "King of the Jews" by killing Jewish boys in the Bethlehem area (2:2, 16-18); the Pharaoh's attempt to solve Egypt's "Jewish problem" by drowning Hebrew boys looms in the background. Matthew is the only Gospel that tells of Joseph and Mary taking the Baby with them to Egypt to elude Herod, and thus the only one who tells of their "exodus" from Egypt (2:15) back up to the Land of Promise. But unlike the first son, Israel, whom God called out of Egypt (Hos. 11:1-3), this Son, Jesus, lives a life of faithful covenant obedience.

There is no better evidence of Jesus' faithfulness to the God of the covenants than in His 40-day period of fasting and praying in the wilderness, fighting with temptation, all of which obviously parallels Israel's 40 years' of wandering in the wilderness. This wilderness area most likely would have been the dry desolation that overlooks the Dead Sea, stretching between the Jordan River (where Jesus was baptized) and Jerusalem. In the Hebrew Scriptures, this area of about 500 square miles is called Jeshimmon, meaning "devastation." It is extremely rough country: nothing but the sun beating down on dust, limestone, and jagged rocks. And here Jesus once again embodied the history of His people, wandering out in that wilderness to be tempted.

It is important to recognize two points about Jesus' temptations if we are to take these experiences truly as *tempting* for Him: (1) the options must have been appealing; and (2) the options must have been truly possible for Jesus to yield to. In order for the covenantal possibilities of relationship to be respected as well as fulfilled, it must be the case that Jesus *could have yielded to temptation.* Jesus truly had to make real choices out in that desert, and throughout His ministry, including that long night in Gethsemane that was to come. Yielding to those temptations, or sinning, had to have been a real possibility—or else Jesus' wilderness testing, not to mention His whole life and ministry, is nothing but a sham, a puppet show put on for our inspiration. If, however, we take Jesus' temptations seriously, it appears that the root issue with which He dealt in the wilderness, coming as it did immediately after His baptism and anointing of the Holy Spirit to do the work of the Messiah, was the method and means by which He was to fulfill God's calling and mission for Him.

The first temptation (Matt. 4:2-4) concerned turning stones, of which there were plenty, into bread. Jesus' own hunger pangs raised the issue of whether His mission would involve social reform and gaining followers by feeding their stomachs. Of course, there is nothing wrong at all, and much that is right, about feeding people; it is simply that, by itself, it is insufficient—for "man does not live on bread alone, but on every word that comes from the mouth of God" (4:4, NIV). But there is more going on here, the "more" of Israel's history in the wilderness. When Jesus quoted Moses' statement about living not only on bread but on the divine Word (Deut. 8:3), He was citing words that were "not, in their own context, addressed to an individual but to a whole covenant-people. . . . If Israel had been allowed to hunger, to be humbled, and to be fed with no ordinary food [but rather with manna], then ought not he who was repeating that experience also endure the same trials?"[2]

Jesus' second temptation (4:5-7) appears to have involved the appeal to achieve recognition and a following through sensationalism, through marvelous wonders that would catapult Him to popularity. Jesus again quoted the words of Moses, "Do not put the Lord your God to the test" (NIV), which in the original context (Deut. 6:16) refer back to Israel's wilderness experience of doubt in God's presence with them at Massah (Exod. 17:6-7). The appeal to sensationalism (the *National Enquirer* mentality applied to religious faith) does "put . . . God to the test" because it is rooted in unbelief, in doubt concerning God's covenantal faithfulness to be with us. Even in the wilderness, Jesus refused to put God to that test.

Finally, Jesus was tempted to compromise with evil in order to gain political and material power (4:8-10). William Barclay puts it well: "What the tempter was saying was, 'Compromise! Come to terms with me! Don't pitch your demands quite so high! Wink just a little at evil and questionable things—and then people will follow you in hordes.'"[3] Jesus once again responded to temptation with words from Moses, addressed to the people Israel, "Worship the Lord your God, and serve him only" (NIV; cf. Deut. 6:13). In this case, the words from Moses immediately preceding the quotation are worth consideration:

> When the Lord your God brings you into the land he swore to your fathers, to Abraham, Isaac and Jacob, to give you—a land with large, flourishing cities you did not build, houses filled with all kinds of good things you did not provide, wells you did not dig, and vineyards and olive groves you did not plant—then when you eat and are satisfied, be careful that you do not forget the Lord, who brought you out of Egypt, out of the land of slavery (*Deut. 6:10-12, NIV*).

---

2. W. F. Albright and C. S. Mann, *Matthew,* in *The Anchor Bible* (Garden City, N.Y.: Doubleday & Co., 1971), 36.

3. William Barclay, *The Gospel of Matthew, Vol. 1* (Philadelphia: Westminster Press, 1975), 70.

In responding to this third temptation, then, it appears that Jesus was reaffirming God's gracious gifts, given to whom God pleases and when He pleases. Jesus refused to do some secular calculation about how He might bring about better results in His ministry. In trusting in the goodness of the Father's will, Jesus refused to compromise and so simply allowed God in His good time and pleasure to bestow upon Jesus "all authority in heaven and on earth," which apparently was given to Jesus only after His death and resurrection (Matt. 28:18, NIV).

The inevitable question is, How was Jesus able to resist temptation to sin, not only during this 40-day period of fasting and prayer, but throughout His life and ministry? This is an important question for Christology, one that we shall take up in subsequent chapters. But for now, let us recognize that, just as Jesus embodied Israel and relived its experience in the wilderness, even more significantly He lived as a faithful son in that wilderness. For Matthew, Jesus was a new Moses, delivered from the Pharaoh's hand and brought forth out of Egypt; but Jesus was also the covenant Son of Israel, choosing to rely on the words of Moses—and unlike the wandering Israelites to whom the words were first spoken, Jesus *lived faithfully* by those wilderness words. Unlike the Israelites who wandered for 40 years and so often rejected God's Word spoken through Moses, Jesus relied on that Word and lived the life of a faithful, obedient Son.

We would do well to remember, too, that the Synoptic Gospels all report that Jesus faced His wilderness temptations under the leadership and empowerment of the Holy Spirit, by whom He was conceived and with whom He was anointed at His baptism. This enablement of divine **ruach** must not be forgotten when considering Jesus' life above sin—but such considerations move us to the following chapter.

17

Jesus Christ, "Truly Man": Spirit Christology

"In the beginning was the Word, and the Word was with God, and the Word was God. . . . And the Word became flesh, and dwelt among us" (John 1:1, 14).

"Jesus the Nazarene, a man attested to you by God with miracles and wonders and signs which God performed through Him in your midst" (Acts 2:22).

The above quotations represent two recognizably distinct approaches the Early Church took in telling the story of Jesus. One approach presents Him as God's "Word bec[o]me flesh," and the other as "a man appointed [and anointed] by God." While not inherently contradictory to one another, certainly these two ways of thinking about Jesus exist in dynamic tension with one another. Traditionally, the Gospel of John with its Eternal Word (Gr., **logos**) Christology has been thought to place the primary accent on Jesus' deity, while the Synoptic Gospels and Acts have been seen to emphasize His humanity. Or, in the parlance of contemporary theology, John's prologue gives us Christology "from above" (i.e., from God's perspective as the Eternal Word descends into our world in Jesus), while Acts gives us Christology "from below" (i.e., from the perspective of the disciples who were witnesses to Jesus' words and deeds). Like the strands of a rope that, twisted around each other, provide a strong cord, these two perspectives compose the strands of the theological tightrope of Christology: affirming that Jesus is *fully God* and *fully human*.

If we take seriously the historical and covenantal context for Christ as outlined in the previous chapter, though, it appears that neither "from above" nor "from below" is sufficient. Rather, in this style of thinking we call narrative theology, we must emphasize an approach to Christology that might be characterized as "from before."[1] In other words, an indispensable dimension of understanding and telling the story of Christ is to appropriate and appreciate the history of the people of Israel in relationship to God—a story and history that comes "before" the birth of Jesus, and in fact paves the way for His coming. We have seen that this was especially the approach to Christology taken in Matthew's Gospel, but the same principle holds true generally throughout the New Testament.

It is out of this concern to keep Christ in historical and covenantal context, as well as the concern to walk on the tightrope of Christology, that some contemporary theologians are arguing that a most fruitful approach to thinking about Jesus is what is called *Spirit Christology*. This theme, prominent in the Synoptic Gospels, is that Jesus' life and ministry are best understood in terms of the dynamic presence of God's Holy Spirit at work in and through Him in a unique and decisive fashion.

It is instructive to keep in mind that the biblical word "spirit" is a translation of the Hebrew term **ruach** and (in the New Testament) the Greek term **pneuma**, both of which mean wind, breath, or air in motion. The phrase "the Spirit of the Lord" in the Hebrew Scriptures, then, connotes God's own life-giving breath. Genesis tells us that God's breath-spirit, blown into the man, brought him to life (2:7). God's Spirit also brought life to the Israelite people, dividing the threatening waters of the sea during their Exodus (Exod. 14:21; 15:8). But the life-giving activity of God's **ruach** extends beyond the borders of Israel or even the existence of human beings, for indeed the Spirit brings order and life to all of creation: God's **ruach** moved over the surface of the dark, chaotic waters in the creation narrative (Gen. 1:2); again, God's **ruach** passed over the watery chaos of the Flood to allow the land to appear once more (8:1). No wonder the Psalmist, in reflecting upon God's relationship to the creatures of the earth, wrote,

> They all wait for Thee,
> To give them their food in due season.
> Thou dost give to them, they gather it up;
> Thou dost open Thy hand, they are satisfied with good.
> Thou dost hide Thy face, they are dismayed;
> Thou dost take away their spirit [**ruach**], they expire,
> And return to their dust.
> Thou dost send forth Thy Spirit [**ruach**], they are created;
> And Thou dost renew the face of the ground. (*104:27-30*)

---

1. Gabriel Fackre, in the revised edition of his book *The Christian Story* (Grand Rapids: Wm. B. Eerdmans Publishing Co., 1984), has already suggested that a narrative approach to Christology "might be characterized as Christology 'from before' rather than 'from below' or 'from above'" (p. 101).

The Spirit, then, is God's own life-giving presence, bringing order out of chaos—and chaos, as we have seen, is most often represented in the Bible by the image of chaotic, deep, and dark waters. The **ruach** is God's own Breath blowing over this formless void to bring the "solid ground" of life, structure, and the possibilities of relationship between God and human beings. It is precisely this same Spirit of God, according to the Synoptic Gospel writers, who was uniquely and especially at work in the person and ministry of Jesus. The title "Christ," in fact, means "anointed one" and suggests primarily the anointing of God's Spirit-breath-wind.

Keeping this background in mind, one discovers a rich Spirit Christology taking shape in the Synoptic Gospels, particularly in some of the most critical junctures of Jesus' ministry. Let us explore these moments in the story of Jesus as they shed light on the question of who Jesus was and is:

1. *Jesus' birth of a virgin through the work of the Spirit* (Matt. 1:18-23; Luke 1:34-35). The miracle of the Spirit's life-bestowing power is no more evident than in Matthew's and Luke's accounts of the Virgin Mary's conception of the Child who would be called Jesus. According to Luke, the angel Gabriel announced to this young Jewish maiden, "The Holy Spirit will come upon you, and the power of the Most High will *overshadow* you" (1:35, italics added). The verb translated "overshadow" would have reminded Luke's original readers of the Genesis creation story, where the Spirit was "brooding over" the chaotic waters. The second-century theologian Irenaeus recognized this imagery when he stated that, just as the Spirit of God brooded over the face of the deep, so also that same Spirit brooded over the womb of Mary to bring about the new creation, a new beginning for humanity through Jesus Christ.

Thus, it was God's own mighty and creative Spirit, the Source and Giver of life, who initiated new life in this obedient Jewish maiden. In recognizing this miraculous work of God's Holy Spirit, we are reminded that Jesus truly is God's gracious Gift to us, initiated by the will and work of God. Truly, the conception and birth of Jesus by the Virgin Mary is God's sign that He is "Immanuel," or "God with us" (Matt. 1:23). Jesus is not simply the best man the human race has to offer; rather, Jesus is the very fruition and fulfillment of God's redeeming activity in human history! To put it simply, the virgin birth of Jesus reminds us that it is by grace that we are saved, and not by human effort (Eph. 2:8-9).

Some philosophers and theologians have objected, however, that the doctrine of the Virgin Birth compromises belief in Jesus' real and full humanity, an important teaching of Christian faith and the focus of this chapter. Both the New Testament and Christian tradition have insisted that Jesus must have fully shared in our human estate, or He could not be our Savior. Consequently, some critics of the doctrine argue that it makes Jesus more than (or perhaps less than) human, or that it appears to remove Him from the stream of human history.

Perhaps the most fitting response to this criticism is that the two Gospels that tell of Jesus' birth of a virgin, Matthew and Luke, are also the two Gospels that include the human genealogies of Jesus. It is interesting that the two Gospels that go to great lengths to establish the real "family" connections between Jesus and His fellow Jews (Matt. 1:1-17) and between Jesus and the human race in general (Luke 3:23-38) are also the two that testify to His miraculous conception. Apparently the biblical writers saw no contradiction between Jesus' birth of a virgin and Jesus' real kinship with us!

It is interesting to note, too, that the Early Church placed as much emphasis upon the simple fact that Jesus was *born,* period, as upon the claim that He was born of a virgin. This was an issue because there were people who called themselves *gnostics* (Gr., **gnōsis** = knowledge) who denied that Christ, the Son of God, could have undergone such a bloody, traumatic, thoroughly human experience like childbirth. Gnostics denied the goodness of the created material order, and believed that Jesus, the spiritual Deliverer, only appeared to be human so as not to scare or to shock us creatures of flesh and blood. This sort of denial of Jesus' authentic humanity is called *docetism* (Gr., **dokeō**, to seem or to appear, as in Jesus seeming to be human). The Early Church, in insisting on Jesus' real birth of a woman at the end of the gestation process, was roundly rejecting the docetist claim.

Those early Christians found additional strong support for Jesus' real solidarity with us in the Gospel of Luke especially. For Luke also mentions that Jesus was circumcised in accordance with the covenants established with Abraham and Moses, and also that, as He grew up, He "kept increasing in wisdom and stature, and in favor with God and men" (2:52). We find, then, that Jesus underwent the normal physical, emotional, and social development of a first-century Galilean Jewish male, even as He sought and nurtured a unique and intimate relationship with God (Luke 2:49).

2. *Jesus' baptism as the initiation of His active ministry, and the wilderness temptations* (Mark 1:9-13). All four Gospels tell of Jesus' baptism by John in the Jordan River, and the dramatic anointing of Jesus by the Holy Spirit. In this regard, Jesus' baptism is reminiscent of the judges, prophets, kings, and even artisans of Israel's history, whose initiation into ministry often involved a decisive anointing by the Spirit of God. Even so, only Jesus is properly called the Christ, or God's

Anointed, God's Son in whom God is well-pleased (Matt. 3:17). It was probably Jesus' experience during baptism that Peter had in mind when he preached, "You know of Jesus of Nazareth, how God anointed Him with the Holy Spirit and with power" (Acts 10:38). The baptism of Jesus, though, was not an end in itself, but the initiation of His public ministry; Peter continues, ". . . and how He went about doing good, and healing all who were oppressed by the devil; for God was with Him."

The power of narrative symbol in the Gospels becomes apparent when one considers the possible meanings of the Spirit's descent in the form of a dove. The dove, along with the flame, has become a prominent symbol of the Spirit in Christian art and architecture. Less attention, however, has been devoted to possible symbolic meanings of the dove. One interesting biblical image harks back to the story of Noah, whose release of a dove signaled salvation for the ark's inhabitants. In this interpretation, just as the ark's emergence from the chaotic floodwaters was greeted by the dove, so, too, Jesus, emerging from Jordan's waters, was greeted. In both cases, too, the presence of the dove foreshadowed the dawning of a new covenant—the first marked by Noah's sacrificial offering and God's reply in the rainbow, the second by Jesus' offering on the Cross and God's reply in the empty tomb.

Another fascinating possibility for interpreting the Spirit's form as a dove is rooted in the primeval overcoming of chaos as proclaimed in Genesis 1. Jewish commentators had long compared the "moving" or "brooding" over the surface of the waters by the Spirit of God to a nurturing mother bird over her young in the nest. Based on the language of Genesis, in fact, the rabbis developed the imagery of the "wings of the Shekinah" (Heb., **shakhan,** to dwell; God's dwelling presence or Spirit), suggesting that God's Spirit was "brooding over the face of the water . . . as a dove broods over its nest."[2]

In this case, the imagery of the Spirit's dovelike descent upon Jesus draws the imagination toward the parallels between God's original creation of the world and His new creation initiated in Christ. God's Spirit-breath brings to life new possibilities for the redemption of the fallen creation. One might extend this parallel so that Jesus is interpreted as the new Adam, God's new Man, the re-creation of humanity in God's image through the life-giving anointing of God's **ruach.** Certainly this fits particularly well with Luke's genealogy, which is strategically placed immediately following the baptism narrative (3:23-38). A comparison of the genealogies of Matthew and Luke may be instructive at this point. For while Matthew begins Jesus' genealogy with

---

2. Talmud, Haggigah 12a.

Abraham and moves forward through Israel's history (see chap. 16), Luke's begins with Jesus and moves backward all the way to Adam, whom Luke boldly calls "the son of God" (3:38). It would seem, then, that Luke was inviting his readers to understand Jesus as a new Adam, the Son of God in whom God has begun creation anew.

The Synoptic Gospels tell us that Jesus' time of testing in the wilderness followed immediately after His baptism. While we have already suggested that the history of Israel's wilderness wanderings and testing provided the background for Matthew's narrative, it is likely that Luke, seeing Jesus as the new Adam who renews humanity, had the temptations of Eden in mind. In either case, the Synoptics all agree in emphasizing that the Holy Spirit provided empowerment and leadership to Jesus in this time of testing, and in fact it was the Spirit who led Jesus into the wilderness for that very reason. It is appropriate to suggest, then, that it was because Jesus was "full of the Holy Spirit" (Luke 4:1) that He was empowered to resist the temptations to compromise His messianic calling.

3. *Jesus' mighty ministry of deliverance* (Luke 4:18; 11:20). Luke, having repeatedly mentioned the decisive importance of the Holy Spirit's presence and power in Jesus' life and ministry, includes a story unique to his Gospel about Jesus' hometown sermon in the Nazareth synagogue. He has returned to Galilee "in the power of the Spirit" (4:14) and attends the Jewish worship service "as was His custom" (v. 16). Here He is given the opportunity to preach, and the passage He reads must be considered a central one for His own self-understanding. His text is Isa. 61:1:

> The Spirit of the Lord is upon Me,
> Because He anointed Me to preach the gospel to the poor.
> He has sent Me to proclaim release to the captives,
> And recovery of sight to the blind,
> To set free those who are downtrodden,
> To proclaim the favorable year of the Lord.
>
> *(4:18-19)*

Here, it seems, we are given a glimpse into Jesus' own self-understanding, His own consciousness of the meaning and motive of His mission. His is to be a ministry of deliverance, release, enablement, and healing—a liberating ministry empowered by the Spirit of Yahweh. Jesus' own understanding of himself and His ministry cannot be incidental to our own attempts to understand Him in Christology; hence, Jesus as the Servant of God, anointed by God to fulfill God's purposes, should be a key Christological theme (Matt. 12:18-21). No wonder the apostles in an early prayer referred to "Thy holy servant Jesus, whom Thou didst anoint" (Acts 4:27).

Similarly, when challenged by the Pharisees, Jesus described His works of exorcism in terms of the activity of God's Spirit (Matt. 12:28; Luke 11:20). Accused of having cast out demons by the prince of demons—a failure of logic if ever there was one, as Jesus himself pointed out!—He replied, "But if I cast out demons by the Spirit of God, then the kingdom of God has come upon you." Reasoning on the basis of Matthew's text, one may safely assume that the Spirit of God was the power at work not only in Jesus' exorcisms but in His healings and His teachings too—for He told His disciples that, in delivering their testimonies, "It is not you who speak, but it is the Spirit of your Father who speaks in you" (Matt. 10:20). Thus, the Holy Spirit is understood to be the animating power of the whole of Jesus' life and ministry. And it is by the power of the Spirit that God's kingdom comes, triumphing over the dark forces of hell.

It is interesting that the parallel passage in Luke 11:20 has the words "I cast out demons by the *finger* of God" (italics added) rather than Matthew's phrase "Spirit of God." This is surprising, since Luke generally is recognized as the Gospel that refers most often to the Holy Spirit. Perhaps Luke was attempting to stir a memory of "the finger of God" that the Pharaoh's magicians reluctantly recognized in the plagues (Exod. 8:19). In that case, Luke may be suggesting that the Pharisees who refused to acknowledge "the finger of God" active in the liberating ministry of Jesus come off looking worse than the Egyptian servants of Pharaoh. Finally, though, the phrases "Spirit of God" and "finger of God" are not essentially different, since both refer to God's own active presence in Jesus' ministry and, for that matter, in the Exodus event centuries prior to Jesus. In fact, the laws of the Sinai covenant were said to have been written by "the finger of God," which is, according to mid-20th-century Nazarene theologian H. Orton Wiley, "an expression which is interchangeable with 'the Spirit of God.'"[3] Phrases such as these all denote the powerful, living presence of God himself at work in our world. To say, then, that Jesus lived and moved in the power of the Spirit of God is to say that, when we look at His words and deeds, we see who God is and what God is doing to deliver human beings from the powers of oppression.

4. *Jesus' self-offering on the Cross, and His resurrection* (Heb. 9:14; Rom. 8:11). There is admittedly very little in the Scriptures that links Jesus' crucifixion with the power of the Holy Spirit. But if the claims of a Spirit Christology are correct, and the whole of Jesus' life and ministry can be rightly understood as having been empowered by the Spir-

---

3. H. Orton Wiley, *Christian Theology*, 3 vols. (Kansas City: Beacon Hill Press of Kansas City, 1940-43), 2:307.

it of God, then His self-offering on the Cross can, indeed must, also be seen as a deed done in the power of the Spirit. For Jesus' death on the Cross is not a sudden, absurd end to His life; rather, it is the zenith point, the eminently appropriate symbol of His entire ministry of sacrificial love. And here, as nowhere else, we witness that the nature of the power of the Spirit is not power according to the world's standards, which thrives on manipulation and heavy-handed enforcement of the desires of the one "in power." Rather, the power of God's Spirit finds its clearest expression in the bleeding, vulnerable figure of the Crucified.

Heb. 9:14 states, "Christ . . . *through the eternal Spirit* offered Himself without blemish to God" (italics added). In the words of the Scottish theologian Alasdair Heron, the Holy Spirit "is the motive and power of his dedication to the Father, which culminates and is sealed upon the cross. . . . The decisive actualization of the presence of God's Spirit in human life and history is encompassed in [Jesus'] offering of himself."[4] Jesus—living, moving, and giving himself through the power of God's own Spirit—thus *incarnates* or embodies God in the world, God's own long-suffering in behalf of the world.

But the New Testament rarely speaks of Jesus' death without also moving triumphantly to His resurrection, the overcoming of death's dominion. Jesus' resurrection from death was the heart and center of the Early Church's gospel message, and the glorious event that is celebrated every Sunday ("the first day of the week") when Christians gather for worship. Once again, in the New Testament we find a recognition of the role of God's Spirit in raising Jesus, for it is God "who gives life to the dead and calls into being that which does not exist" (Rom. 4:17). Paul, in fact, begins his letter to the Romans by identifying Jesus as one "born of a descendant of David according to the flesh, . . . [and] declared the Son of God with power by the resurrection from the dead, *according to the [S]pirit of holiness*" (1:3-4, italics added). Later in the same letter, Paul tells the Roman Christians that the Spirit of God (also called "the Spirit of Christ" in the same verse) dwells in them (8:9), assuring them that "if *the Spirit of Him who raised Jesus from the dead* dwells in you, He who raised Christ Jesus from the dead will also give life to your mortal bodies through His Spirit who indwells you" (8:11).

Paul makes it clear that the same life-giving Spirit who was active in creation, covenant, and Exodus, and who worked mightily in the conception, life, ministry, and self-offering of Jesus, also raised Jesus to new life and now bestows that resurrection life to those who open

---

4. Alasdair I. C. Heron, *The Holy Spirit* (Philadelphia: Westminster Press, 1983), 58.

themselves to the Spirit's presence, power, and leadership (8:14). The Holy Spirit is the very deepest self of God (1 Cor. 2:10-12) shared with us, poured out within us, to bring us new life and spiritual vitality. It is by this presence and power that, just as "Christ was raised from the dead through the glory of the Father, so we too might walk in newness of life" (Rom. 6:4).

We shall have occasion later to think more on the nature of the Resurrection (chap. 28). But in the context of Spirit Christology it is worthwhile to note that Paul, in his classic treatment of resurrection life in 1 Corinthians 15, writes that in His resurrection Jesus as "the last Adam became a life-giving spirit" (v. 45). Thus, Jesus' resurrection was not the resuscitation of a corpse to ordinary human life; rather, it was a *transformation* of Jesus by the Spirit of life into God's dimension of spirit, "the image of the heavenly" (v. 49). The Resurrection is the act of God's Spirit whereby Jesus became life-giving Spirit—and each of us after Him, according to Paul, shall likewise be transformed into a "spiritual body" (v. 44).

But in this chapter dealing with Jesus as a human being, it is important to stress that this transformation of Jesus in resurrection as "the first fruits of those who are asleep" (v. 20) does not involve a dehumanizing of Jesus. It is Jesus the first-century Galilean Jew who is raised and transformed, but not in such a way that His true humanity is lost or denied. The Book of Hebrews assures us repeatedly that "we do not have a high priest who cannot sympathize with our weaknesses" (4:15); hence, we know that Jesus has not forgotten or entirely left behind His experience as a suffering, struggling human being (5:7). A most powerful symbol of Jesus' continuing human presence with us—even as resurrected, spiritually transformed presence—is that the Gospels tell us that the resurrected Christ's wounds were still visible (John 20:27), still borne by our fellow Victor over death. The one who interceded from the Cross, "Father, forgive them; for they do not know what they are doing" (Luke 23:34), yet even now as the life-giving Spirit intercedes for us (Rom. 8:34). The poetry of Charles Wesley's great hymn "Arise, My Soul, Arise" says it so well:

> *He ever lives above For me to intercede,*
> *His all-redeeming love, His precious blood to plead.*
> *His blood atoned for all our race, His blood atoned for all our race,*
> *And sprinkles now the throne of grace.*
>
> *Five bleeding wounds He bears, Received on Calvary.*
> *They pour effectual prayers; They strongly plead for me.*
> *"Forgive him, O forgive," they cry. "Forgive him, O forgive," they cry.*
> *"Nor let that ransomed sinner die."*

The material of this chapter demonstrates that an important way in which Christians of the New Testament era understood Jesus and His ministry was in terms of the presence and power of God's holy, creative and re-creative, life-giving Spirit. The Spirit is God himself present and at work in the world—but in the life and ministry of Jesus of Nazareth, that Spirit is present and active in a unique and absolutely exemplary fashion. In witnessing the words and works of Jesus, *truly we see God.*

This chapter began with a quotation from Peter's sermon at Pentecost and will close with the same sermon. On that great day of the Church's beginning, Peter chose his text from the prophet Joel:

> . . . this is what was spoken of through the prophet Joel:
> "And it shall be in the last days," God says,
> "That I will pour forth of My Spirit upon all mankind;
> And your sons and your daughters shall prophesy,
> And your young men shall see visions,
> And your old men shall dream dreams;
> Even upon My bondslaves, both men and women,
> I will in those days pour forth of My Spirit."
>
> *(Acts 2:16-18)*

It is God's intention to give of His very self, His own Spirit, to all people. But God accomplishes His universal purposes through particular means, and Peter states that His means is Jesus! "This Jesus God raised up again, to which we are all witnesses. Therefore having been exalted to the right hand of God, and *having received from the Father the promise of the Holy Spirit,* He has poured forth this which you both see and hear" (Acts 2:32-33, italics added). There is no better summary statement of the purpose of this chapter, than that God's promise to pour out His Spirit upon all people finds its primary focus and fulfillment in the person of Jesus. It is He who first and best has "received from the Father the promise of the Holy Spirit"!

18

Jesus Christ, "Truly God": Logos Christology

The Church has reasoned well that Jesus had to have been fully human in order that we humans might be fully redeemed, but that He equally had to have been fully God in order truly to be our Redeemer at all. Thus, the logic of Christological reflection has been essentially motivated by *soteriology,* or the doctrine of salvation. It is because Jesus is our *Savior* that He must be truly God and truly human.

But in the New Testament, Jesus is not only Savior but also Lord. Probably the most profound instance of such Lordship Christology is in Philippians 2, Paul's famous *kenosis* (Gr., "emptying") passage. Here it is:

> If you have any encouragement from being united with Christ, if any comfort from his love, if any fellowship with the Spirit, if any tenderness and compassion, then make my joy complete by being like-minded, having the same love, being one in spirit and purpose. Do nothing out of selfish ambition or vain conceit, but in humility consider others better than yourselves. Each of you should look not only to your own interests, but also to the interests of others. *Your attitude should be the same as that of Christ Jesus:*
>
> > Who, being in very nature God,
> > > did not consider equality with God something to be grasped,
> > but made himself nothing,
> > > taking the very nature of a servant,
> > > being made in human likeness.
> > And being found in appearance as a man,
> > > he humbled himself
> > > and became obedient to death—
> > > > even death on a cross!
> > Therefore God exalted him to the highest place
> > > and gave him the name that is above every name,
> > that at the name of Jesus every knee should bow,
> > > in heaven and on earth and under the earth,

and every tongue confess that Jesus Christ is Lord,
to the glory of God the Father.

(vv. 1-11, NIV, italics added)

Many scholars believe that, in this passage describing Christ's glorious humility, Paul is quoting from a hymn of the Early Church. If this is so, it seems quite possible that the hymn itself was a song of adoration remembering a narrative in John's Gospel concerning Jesus during His last night together with His disciples. Especially if we remember that John's Gospel is a *logos Christology* in which Jesus' every word and deed, Jesus' very *being*, manifests God's nature, then the parallels between John 13 and this hymn that Paul quotes become fascinating indeed:

John 13	Philippians 2
Jesus . . . having loved His own who were in the world, He loved them to the end. . . .	Have this attitude in yourselves which was also in Christ Jesus,
. . . knowing that the Father had given all things into His hands, and that He had come forth from God, and was going back to God.	who being in the very character of God, did not regard equality with God something to be seized,
rose from supper, and laid aside His garments; and taking a towel, . . .	but emptied himself, taking the very character of a bond-servant,
He poured water into the basin, and began to wash the disciples' feet . . .	. . . [he] humbled himself by becoming obedient to the point of death, even death on a cross.
	Therefore also God highly exalted him, and [graciously] bestowed on him the name which is above every name, that at the name of Jesus every knee might bow . . . and that every tongue might confess that Jesus Christ is Lord . . .
You call Me Teacher and Lord; and you are right, for so I am.	
"If I then, the Lord and the Teacher, washed your feet, you	

also ought to wash one another's feet. . . .

"Truly, truly, I say to you, he who
receives whomever I send receives Me; and he who receives
Me receives Him, who sent   to the glory of God the Father.
Me."
(vv. 5-11)
(vv. 1, 3-5, 13-14, 20)

In John's account of Jesus' last supper with His disciples, he portrays the very Son and Word of God on His knees, washing His disciples' feet—including the feet of a traitor! This is the One who has "explained" or "interpreted" the invisible and mysterious God of all creation to us (John 1:18), the One who makes God known in His words and actions. Simply stated, the revolutionary portrait John offers us is of a Creator and Sustainer who is humble and gentle, a God with a servant's heart. This, in fact, is also the thrust of the Philippians passage under our consideration. Let us, in fact, return our attention to Paul's reflections.

Paul first of all appeals to the Philippians' sharing (Gr., **koinōnia**) in the Spirit of God (2:1). The same Spirit who anointed and empowered Jesus himself, the Spirit who is God's own outpoured and dynamically shared self, is given equally and shared among the Philippians (cf. Joel 2:28-29; 1 Cor. 2:10-12). The Holy Spirit, amazingly enough, is God's own deepest self poured out and shared among us. That same Spirit, writes Paul, is given to, and is at work in, every Christian. When God gives himself, when God pours himself out, He gives himself—His own Spirit! Koinonia is at the very heart of who God is, and the heart of who God is has been poured out upon Christ's disciples. Certainly, Paul is saying, the result should be that Christians, in whom this Spirit is at work, also now will live the life of koinonia.

Paul then offers an illustration of the kind of life he means—and the illustration is Christ himself. It is important to keep in mind that this passage, highly celebrated as one of the central New Testament texts to proclaim Christ's deity, is as much an ethical injunction for the Church, grounded in Christ's example, as it is a theological treatise. There is no better model of the poured-out, shared life of **koinōnia** than what is revealed in Jesus Christ.

Most significantly, Paul suggests it was *precisely because Christ shared in the divine nature that He emptied himself, poured himself out.* Some biblical translations suggest that Christ did this "although" He existed in the divine nature, but the Greek text makes it plain that this self-emptying, this laying down of His life, was not contrary to God's heart but in fact expressive of God's heart! Christ, being in the **morphē**

(Gr., "form") of God—the essential nature and character of God, the deepest being of God, or what God truly is—emptied himself! Precisely *because* He was in the form of God, He reckoned equality with God not as a matter of selfish grabbing but of openhanded giving! Or, to put it in terms of John's Passover supper story, it is precisely because Jesus knew "that the Father had given all things into His hands, and that He had come forth from God, and was going back to God" (13:3), that He "laid aside His garments . . . and began to wash the disciples' feet" (vv. 4-5)—the most menial servant's task.

The 19th-century Danish philosopher Søren Kierkegaard, in his classic little work *Philosophical Fragments,* compared the self-emptying love of God for humanity to a great king's love for a humble maiden. How might the king communicate his love without overwhelming the poor girl? But how much more the challenge facing God to show His love for us! Perhaps the king could get close to the maiden by putting on the garments of a poor beggar; but what about God Almighty? Kierkegaard's words are worth our while:

> In order that the union may be brought about, the God must therefore become the equal of such a one [as the object of His love], and so he will appear in the likeness of the humblest. But the humblest is one who must serve others, and the God will therefore appear in the form of a *servant.* But this servant-form is no mere outer garment, like the king's beggar-cloak, which therefore flutters loosely about him and betrays the king; . . . It is his true form and figure. For this is the unfathomable nature of love, that it desires equality with the beloved, not in jest merely, but in earnest and truth. . . . This is the God as he stands upon the earth, like unto the humblest by the power of his omnipotent love. . . . But the servant-form is no mere outer garment, and therefore the God must suffer all things, endure all things, make experience of all things. He must suffer hunger in the desert, he must thirst in the time of his agony, he must be forsaken in death, absolutely like the humblest—behold the man! . . . Is it then only the omnipotent wonder-worker that you love, and not him who humbled himself to become your equal?[1]

Yes, in emptying himself by taking the form or nature (Gr., **morphē**) of a servant, He was *precisely* in the form or nature (**morphē**) of God— the nature of a Creator who in love allows there to be a world that is truly "other" to God, a Creator who fashions human beings in His own image, creatures who can actually rebel against God and cause Him pain. It is the same God who stalked Eden with the question "Where

---

1. Søren Kierkegaard, *Philosophical Fragments* (Princeton, N.J.: Princeton University Press, 1967), 39-42.

are you?" and whose question finally became flesh and dwelt among us as a humble servant, washing the feet of a traitor.

Think of it: The Word that become flesh was born in a barn to poor folks, and in fact under the suspicion of illegitimacy. Yes, angels sang at His birth, but to whom? To dirty old shepherds, a low working class who were so distrusted that their word was not acceptable in a court of law! He began His public ministry by submitting to baptism—a baptism for sinners, signifying their repentance—and spent the bulk of His ministry rubbing shoulders with the sinners and outcasts of respectable Jewish society. In fact the Pharisees, whose identity hung more than anything else on with whom they would eat and with whom they wouldn't, were incensed at His willingness to sit down at the table to eat and fellowship with just about anybody! It was He who opened His arms wide and said, "Come unto me, all who labor and are heavy laden, and I will give you rest. . . . For I am gentle and humble in heart" (Matt. 11:28-29). It was He, as John reminds us, who took upon himself the lowliest task as an example to His disciples, that of washing their feet. It was He who, only a few hours later, was on His face in the Garden of Gethsemane, falling on His face in despair as He cried out in pain to His inner circle of disciples, "My soul is deeply grieved, to the point of death; remain here and keep watch with Me" (26:38).

And finally, it was He who trudged up Calvary alone, abandoned by His friends, carrying His cross. Crucifixion was an unspeakably harsh capital punishment the Romans reserved for the lower classes, mainly slaves. It was cruel and degrading, and the Jewish historian Josephus called it "the most wretched of all ways of dying." The victim was stripped naked, whipped until his flesh was bleeding and raw, forced to carry the horizontal beam of his own cross, and nailed hand and foot to its beams. He suffered from exposure, loss of blood, maltreatment by sadistic spectators, torture by insects, and impaired circulation, all of which together caused excruciating (Lat., **cruciare**, "to crucify") pain. It was a slow, agonizing, unimaginably torturous way to die. Crucifixions were marked by screams of rage and pain, wild curses, and the shouts of indescribable despair by the unfortunate victims.

Lowly birth, humble life, crucified, dead, and buried: at every fork in the road, Jesus took the path of servanthood. He emptied himself, made himself nothing, humbled himself, and was obedient to the point of death—even death on a cross. And the point of Philippians 2 is that this utterly downward outpouring of self reveals God's very nature. No human being can be dragged so low as to descend lower into pain and humiliation than Jesus has been. As we confess in the Apostles' Creed, "He was crucified, dead, and buried. He descended into hell." Jesus can go no lower, can empty himself no more, than what He has done. And though the usual confession of the Church is that Jesus is God, it is more precisely the case that *God is Jesus!* God shares himself with us, He descends to us, and He reveals His very nature in the self-emptying and humiliation of the Crucified One.

It is precisely at that lowest point, and from that lowest ebb, that God raised up Jesus; as Paul writes in Phil. 2:9, *"Therefore* also God highly exalted Him" (italics added). It is because He emptied himself, poured himself out, and continued to pour himself out in servanthood till He poured out His own blood on the Cross—it is because of this obedience unto death—that God has raised Him, and glorified Him, and graciously given Him the name above all names. The context suggests that this name or title that God has graciously and lavishly bestowed upon Jesus is "Lord"—Lord of all.

Jews of Paul's time used this word Lord (**kurios**) to refer to the Almighty, to Yahweh, to the one God of Israel. But Paul (again, perhaps quoting a hymn the Philippians sang) says that God has given that name to this humble Servant Jesus; essentially, the message is that God himself has poured out His own honor, name, and authority upon this One who was obedient unto death. Jesus bears the name of Lord because it has been conferred on Him by the Father, that at His name all will bow and confess that He is Lord, but most significantly, and often overlooked, that He is Lord *to the glory of God the Father!* In other words, God has bestowed the title of Lord upon the humble Jesus, but Jesus' own Lordship itself points back to God the Father and God's glory! Finally, the very attitude that Paul calls the Philippians to have toward one another is supremely exemplifed in the very relationship of mutual humility and self-giving between God the Father and our Lord Jesus Christ. Such lives of mutual love and servanthood can be enabled and empowered only as the same Spirit that bonds the Father and Son in love bonds the Church in love too; it is possible only if there is "any fellowship of the Spirit" (Phil. 2:1). In such reflections, it becomes apparent that the Church's confession of God as Triune—as Father, Son, and Spirit—is a commentary on what God has done through Jesus Christ to draw fallen humanity back into intimate fellowship with himself in the Holy Spirit.

It is on the basis of this Christian conviction that it is *truly God* who "in Christ was reconciling the world unto himself" (2 Cor. 5:19) that the Church from its youth has striven heartily with Christological heresies. Well-meaning Christian thinkers repeatedly have fallen off the tightrope of Christology in their attempts to describe precisely how it is that Jesus is both divine and human. Already in the late first and early second centuries, in fact, Christian teachers had to fend against the *docetists* on the one hand, who denied Jesus' true and full humanity, and the *adoptionists* on the other hand, who denied Jesus' deity and argued that He was a good man "adopted" by God by the anointing of the Holy Spirit at His baptism. To insist on Jesus' deity apart from an equal recognition of His humanity leaves Christians with God masquerading in human form, essentially unrelated (and irrelevant) to our human weaknesses and struggles. But to insist on Jesus' humanity apart from an equal recognition of His deity leaves us with a good teacher and example who perhaps reminds us of God—but who is not, and cannot be, our Redeemer.

We can briefly illustrate this important point by observing the pattern of Christological controversies the Church faced in its first few centuries. In the Church's first ecumenical council, at Nicea in A.D. 325, an influential preacher named Arius was condemned for teaching that the Word that became flesh in Jesus was not truly divine, but the first and highest of God's creatures. His theological opponent, Athanasius (296-373), the champion of Nicea, countered by arguing that if the Word does not share in the divine nature, then it is not truly God who has reached out to fallen humanity in Jesus Christ; we deal only with another creature, a being lesser than our Creator. It is only the One who created us who can also re-create us and redeem us from sin. Hence, Athanasius argued, if Christ is not God, then we are not saved—and we are also guilty of idolatry, since we worship that which is less than, and other than, God. It was on the basis of Athanasius' astute arguments that the Nicene Creed, written during this church council, affirmed, "We believe . . . in one Lord Jesus Christ, . . . God of God, Light of Light, . . . consubstantial [of one nature] with the Father, . . . who for us men and for our salvation came down and was incarnate, [and] became man."

In another council at Constantinople in 381, though, a young friend and aide of Athanasius was condemned as a heretic for having gone too far in his emphasis upon Christ's deity. Apollinaris probably differed little from Athanasius in his teaching about Christ; he probably was simply a little more explicit in his attempts to describe the interaction of the divine and human natures in Christ. Essentially, Apollinaris taught that while Jesus had a human body, His mind or reason was that of the divine Logos, so that He did not possess a human mind. While this appeared to solve the problem of the relation of the divine and human in Jesus, the Church's theologians perceived that it also severely compromised Jesus' real humanity. Jesus could not be part human and part God, like some heavenly half-breed; instead, the Church insisted that Jesus was (and is) *fully human and fully God* at the same time. For, as the great fourth-century theologian Gregory of Nazianzus insisted, our humanity is not redeemed in its entirety (body, soul, and spirit) unless the Word, God's Son, takes unto himself our humanity in its entirety. "If anyone has put his trust in [Christ] as a man without a human mind," Gregory wrote, "that person is himself really bereft of mind, and quite unworthy of salvation. *For that which [Christ] has not assumed he has not healed;* but that which is united to his Godhead is also saved" (italics added).[2]

One can trace this back-and-forth tension in the Church's attempts to safeguard the saving identity of Jesus in its subsequent condemnations of Nestorius in 431 (who apparently so emphasized the distinction between Jesus' human and divine natures as to end up affirming that there were actually two persons or minds in Jesus' consciousness), and of Eutyches in 451 (who taught that the divine nature in Christ "overwhelmed" or "swallowed up" the human nature in such a way that Jesus was God with a deified body). On the one hand, Christian teachers insisted, Jesus must be truly God in order to *save* us; on the other hand, Jesus must be truly human so that He might fully save *us*. Thus it was that the council at Chalcedon in 451 elaborated on the Nicene Creed of the previous century: "We confess one and the same our Lord Jesus Christ, . . . the same perfect in Godhead, the same perfect in manhood, truly God and truly man, the same of a reasonable soul and body; consubstantial with the Father in Godhead, and the same consubstantial with us in manhood, like us in all things except sin; . . . begotten before ages of the Father in Godhead, the same in the last days for us; and *for our salvation* born of Mary the virgin mother of God in manhood, one and the same Christ, Son, Lord, unique" (italics added).

While we must respect and appreciate the efforts of the Early Church to protect and define the identity of Jesus Christ as both our Savior and Brother, it is clear that the Church tended, at least in its creedal statements, to abandon the biblical pattern of narrative in favor of philosophical categories adapted largely from Greek thought. This in itself was not an evil; however, we should be aware of this shift as we attempt to understand the development of Christology. To their credit, it is arguable that the Church's theologians were attempting primarily to fashion a doctrine of Christ that would answer both the claims of the New Testament and the needs of the human heart. Both are addressed, for example, in the Tome of Pope Leo, a tract that was deeply influential in the above-quoted Christological formulation developed at Chalcedon. Leo's words are an eloquent commentary on Philippians 2, with which we began this chapter, and thus provide an appropriate closure:

---

2. Gregory of Nazianzus, "Letters on the Apollinarian Controversy," in *Christology of the Later Fathers*, Library of Christian Classics, vol. 3. (Philadelphia: Westminster Press, 1954), 218.

He assumed "the form of a servant" without the defilement of sin, enriching what was human, not impairing what was divine: because that "emptying of himself," whereby the Invisible made himself visible, and the Creator and Lord of all things willed to be one among mortals, was a stooping down in compassion, not a failure of power. Accordingly, the same who, remaining in the form of God, made man, was made man in the form of a servant. . . . For the selfsame who is very God, is also very man; and there is no illusion in this union, while the lowliness of man and the loftiness of Godhead meet together. For as "God" is not changed by the compassion exhibited [in the Incarnation], so "Man" is not consumed by the dignity bestowed [in the Incarnation]. . . . And as the Word does not withdraw from equality with the Father in glory, so the flesh does not abandon the nature of our kind. For, as we must often be saying, he is one and the same, truly Son of God, and truly Son of Man.[3]

---

3. The Tome of Leo, as quoted by William Placher, *Readings in the History of Christian Theology* (Philadelphia: Westminster Press, 1988), 1:74.

19

Jesus Christ,
Resurrected One

It may seem strange to place a chapter on Jesus' resurrection before a chapter on His crucifixion; there is, to be sure, no question about which comes first! Especially in an attempt at narrative theology, with its concern for *telling the story,* it may appear awkward to begin with the empty tomb before proceeding to the Cross. Yet this is one of those rare instances where the real intent of the narrative is best served by starting at the *end* rather than the beginning. For in fact, as far as the apostles were concerned, the Resurrection truly and profoundly is the beginning of the story of Jesus as the Christ, God's uniquely anointed Agent of salvation.

The apostle Paul demonstrates the absolute centrality of the resurrection of Jesus with a bit of narrative theology of his own in his letter to the Romans. In chapter 4, Paul speaks of Abraham's justification in God's sight by virtue of having believed God's promise to make him the father of many nations (see chap. 12 of this text). Though Abraham was old and deteriorating—"as good as dead," Paul says (4:19)—his faith remained sturdy. In the interests of making his theological point, Paul conveniently forgets Abraham's hesitations and even laughter at the idea of being such an ancient daddy; he simply asserts that Abraham "did not waver in unbelief, but grew strong in faith, giving glory to God, and being fully assured that what He had promised, He was able also to perform" (vv. 20-21). Abraham, even in his moments of doubt, believed God's promise, and "therefore . . . it was reckoned to him as righteousness" (v. 22). Then Paul makes the point of application to his readers:

> Now not only for his sake was it written, that it was reckoned to him, but for our sake also, to whom it will be reckoned, as those who believe in Him who raised Jesus our Lord from the dead, . . . who was delivered up *because of our transgressions,* and was raised *because of our justification* (vv. 23-25, italics added).

Here we find the heart of the gospel: Jesus on the Cross because of our sin, because of our rejection of God's love for us and His call upon our lives to love; *and* Jesus raised from death by God as *the* sign of our justification, or God's willingness to continue to love us even in our rejection, and to offer forgiveness and reconciliation to us. With this in mind, perhaps we can explore Paul's bit of narrative theology on Abraham a bit further.

Paul suggests that Abraham was *justified,* or brought into proper relationship with God, by believing God's promise to him. That is, the relationship between God and Abraham, like that between God and every human being, was a personal relationship grounded in Abraham's trust in God's word. Of course, any personal relationship depends upon a mutual trustworthiness, a belief by each person that the other is reliable. Paul then shifts from the Abraham story to the Jesus story, and tells us that, just as Abraham was brought into right relationship with God by believing His promises, so we by the same process are brought into right relationship with God. That is, God has made promises of grace and forgiveness to humanity, promises of love and long-suffering, through the person of Jesus of Nazareth.

If Jesus' life and ministry ended upon the Cross, then it would seem that Jesus' message ended there too. But God's resurrection of His Son validates Jesus' proclamation of a loving and forgiving God and in fact validates Jesus himself as God's *Logos*, God's Word of promise, to us. "For as many as may be the promises of God," writes Paul in another context, "in [Christ] they are yes; wherefore also by Him is our Amen to the glory of God through us" (2 Cor. 1:20). Jesus embodies the promises of God to us, thereby bearing the very validation of God's trustworthiness.

Paul is saying the resurrection of Jesus can make us certain of God's faithfulness. When Jesus died on the Cross, by all human calculations it was the horrid death of a blasphemer, the utter defeat of a charlatan's charade—or at best the tragic ending of an innocent and naive man's life. But if indeed Jesus has been resurrected to divine glory, then everything He said and did during His earthly ministry is divinely validated: His forgiveness of sins; His associations with tax collectors, prostitutes, and other assorted sinners; His kindnesses to despised women, Samaritans, lepers, and other "undesirables"; his breaking of Sabbath laws for the welfare of human beings; His teachings about a God by whom even the hairs of our heads are numbered; and even His accursed death on the Cross. The God who is faithful to the tortured Jew on Calvary has thereby proven His faithfulness to all of humanity. Jesus is raised *because of our justification* by God, because God is willing, in His Son Jesus, to take us in and love us with an everlasting love. The resurrected Christ is the validation of God's trustworthy word of promise!

In this regard, it is important to note that the Resurrection is always regarded by Paul, and almost unanimously throughout the New Testament, to be God's doing. In fact, once again we see God's work as Creator of all things through the prism of His historical acts of deliverance; He is characterized by Paul in Rom. 4:17 as the One "who gives life to the dead [Abraham in his old age; Jesus in His grave] and calls into being that which does not exist [the created order out of chaos]." Similarly, the very Creator and Sustainer of all things is characterized simply as He "who raised Jesus our Lord from the dead" (v. 24), and salvation is characterized simply as believing in Him who raised Jesus. The point is, God is identified first of all by His decisive act in history to save us—His raising of Jesus from death—rather than in some more speculative or general way. The God of the universe is known first of all through His Story of deliverance!

The gospel proclamation of the Early Church, as it is reflected in the Book of Acts, invariably holds the Cross and Resurrection together almost as a single event—the event of God's saving and liberating power in the person of Jesus. But there is no question that the accent falls primarily upon the Resurrection. For example,

> Men of Israel, listen to these words: Jesus the Nazarene, a man attested to you by God with miracles and wonders and signs which God performed through Him in your midst, just as you yourselves know—this Man, delivered up by the predetermined plan and foreknowledge of God, you nailed to a cross by the hands of godless men and put Him to death. *And God raised Him up again,* putting an end to the agony of death, since it was impossible for Him to be held in its power (2:22-24, *all italics added*).

> If we are on trial today for a benefit done to a sick man, as to how this man has been made well, let it be known to all of you, and to all the people of Israel, that by the name of Jesus Christ the Nazarene, whom you crucified, *whom God raised from the dead*—by this name this man stands here before you in good health (4:9-10).

> You know of Jesus of Nazareth, how God anointed Him with the Holy Spirit and with power, and how He went about doing good, and healing all who were oppressed by the devil; for God was with Him. . . . And they also put Him to death by hanging Him on a cross. *God raised Him up on the third day* (10:38-40).

> Having overlooked the times of ignorance, God is now declaring to men that all everywhere should repent, because He has fixed a day in which He will judge the world in righteousness through a Man whom He has appointed, having furnished proof to all men *by raising Him from the dead* (17:30-31).

And finally, Paul states it most simply before King Agrippa: "Why is it considered incredible among you people if *God does raise the dead?*" (26:8). And wherein does God raise the dead? Very specifically, in Jesus! This is the heartbeat of Peter's and Paul's preaching in Acts: God is the Life-Giver; God raises the dead; God has revealed himself to be so in Jesus. The importance of Jesus' resurrection for Christian faith is most obvious in 1 Corinthians 15, the *locus classicus* of New Testament passages on the Resurrection. There Paul writes,

> Now if Christ is preached, that He has been raised from the dead, how do some among you say that there is no resurrection of the dead? But if there is no resurrection of the dead, not even Christ has been raised; and if Christ has not been raised, then our preaching is vain, your faith also is vain. Moreover *we are even found to be false witnesses of God, because we witnessed against God that He raised Christ, whom He did not raise, if in fact the dead are not raised.* For if the dead are not raised, not even Christ has been raised; and *if Christ has not been raised, your faith is worthless; you are still in your sins.* Then those also who have fallen asleep in Christ have perished. If we have hoped in Christ in this life only, we are of all men most to be pitied (*vv. 12-19, italics added*).

What a proclamation! If Christ is not raised, then Paul and the other apostles are liars about God, because they have characterized Him as the One who raises the dead, beginning with Jesus. Conversely, if Christ is not raised, then those to whom the apostles have preached are still in their sins! When it comes to the doctrine of *atonement*, traditional theological reflection, at least in the Western traditions of Christianity, has tended to stay near the Cross; but here, Paul reminds his readers that, apart from the Resurrection, there is nothing particularly unique or salvific about Jesus' death. He goes on in the same chapter to call Jesus the Guarantee, the "first fruits," of a general resurrection of the dead.

This may be the proper time to acknowledge that neither Paul nor anyone else understands precisely what is entailed in resurrection, other than that it is God's own doing (1 Cor. 15:38). It is not simply the resuscitation of a corpse, along the lines of Jesus' raising of Lazarus. Rather, Paul states that Jesus has been raised with a "spiritual body," that Jesus as the last Adam has become "a life-giving spirit" (vv. 44, 45). The Resurrection narratives of the Gospels suggest that the resurrected Jesus certainly is the same Person who was crucified—especially when it comes to His wounds!—and yet in resurrected glory He is no longer limited in space and time (Luke 24:31; John 20:19, 26). It is the same Jesus, but transformed and glorified by God's life-giving power.

Perhaps more important, the disciples interpreted Jesus' resurrection as His vindication, as already mentioned. Most particularly, the Resurrection was seen as God's vindication and acceptance of Jesus' twisted and torturous death on the miserable and shameful Roman cross. After all, according to Jewish tradition, to die by crucifixion was essentially to die an accursed man. How could the Messiah be crucified? Paul wrote that this was a stumbling block to the Jewish people, precisely because, as a rule, messiahs do not go around getting crucified! Thus the Resurrection was, most profoundly, the divine vindication of Jesus' Messiahship.

In those earliest Christian sermons as recorded in the Book of Acts, there is not any developed theology of the significance of Jesus' cross, other than that it occurred according to God's own purposes, and that God had overcome human perversity and murder of this innocent Man by raising Him from the dead. But in Paul's letters we begin to read of Jesus' death as having been "for us," "for our sins," "in our behalf," and the Cross becomes Christ's deepest expression of love for us. But such considerations move us toward the following chapter.

20

Jesus Christ, Crucified Lord

Apart from faith in Jesus' resurrection, His forlorn and confused disciples certainly would never have thought of His cross as anything but an absurd and tragic ending to a great rabbi's life. In and of itself, there was nothing particularly unique about Jesus' being crucified; thousands of Jews suffered this most brutal form of capital punishment under the Romans. For that matter, at least two others were crucified with Jesus on His day of death.

But Jesus' shockingly unexpected continuing presence with His disciples, especially at the least likely of times and places (John 20:10—21:14), meant that the Jewish expectation of resurrection of the dead had begun to be fulfilled. The end of the age was upon them! Jesus' resurrection meant that nothing would be the same for them, that all was transformed and now seen in the new light of Christ's resurrection life. All was transformed, indeed, including and especially Jesus' horrible death on the Roman execution stake. What had been the unspeakable murder of an innocent man by the representatives of a politics of power on "the wooden instrument of a dreamer's death" now became the unique act of God's love, "the supreme altar of the Christian faith."[1] It will be our task in this chapter to probe the ways in which the apostles, and the Christians after them, have attempted to interpret the mystery of a Messiah crucified, the gracious horror of their Friend and Lord bleeding on the Cross.

Down through the centuries of the Church, theologians have continued to wrestle with this deepest of mysteries. It is noteworthy that there has never been a single "official" doctrine of the Atonement approved by church council or creed; rather, what we find are many dif-

---

1. H. Wheeler Robinson, *The Christian Experience of the Holy Spirit* (New York and London: Harper & Brothers, 1928), 78.

ferent attempts to view the cross of Jesus from differing angles and from within different historical and social contexts. Nevertheless, there has been a common thread running through the Church's understanding of Christ's *atonement* ("at-one-ment," being in accord): sin breaks relationship with God, but His love, a reconciling and forgiving love, restores the possibility or capacity for relationship. Holding tightly to this common thread, we will survey four dominant models in New Testament reflection upon Christ's atonement for humanity: reconciliation, propitiation, liberation, and participation. Corresponding to each of these models, we might suggest that Jesus is seen in a different light: Prophet, Priest, Prince, and Presence. This is a slight modification of the traditional offices of Christ of Prophet, Priest and King, a triad of titles that were important in John Wesley's understanding of Christ's atoning ministry. In this chapter we are adding a fourth dimension that has been the dominant image of atonement in the Orthodox traditions of Eastern Christianity.

First, *reconciliation* and *Jesus as Prophet.* To be reconciled is to be brought back into harmonious relationship, and the gospel proclaims that we have been reconciled to God—by God. There is never a hint that it is God who needs to be reconciled; it is always *we* who need it. The language of reconciliation, of mended and restored relationship, runs deep and strong in Paul's theology. For example,

> For if while we were enemies, we were reconciled to God through the death of His Son, much more, having been reconciled, we shall be saved by His life. And not only this, but we also exult in God through our Lord Jesus Christ, through whom we have now received the reconciliation *(Rom. 5:10-11).*

Paul even proclaims that God enlists human cooperation in the divine task of reconciliation:

> Now all these things are from God, who reconciled us to Himself through Christ, and gave us the ministry of reconciliation, namely, that God was in Christ reconciling the world to Himself, not counting their trespasses against them, and He has committed to us the word of reconciliation *(2 Cor. 5:18-19).*

Jesus as *Prophet* is an appropriate image here because the prophet speaks God's reconciling word to God's people. Jesus is Prophet *par excellence* because He not only spoke God's word, but He lived and embodied that word; He is, in John's prologue, that very Word of God in the flesh (John 1:14). Thus, as we follow closely the words and example of this Prophet, we find Him proclaiming in word and deed a God who actively seeks the lost, who loves even the (apparently) most hopeless sinner, who tenderly gathers the wandering sheep. And on the Cross, when this One gasps the prayer, "Father, forgive them; for they do not know what they are doing" (Luke 23:34), can there be a greater demonstration of God's reconciling love? If at the extremity of the Cross Jesus could whisper a prayer of forgiveness, is there ever a place or time when God's heart is not open, His arms not ready to embrace His wayward creatures?

In the history of Christian theology, one of the great representatives of this model has been the brilliant Peter Abelard (1079-1142), who is usually identified with what is called the "moral influence" theory of atonement. Essentially, Abelard argued that the greatest problem threatening people's relationship to God was their unnecessary fear of God, or thinking of Him as a vengeful monster who could hardly wait to smash them with heavy-handed justice. Abelard believed that Jesus' life, and particularly His death on the Cross, was intended to bridge the chasm created by human fear. The Cross was, for Abelard, a revelation of God's eternal love that holds the possibility of overcoming human fear of God. Thus, it was a moral influence in that, as we perceive the matchless love revealed in the cross of Jesus, we might be swayed likewise to love God and others. Jesus speaks a word of love, Jesus *is* God's Word of Love, and that Word, said Abelard, is sufficient to melt our fears and embolden our hearts to love.

Abelard's understanding of reconciliation is attractive for many because it celebrates the love of God, but others point out that it says little about the problem of sin. Jesus' death is said to be a revelation of God's love, but Abelard, his critics argue, never specifies *why* the Crucifixion bespeaks love. If it is not a death in which our sin is borne, then why is it a demonstration of love? If His death does not save us from sin in some way, but rather only calms our fears, is that a sufficient addressing of the human problem of rebellion and self-will?

Perhaps better to appreciate Abelard's theory, it will help to see it against the backdrop of the theory against which he was most clearly reacting: that of Anselm, whom we have met before in the context of the ontological argument for God's existence (chap. 3). Anselm's theory appears to depend most heavily upon the New Testament theme of *propitiation* (Lat., **pro** = forward, **petere** = go toward; to approach with favor), which fits well with the second model of *Jesus as Priest*. It is another word having to do with relationships between persons, for to propitiate someone else is to appease, to win over, to avert that person's anger. (Anyone who has ever made an emergency trip to the floral shop knows something about propitiation!) In the history of religions, propitiation usually has played an important role as those acts, prayers, or sacrifices whereby human beings made the deity or deities kindly disposed toward them, so that the worshipers would enjoy good crops, weather, or any number of other blessings. For the ancient Hebrews, propitiation was closely associated with the mercy seat in the Tabernacle, where a sacrifice was offered to God for the forgiveness of sins.

Again, what is significant and even revolutionary about the gospel is that it proclaims that it is *God* who does the offering! It is God who makes propitiation. Atonement does not mean that Jesus "buys God off" or persuades Him not to smash us; atonement is God's own offering of propitiation, God's own provision of a mercy seat, whereby we are offered grace. "In this is love, not that we loved God, but that He loved us and sent His Son to be the propitiation for our sins" (1 John 4:10). Here the depth of our sin is taken more seriously, and thus Jesus' death truly becomes the place where God deals mercifully and lovingly with us in our sin.

Anselm attempted to work this theme of propitiation into his theory of atonement in an extended essay titled *Cur Deus Homo,* or *Why God Became Man.* In order to do so, he spoke of God in terms reminiscent of the feudal lords of the time, a King and Judge who is deeply dishonored by human sin, and who demands satisfaction before He can forgive. Simply to forgive human sin, Anselm argued, would lead to "irregularities" in God's rule of the universe. Human beings owe complete obedience to God but in their sin have not paid what is due. Indeed, they cannot pay, but God cannot simply cancel the debt either. Essentially, as Anselm saw the problem, only human beings could rightly pay the debt, but only God himself was capable of doing so. Hence, said Anselm, the God-Man came and rendered the honor and obedience to God that was due Him; God in Christ "covers the debt."

Here the notion of *Jesus as Priest* comes to the fore because Jesus is seen as the intermediary Figure between God and human beings. "For there is one God, and one mediator also between God and men, the man Christ Jesus" (1 Tim. 2:5). His cross becomes the mercy seat, the point of contact and forgiveness. This theme of Jesus' priesthood is especially important, for example, in the Book of Hebrews:

> Therefore, brothers, since we have confidence to enter the Most Holy Place by the blood of Jesus, by a new and living way opened for us through the curtain, that is, his body, and since we have a great priest over the house of God, let us draw near to God with a sincere heart in full assurance of faith, having our hearts sprinkled to cleanse us from a guilty conscience *(10:19-22, NIV).*

Anselm's theory surely did take human sin seriously, and so understood Jesus' obedience, even unto death on a cross, as a priestly act of propitiation. In that regard, his understanding of atonement seems to have it over Abelard's. However, there is a danger here of making

God into a bit of an ogre who will not rest till every last drop of debt is squeezed out of humanity; it is the danger of thinking of God as One who can be propitiated, or rendered merciful, by human offerings or sacrifices. If it is kept in mind that the debt is one that God actually takes upon himself in Christ (something that, in the course of his argument, Anselm almost seems to forget), then perhaps this is no real problem. But Anselm's elaborate atonement scenario has given rise, unfortunately, to images of a vengeful God who must be constantly defused by a compassionate Christ who begs the Father to be merciful. It was precisely such images that had instilled such fear of God in the human heart, according to Abelard. Just as Abelard might profit from a dose of Anselm's recognition of human sin, so Anselm perhaps could use a touch of Abelard's appreciation for divine love.

A third approach to the doctrine of atonement is *liberation,* with *Jesus as Prince.* Here the imagery is that of deliverance, of freedom from bondage to sin, accomplished by a victorious royalty. Jesus has won a decisive victory over Satan, sin, oppression, rebellion, and apathy—and His weapon is, of all things, His cross! This is a dominant theme in New Testament writings, but perhaps most powerfully expressed in the letter to the Colossians:

> The Father . . . has rescued us from the dominion of darkness and brought us into the kingdom of the Son he loves, in whom we have redemption, the forgiveness of sins. . . . When you were dead in your sins and in the uncircumcision of your sinful nature, God made you alive with Christ. He forgave us all our sins, having canceled the written code, with its regulations, that was against us and that stood opposed to us; he took it away, nailing it to the cross. And having disarmed the powers and authorities, he made a public spectacle of them, triumphing over them by the cross (1:12-14; 2:13-15, NIV).

Here Jesus is the Prince, the royal Fighter in God's kingdom, our Liberator through whom all forces that oppose us are defeated. This model, to be sure, has always had great appeal in the telling of God's Story, for it engages us with its sense of drama and excitement. It has earned the title of *Christus Victor,* the victorious Christ, and has been celebrated in a book bearing that title and written by the 20th-century Swedish theologian Gustaf Aulén.

Aulén, in turn, cites one of the early fathers of the Church, Irenaeus (ca. 125-ca. 200), as having been a seminal figure in developing the *Christus Victor* model of atonement. Irenaeus spoke of Jesus as the Second Adam who, in His life and death of obedience, undoes or reverses the sin of the first Adam. It is clear that this understanding of atonement is essentially an extended commentary on Paul's comparison of Adam and Christ in Rom. 5:12-21; for example, "Just as through the disobedience of the one man the many were made sinners, so also through the obedience of the one man the many will be made righteous" (v. 19, NIV). In Jesus, then, there is a recapitulation of all things or, more simply, a restatement of the theme of what it means to be a faithful human being living for God and before God. Irenaeus, for example, pointed out that just as Adam had sinned by grasping at what was not rightly his on the tree of the knowledge of good and evil, so Jesus had poured out what was rightly His on the tree of His cross. Thus, Jesus provides in His faithful life and death a victory over sin, death, and the devil by undoing their power; He provides a restoration and even perfection of all creation, but beginning especially with those human beings who appropriate His victory through faith in Him and eating at His table.

This atonement model has particular promise for understanding Jesus' entire ministry, not simply His cross. Jesus is God's victorious Prince who conquers sin not in the forceful, violent fashion typical of earthly conquerors fighting battles. Though it is clear that many of His contemporaries in first-century Palestinian Judaism anticipated a heroic conqueror wielding coercive power, Jesus fulfilled a role precisely opposite: that of a suffering servant. If sin breeds sin, if violence begets further violence, then truly the only way to overcome the destructive downward spiral of sin in human life and society was precisely the route Jesus took. In the words of 1 Pet. 2:23, "while being reviled, He did not revile in return; while suffering, He uttered no threats, but kept entrusting Himself to Him who judges righteously." In other words, rather than becoming a participant in humanity's snowballing tendency toward hatred, suspicion, envy, and violence—in short, *sinfulness*—Jesus absorbed it all within His own person, and throughout his ministry, without lashing back. Thus, "He Himself bore our sins in His body on the cross" (v. 24), carrying our sin rather than contributing to its destructive force in human existence. All of sin's violence was spent and exhausted on this holy, loving, solitary Man.

In itself, this would simply mean the tragic murder of a guiltless saint. But the Resurrection signals that this Figure truly is God's victorious Prince and Son and that He lives to impart His sin-conquering power to those who seek Him. "For since He Himself was tempted in that which He has suffered, He is able to come to the aid of those who are tempted" (Heb. 2:18; cf. Rom. 6:8-11). If Jesus' ministry of self-emptying love, culminating in His crucifixion, brought a halt to the momentum of human sinfulness, how much more does His resurrection let loose a divine power in the world for the aggressive conquering of sin and death! It is no wonder that this atonement model of Jesus as Prince has exercised considerable power in the faith and imaginations of Christians throughout the centuries.

A fourth approach to atonement, bearing some relation to the third just mentioned, is that of *participation,* with *Jesus as Presence.* Here we encounter a model that has been most at home in the Greek and Russian Orthodox traditions of Christianity, but one that continues to exercise a justly considerable influence upon Christian theology in general. In this model, it is not so much Jesus' death as it is the *Incarnation itself* that brings about atonement. For the Incarnation points to the reality of "Immanuel," "God with us" (Matt. 1:23), of God's gracious "descent" into human finitude and suffering. God, in Christ, actually takes human nature upon himself and, in so doing, redeems it. Again, the Book of Hebrews seems to hint at such a view in these words:

> Since the children have flesh and blood, he too shared in their humanity so that by his death he might destroy him who holds the power of death—that is, the devil—and free those who all their lives were held in slavery by their fear of death *(2:14-15, NIV).*

One of the most prominent theologians to speak of the Incarnation itself as the saving act of God, whereby He brings healing to our humanity corrupted by sin, was Athanasius. As we learned in chapter 18, Athanasius was instrumental in helping the Church come to its earliest official statement in Christology, at the Council of Nicea (325). Here, and in subsequent statements, it was affirmed that by virtue of His deity, Jesus brings salvation and eternal life, and by virtue of His incarnation *as* a human being, He brings these blessings *to* human beings. Through the participation of the divine-human presence in and with the human race, God in Christ brings healing to our wounded existence.

Jesus as Prophet, Priest, Prince, and Presence; atonement as reconciliation, propitiation, liberation, and participation: these are the primary models by which the Church through the centuries has attempted to grasp the mystery of the Atonement, but even these do not comprise an exhaustive list. The great lesson here is that the mystery finally eludes us, for here, Christians have confessed for centuries, we come closest to a bare demonstration of the matchless love of God. How could such love be boxed in? Happily, we need not feel confined to choose one or two of the models to the exclusion of the others, for in fact it has been suggested often that they work best when held together in creative tension.

It is, nonetheless, no small miracle of history that this terrible instrument of torture and death, the Roman cross, has become to Christians the most profound symbol of divine love that will not let us go. In the symbol of Calvary's tree, Christians have confessed that ultimate Reality is laid bare, that God is revealed as the One who gives up himself, who empties himself, who pours out His life, and they have said in amazement, *"For me*—it is for me." Here is the great historical event in which, and by which, we confess with John, "God is love" (1 John 4:8, 16).

> We know love by this, that He laid down His life for us; and we ought to lay down our lives for the brethren. . . . In this is love, not that we loved God, but that He loved us and sent His Son to be the propitiation for our sins. Beloved, if God so loved us, we also ought to love one another (*3:16; 4:10-11*).

And so finally, the Cross is not merely the historical manifestation of the love and mercy of God but also the central symbol in the Story of God. It also symbolizes the attitude and direction of the Christian walk, of the Christian orientation toward others. To walk the way of the Cross is to walk in self-emptying love, in humility, in servanthood, in vulnerability. It is to consider oneself "dead to sin, but alive to God in Christ Jesus," just as Jesus himself "died to sin, once for all," but now "lives to God"! (Rom. 6:10-11).

PART VI

LIVING IN GOD'S STORY: THE DOCTRINE OF THE CHURCH

When we turn our attention to the doctrine of the Church, or *ecclesiology* (Gr., **ekklēsia,** called-out ones), we are asking questions about our present location in the Story of God. For it is within the context and historical traditions of the Church that we find ourselves in this moment, seeking to trace the flow, direction, and meaning of God's Story. It is, indeed, because of the historical Church that we have even been encountered by the main Character. The Church, before it is anything else, is a body of believers that, throughout the ebb and flow of historical circumstance, is gathered together by the God of all grace to recite the story of salvation and to worship the One around whom the story revolves.

The Church, this body of believers gathered to tell, hear, and live God's Story, transcends the normal human boundaries of generation and geography. It includes within itself people of widely divergent denominations, languages, cultures, colors, and historical eras. This variety makes for an incredible richness and diversity of expression in the Church's worship of the living God. Whatever we shall say in the following pages about the Church, its sacraments, and its transforming moments of encounter with God through Christ, it would behoove us to keep an appreciation for this diversity firmly in mind. The rallying point of the Church is not a common worship style or cultural expression, but none other than the God who has acted for our salvation in Jesus Christ and who has gifted the Church with His own Spirit.

It may be worth noting, too, that in Part VI, dealing with the doctrine of the Church, there are chapters dealing with the topics of salvation through faith in Christ, entire sanctification, and Christian existence or ethics. Furthermore, these topics will follow our reflections upon the Church. There are intentional reasons for taking this approach: first, it reminds us that the Church as God's society of the redeemed should have priority over our more normally individualistic concerns, particularly in light of an overemphasis upon the concept of the individual and his or her rights in modern Western societies; second, it reminds us that, whatever we might say about the individual Christian's experience of God, such experience occurs and must continually be understood as occurring within that larger society of believers in Christ, the Church.

21

Pentecost: Reversing Babel

We have already seen in chapter 17 that, according to Peter in his Pentecost sermon, Jesus is the One in and through whom God's promise to pour out His Spirit upon all people is fulfilled first and primarily: "And having received from the Father the promise of the Holy Spirit, He [Jesus] has poured forth this which you both see and hear" (Acts 2:33). For Peter, it is God's Holy Spirit, outpoured in and through the resurrected and glorified Christ, who creates and animates the Church. God is the Church's Origin, the resurrected Christ its Center, and the outpoured Spirit its vitalizing Power.

One finds essentially the same truth embodied in one of John's post-Resurrection appearance narratives. John tells us that on the evening of Jesus' resurrection day—"the first day of the week," which was to become the Church's day for gathering to celebrate Christ's risen presence—Jesus appeared in the midst of a locked roomful of disciples.

> "Peace be with you; as the Father has sent Me, I also send you." And when He had said this, He breathed on them, and said to them, "Receive the Holy Spirit. If you forgive the sins of any, their sins have been forgiven them; if you retain the sins of any, they have been retained" (John 20:21-23).

Here we find the living Jesus in the midst of His disciples, bestowing God's **shalom** upon their gathering. Then, just as the Creator had breathed into Adam with the **ruach** of life in the Genesis story, so the resurrected Jesus, "the life-giving spirit" (1 Cor. 15:45), breathes upon the disciples to grant them the life and power of God. As the Father sent the Son to be His ultimate Representative, so the Son sends the disciples in the Spirit's power to continue the mission of representing the Father. Indeed, Jesus appears to bestow a responsibility upon His disciples that Protestants have been reticent to recognize: the power to forgive sins! In any event, in the New Testament the Church is understood to be that gathering of believers who celebrate the resurrection of Jesus, who experience His living presence through the Holy Spirit whom He bestows, and who continue in the mission of service to the Father that Jesus has begun.

A number of biblical scholars and theologians have pointed out that the story of the Church's beginnings at Pentecost represents a distinct antitype to another biblical narrative, that of the Tower of Babel. It is not difficult to spot the parallels:

BABEL	PENTECOST
Now the whole earth used the same language and the same words. . . .	
And they said, "Come, let us build for ourselves a . . . tower whose top will reach into heaven, and let us make for ourselves a name; lest we be scattered abroad over the face of the whole earth."	And when the day of Pentecost had come, they were all together in one place. . . . all with one mind were continually devoting themselves to prayer. . . .
And the Lord came down to see . . . the tower which the sons of men had built.	And suddenly there came from heaven a noise like a violent, rushing wind . . .
And the Lord said, . . . "Come, let Us go down and there confuse their language, that they may not understand one another's speech." . . .	And they were all filled with the Holy Spirit and began to speak . . . other [languages, NIV margin], as the Spirit was giving them utterance.
Therefore [the city's] name was called Babel, because there the Lord . . . scattered them abroad over the face of the whole earth.	Now there were Jews living in Jerusalem, devout men, from every nation under heaven. And when this sound occurred, the multitude came together, and were bewildered, because they were each one hearing them speak in his own language . . . "the mighty deeds of God."
(Gen. 11:1, 4-7, 9)	*(Acts 2:1; 1:14; 2:2, 4-6, 11)*

The Babel narrative sets a stage in which human power and fame is predicated upon uniformity in language and locale. Diversity, in fact, is perceived by the protagonists ("the whole earth") to be a threat to the human project. And what is this human project? To build "for ourselves" a skyscraping tower whereby to "make for ourselves a name." This is a portrait, in fact, of the motivations underlying much of human culture: that a people's name, ideas, and accomplishments be preserved and passed on through artifacts and monuments of various kinds (art, architecture, literature, politics, etc.). Further, the picture we find in Babel is common enough: human culture being constructed apart from God, the purely human attempt to build a utopia symbolized in "a tower whose top will reach into heaven." It is important to keep in mind that the basis for Babel's manmade utopia was the embracing of sameness and the rejection of diversity—"lest we be scattered abroad over the face of the whole earth." This, too, is an all-too-familiar theme in human history. One need only to think of the Nazi and Communist attempts to create human utopia in order to recognize the threat of the totalitarian ideal that squelches diversity for the sake of a supposed "common good."

There is an ironic note in the Genesis story, however, in that God must actually "come down" to see this ambitious building project that was intended by its builders to "reach into heaven." Apparently it falls well short of its goal! The narrative graphically teaches that even the best of human efforts to build the ideal community, when undertaken without a recognition of and reliance upon God, fall well short of divine glory.

Significantly, the story attributes the existence of diversity in human language and culture to the very action of God in response to the presumptuous efforts of Babel. One can read the narrative as pronouncing divine judgment upon human pride in presuming to erect a monument to itself. While human beings have busied themselves in the attempt to make a name for themselves, all on the dangerous and tottering foundation of cultural uniformity, God graciously responds by gifting humanity with a marvelous diversity of locale, tongue, and culture. Humanity is scattered abroad, and Babel—symbolizing the human sins of pride and presumption—teeters under judgment.

Let us now shift scenes to Pentecost, following the ministry, death, resurrection, and ascension of Jesus. As the narrative parallels make clear, once again we find a people who have gathered together in a common project. But instead of a concern for making a name for themselves, this group is united by its devotion to God in prayer. Instead of the egotistical drive to build a monument to human ingenuity, at Pentecost we find a gathering of people whose driving concern is for God's will and glory.

Once again God "descends"—this time not in judgment, but in glory. God the Holy Spirit blows mightily through the disciples' midst, the rushing **ruach** bestowing the vitality of a new creation. And whereas at Babel God confused human language and frustrated the human attempt to build utopia, at Pentecost God's Spirit gave the disciples many languages in order to initiate a new people of God. The alienation of Babel is overcome in the reconciling power of the Spirit at Pentecost. Cultural differences are crossed, language barriers are spanned, and Jews from every nation, gathered at Jerusalem for the Jewish festival of Pentecost, hear "the mighty deeds of God" in their native tongues.

The harsh realities of human prejudice, hatred, and bloodshed have taught us that ideal community, the true utopia, seems always to be out of human reach. Cultural, political, racial, linguistic, and religious differences, to name a few, readily become barriers to authentic community. This does not mean that diversity is wrong; indeed, the Babel narrative attributes the development of diversity to Yahweh, the God of history. But it does mean that, apart from the revolutionary, transforming dynamic of God's Spirit in human life and society, the human utopia is only a dream. Peter, in quoting the prophet Joel for his text in his Pentecost sermon, indicates that it is only in the lavish, almost indiscriminately gracious outpouring of God's Spirit "upon all people"—sons and daughters, young and old alike, men and women, even upon slaves—that genuine human community may occur. Indeed, that early Spirit-filled community of believers, responding to the dynamic prompting of divine **ruach,** "had all things in common . . . selling their property and possessions, and . . . sharing them with all, as anyone might have need" (Acts 2:44-45).

It is obvious, though, that the gracious outpouring of God's Spirit did not, and still does not, solve every problem of human societal-communal relationship nor automatically usher in an eschatological utopia. But the New Testament clearly indicates that the gospel creates radically new opportunities for bridging the humanly constructed barriers arising from cultural or racial differences. Hence, while the self-aggrandizement of Babel's tower collapsed in alienation and ruin, at Pentecost God began to construct His own "tower," His own community, His own temple—a temple not made of bricks and mortar, but of human beings in relationship to God through Christ in the Spirit. The most powerful New Testament passage dealing with this profound ecclesiological insight is found in the letter to the Ephesians:

> Therefore remember, that formerly you, the Gentiles in the flesh, . . . were at that time separate from Christ, excluded from the commonwealth of Israel, and strangers to the covenants of promise, having no hope and without God in the world. But now in Christ Jesus you who formerly were far off have been brought near by the blood of Christ. For He Himself is our peace, who made both [Jew and Gentile] into one, and broke down the barrier of the dividing wall, . . . that in Himself He might make the two into one new man, thus establishing peace, and might reconcile them both

in one body to God through the cross, by it having put to death the enmity. . . . for through Him we both have our access in one Spirit to the Father. *So then you are no longer strangers and aliens, but you are fellow citizens* with the saints, and are of God's household, having been built upon the foundation of the apostles and prophets, Christ Jesus Himself being the corner stone, in whom the whole building, being fitted together is growing into a holy temple in the Lord; in whom *you also are being built together into a dwelling of God in the Spirit* (2:11-16, 18-22, italics added).

What is thoroughly remarkable about this passage, and about Ephesians as a whole, is that it is written from the perspective of Paul, a Jew, to Gentile Christians (the "you" throughout the letter). The Jew-Gentile relationship is a fundamental key to understanding the entire letter and this passage in particular, for its message is that, in Jesus Christ, the alienation between Jew and Gentile is overcome. It would be difficult to imagine a more radical message in first-century Asia Minor, for the gulf between Jew and Gentile ran deeply along religious, cultural, and racial lines. Yet the thrust of this letter is that God is erecting a new temple, a new dwelling place of the Spirit, that involves the fitting together of human beings who may be entirely different from one another.

For this reason Paul called the Corinthian congregation *as a whole* "the temple of God" and said that God's Spirit indwelt them together as a single temple (1 Cor. 3:16). In fact, when Paul warned, "If any man destroys the temple of God, God will destroy him, for the temple of God is holy, and that is what you [plural] are" (v. 17), the context makes it clear that God's temple can be destroyed by divisive attitudes within the congregation (vv. 1-4). A similar image arises in 1 Peter, where Christians are addressed as "living stones, . . . being built up as a spiritual house for a holy priesthood" (2:5). At Pentecost, God began building a new kind of temple, a new sort of tower whose top may not reach the heavens, but whose foundation rests on heaven's reach. We call it the Church, and it is still under divine construction.

Because the Church is obviously a human as well as divine institution, it suffers the usual frailties and ambiguities of all human experience and relationship. Nevertheless, Christian theological tradition has insisted that, because it is also a communion created and sustained by God's own hallowed presence, there are and always should be certain characteristics that distinguish the Church from other human gatherings or institutions. These characteristics traditionally are called *the marks of the Church,* and these marks are unity, catholicity, apostolicity, and sanctity. Each of these four marks is, in fact, readily evident in the passage from Ephesians just quoted.

The first **mark** of the Church, *unity,* points to Jesus Christ as the

One in whom all human cultural and racial barriers are overcome; in the words of Ephesians, "He Himself is our peace, who made both [Jew and Gentile] into one, and broke down the barrier of the dividing wall" (2:14). Jesus, says Paul, brings **shalom** to human hatreds, preaching peace "to you who were far away" (i.e., Gentiles), and "to those who were near" (Jews) (v. 17). It is possible that in referring to Christ's having broken down "the barrier of the dividing wall," Paul had in mind the thick and imposing wall that separated the outer court of the Gentiles from the inner courts of the Temple, where only Jews could pray and offer sacrifice. In any case, it represents a hostile barrier, such as, in the suggestive words of Markus Barth, "a ghetto wall, the Iron Curtain, the Berlin Wall, a racial barrier, or a railroad track that separates the right from the wrong side of the city."[1] How fitting that since the time Barth wrote those words, the so-called iron curtain has disintegrated, and the Berlin wall has been dismantled. Yet new hatreds, fears, and prejudices have quickly arisen to fill the vacuum, reminding us that only in Jesus Christ may such dividing walls be demolished, for in His community of believers they have no place. Thus Paul could write to the Galatian believers, "There is neither Jew nor Greek, there is neither slave nor free man, there is neither male nor female; for you are all one in Christ Jesus" (3:28). The normal human conventions for dividing and alienating people from one another are to exercise no role in the Church. Hence, when the Church is being true to its character, one of its distinguishing marks is its unity in Christ.

The second mark of the Church is *catholicity*, or universality, which points to the fact that all people (and peoples) are invited by the gospel to participate in divine grace. This distinguishing mark of the Church helps us recognize and affirm that all the cultural, linguistic, and ritual differences that appear within the many divergent historical expressions of Christian faith have a legitimate place. An urban black Protestant service, for example, is noticeably different from a Russian Baptist meeting. What unites these various groups into a catholic body is, quite simply, that "through Him [Christ] we both [or all] have our access in one Spirit to the Father" (Eph. 2:18). To the Father, through the Son, in the Spirit: this is the theo-logic of Christian worship and prayer in which the Church's universality is grounded.

It is important to note that this "order of worship" of the Church universal is governed by a trinitarian vision of God. More significantly, the Church's doctrine of the Trinity is not first of all an abstract or speculative doctrine having to do with mathematical gymnastics ("one

---

1. Markus Barth, *Ephesians 1—3*, Vol. 34 of the *Anchor Bible* (Garden City, N.Y.: Doubleday & Co., 1981), 263; cf. also 283-85.

in three" or vice versa), but rather the Church's grateful confession concerning how God has acted in history to redeem humanity. Just as God has reached out in love to us in Jesus Christ and gathered us to himself by the drawing power of His own Holy Spirit, so in return Christians render thanks to God through (or in the name of) Jesus Christ and in the same power and presence of the Spirit. The following diagram may help to illustrate the centrality of the doctrine of the Triune God to the Church's experience of prayer and worship:

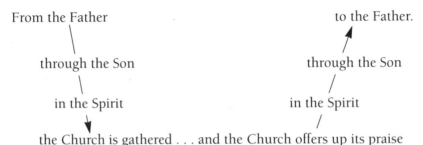

From the Father   to the Father.

through the Son   through the Son

in the Spirit   in the Spirit

the Church is gathered . . . and the Church offers up its praise

This Jesus God raised up again, which we are all witnesses. Therefore having been exalted to the right hand of God, and having received from the Father the promise of the Holy Spirit, He has poured forth this which you both see and hear (*Acts 2:32-33*).

And He came and preached peace to you who were far away, and peace to those who were near; for through Him we [all] have our access in one Spirit to the Father. . . . always giving thanks for all things in the name of our Lord Jesus Christ to God, even the Father (*Eph. 2:17-18; 5:20*).

The doctrine of the Trinity, then, is the Church's story of God as He has labored for our salvation in history. Thus Paul writes to the Corinthian congregation, "Now He who establishes us with you in Christ and anointed us is God, who also sealed us and gave us the Spirit in our hearts as a pledge" (2 Cor. 1:21-22). *It is God himself who has acted decisively for our salvation,* reconciling the world to himself in Christ (5:19) and sharing His own deepest self with us by His Spirit (1 Cor. 2:10-12). No wonder Paul, in reflecting upon the spiritual gifts of the Church, wrote, "Now there are *varieties of gifts,* but the *same Spirit.* And there are *varieties of ministries,* and the *same Lord.* And there are *varieties of effects,* but the *same God who works all things in all persons*" (12:4-6, italics added). The doctrine of the Trinity describes the one dynamic God's self-giving activity whereby He has brought the Church into being and sustains it by the person of the Lord in the presence of the Spirit. And because it is the one Trinitarian God who works throughout the Church's many historical expressions, its catholicity need not and does not depend upon itself or its institutions and traditions, but upon God himself.

The third mark of the Church is *apostolicity*, or its faithfulness to the apostolic preaching of the New Testament. The Church, in the words of Ephesians, is "built upon the foundation of the apostles" (2:20) as those who have rightly interpreted the person, words, and works of Jesus by the inspiration of the Holy Spirit. While Roman Catholic tradition has understood apostolicity to imply a direct institutional line from Peter through the papal line down to the present-day ecclesiastical hierarchy, Protestantism has interpreted it to refer to faithfulness to the apostles' message. Hence, Luther and especially Calvin tended to identify the authentic Church as occurring wherever the Word was rightly preached and the sacraments rightly administered. The "rightly" in both cases was judged on the basis of adherence to New Testament examples. We can therefore "rightly" understand these characteristically Protestant emphases upon Word and sacrament as subsumed under the mark of apostolicity.

Finally, the fourth mark of the Church is *sanctity* or holiness, a sanctity the Church does not have in itself but only by virtue of its relationship to the holy God. Again in the words of Ephesians, "in [Christ] the whole building, being fitted together is growing into a holy temple in the Lord; . . . a dwelling of God in the Spirit" (2:21-22). In biblical thought, a temple is holy both because it is set apart for God's purposes and because it is His place of dwelling. Whatever is set apart by God and used by God is, by virtue of that relationship to God, holy. The Church is the community composed of believers who are urged continually "to present your bodies a living and holy sacrifice" (Rom. 12:1). In the passage that follows that admonition, Paul offers what this holiness means in practical, everyday relationships and living: humility (v. 3), enthusiastic and willing service (vv. 4-8), love, joy, prayer, hospitality, sympathy, peace, and goodness, to name a few characteristics. In sum, the model of sanctity for the Church is none other than Jesus, and it is by a mutual sharing in the one Spirit of God, who also anointed and empowered Jesus, that the Church may indeed "have this attitude . . . which was also in Christ Jesus" (Phil. 2:1-5).

There can be no illusion about the Church perfectly, or even usually very adequately, manifesting these four marks. Certainly these marks indicate the ideal community toward which God calls the Church and empowers it, but the fulfillment of His purposes for His eschatological community awaits the glorious consummation of all things. Nonetheless, in the Church and its fellowship there ought to be a glimpse of heaven, a foretaste of divine glory, in worship, service, and love.

22

Sacraments:
Acting the Story

One of the important themes that resounds throughout the Story of God is that this created order is good—it is the good creation of a good God. Christians join with Jews and Muslims in embracing a doctrine of creation that includes a ringing affirmation that the physical world is not inferior or evil, but in fact manifests the good and loving purposes of God. However, Christians go beyond the doctrine of creation when they confess their belief that, in Jesus Christ, God the Creator has become God our Savior. In the doctrine of the Incarnation—the distinctively Christian belief that the very *Logos* of God, God's Word who shares in His essential being, has become a human being and lived among us—there is an even deeper recognition of the goodness and sanctity of the created order. If God, in Christ, truly has come and shared in our creaturely existence in this world, then flesh and blood, water and bread, dirt, rocks and plants, and everything else really are to be cherished and celebrated. Think again on John's prologue:

> Through him all things were made; without him nothing was made
> that has been made.
> In him was life, and that life was the light of [humanity]. . . .
> The true light that gives light to every man was coming into the
> world.
> He was in the world, and though the world was made through him,
> the world did not recognize him. . . .
> The Word became flesh, and made his dwelling among us.
> We have seen his glory, the glory of the One and Only, who came
> from the Father, full of grace and truth.
>
> *(John 1:3-4, 9-10, 14, NIV)*

The very logic of the Incarnation, as explored in John 1, affirms God's willingness to "rub shoulders" with us within the finite realities of the created order; salvation is not a matter of our escaping the

176

world—it is a matter of God's entering into His world to redeem it, to win it back to himself. The physical world is not to be spurned or belittled but appreciated not only as God's creation but also as the realm in which God has become incarnate in Jesus Christ. The doctrines of both creation and Incarnation tell us it is acceptable and good ("*very* good," in fact) for us to be finite, physical creatures within God's creation.

We are physical beings, and we exist in a physical world—and it is good! The sacraments (Lat., **sacer** = holy) of the Church are an important means by which most Christians affirm that God not only creates the physical realm but also operates in and through it, blessing it with His own holy presence. In the use of the sacraments, most Christians affirm that the created order is not a roadblock or a hurdle to overcome in reaching God; rather, it is His handiwork and thus a way in which the Creator can touch us with grace. No wonder the Anglican Book of Common Prayer, the worship manual John Wesley used, calls the sacraments a "means whereby we receive grace," for surely the creaturely elements of water (in baptism) and bread and wine (in Communion) can become channels of the grace that would touch our lives at a more profound level than a sermon or lecture can. Human beings are more than brains that hear and process words and ideas; we are also physical, emotional, and aesthetic creatures who are capable of physically experiencing love and joy in the deepest reaches of our being. Thus the Book of Common Prayer goes on to say that the sacraments are a "pledge to assure us [of grace]," meaning that they provide a physical reassurance, a bodily promise. They are, we might say, an important means by which God "gets in touch" with us physically.

To be sure, I have mentioned that most Christians understand and practice the sacraments in this way, because not all do. The most prominent Christian group in this category are the Quakers, founded by the 17th-century Englishman George Fox, who believe that practices such as baptism and the Lord's Supper are to be understood and practiced only in spiritual terms and on a spiritual level. On the other extreme, the Roman Catholic church historically has affirmed the sacramental value of many religious rites; the number of sacraments has been as high as 30 but now stands at 7 (baptism, confirmation, the Eucharist or Communion, holy matrimony, ordination, confession or penance, and extreme unction or priestly blessing at the time of death). Most Protestant denominations, including those of the Wesleyan tradition, uphold the recognition of two sacraments: baptism and Communion.

Debating the number of authentic sacraments, however, is not nearly so important as recognizing the importance of what is called *sacramental theology* in the hearing and telling of the Story of God. To those who deny or belittle the importance of Christian participation in these rituals of physical symbolism, a sacramental approach to theology answers that the water and wine and bread of this world draw us into a Story that truly has occurred in this world and in human history. Christianity is not simply a list of spiritual principles or a set of ideals; rather, it involves the recitation and celebration of particular events in our world in which we believe God has acted decisively for our salvation. Far from being empty rituals, those sacraments help us to relive, and to physically experience, those redemptive historical events in this world. In the sacraments we reenact the Story! Sacramental theology encourages us to see that if indeed God has acted decisively in this world for our salvation by actually entering into and sharing in our creaturely existence through Christ, then in some important way[s] the entire created order—all of God's world!—is capable of being transparent to God's creative and redemptive presence, of being at least occasionally a "means of grace" to us if we are open and perceptive. For example, while Protestantism historically has not considered the marriage relationship a sacrament, many Protestant theologians happily affirm the potentially sacramental character of marriage: that husband and wife, in their relationship of mutual love and caring, can serve as means whereby God's gracious, loving presence can deeply touch each other's lives.[1]

Surely Jesus has encouraged a sacramental sensitivity toward God's creation, particularly in His many teachings that drew their illustrations from the created order: mustard seeds and farmers, lilies of the field and birds of the air, sunshine and rain. Jesus obviously felt that the created order was fully capable of providing profound ways of appreciating God's sustaining love and presence (Matt. 5:44-45). And when Jesus taught His disciples that not even a sparrow "will fall to the ground apart from your Father" (10:29), He certainly was affirming the sacramental presence of the Creator throughout all elements of creation, from the greatest to the least.

If there is this larger sacramental sense in which we are encouraged to appreciate all of creation as a potential "means whereby we receive [grace]," a "pledge to assure us thereof," that general sense is for the Christian rooted and grounded in the particulars of Jesus' life and ministry. More specifically, Protestants historically have insisted that a sacrament, in order to *be* a sacrament, must be closely associated with Jesus' own acts and words. Certainly it is for this reason that some

---

1. For example of this tendency in one Wesleyan scholar, and for further reading in this subject in general, see Rob Staples' *Outward Sign and Inward Grace: The Place of Sacraments in Wesleyan Spirituality* (Kansas City: Beacon Hill Press of Kansas City, 1991).

Protestant Christians insist on foot washing as a third sacrament along with baptism and the Lord's Supper (John 13:12-15). We shall, however, focus on these latter two rituals, which have traditionally been identified among Protestants as sacraments and which are identified as such in the Wesleyan theological tradition.

First is *baptism,* which is often called the sacrament of the beginning of Christian life. The most highly developed New Testament theology of baptism is offered by Paul the apostle in his letter to the Romans. There, he argues that baptism is a reenactment of Jesus' own death and resurrection, whereby the believer is united with Christ. In baptism, then, the believer identifies with the story of Jesus' death and resurrection as his or her radically new way of thinking and being. "Therefore we have been buried with Him through baptism into death," he writes, "in order that as Christ was raised from the dead through the glory of the Father, so we too might walk in newness of life" (Rom. 6:4). Jesus' death "to sin, once for all" (v. 10) at Calvary is seen to be the pattern for our own death to sin, and His resurrection signals the transforming reality of our being "alive to God in Christ Jesus" (vv. 10-11).

It would appear that, given this symbolism, baptism by immersion would be the preferred mode. But Paul himself varies his baptismal imagery, writing to the Corinthians that "we were all baptized into one body . . . by one Spirit" (1 Cor. 12:13). Here the picture in Paul's mind is not that of Jesus' death, burial, and resurrection, but of God's outpoured Spirit—an image that is reflected in baptism by sprinkling. These two examples, which could probably be multiplied, suggest a variety in baptismal symbolism, providing a warning against an overly strict or legalistic approach to the questions of baptismal mode. Perhaps this is why the Church, in its majority traditions throughout history, has maintained an openness toward the manner or modes of baptism.

Of course, with either of the above-mentioned Pauline images for baptism, Jesus still is the focus. For if the Romans imagery suggests His death, burial, and resurrection, the Corinthians imagery suggests His own unique anointing by God's Spirit, most powerfully narrated in the Gospels in the baptism accounts. Here, in fact, we find the primary justification for Christian baptism: Jesus himself was baptized and later commanded His disciples to baptize in the name of the Father, the Son, and the Holy Spirit (Matt. 28:19). But if our own baptism involves an identification with Jesus, it is noteworthy that His baptism is, in obedience to the will of His Heavenly Father, an act of identification with us as sinners.

Recall that John the Baptizer, Jesus' cousin, was a wilderness preacher who attracted the city crowds to the Jordan River with his thunderous sermons on repentance from sin. His was, according to Mark's Gospel, "a baptism of repentance for the forgiveness of sins" (1:4). Since up to that point the rite of baptism had been largely reserved for Gentile converts into Judaism, John's was a radical message and demand. "And do not suppose that you can say to yourselves, 'We have Abraham for our father'; for I say to you, that God is able from these stones to raise up children to Abraham," chided the Baptizer (Matt. 3:9). He had retreated into the wilderness as a sign of judgment against the wickedness of the cities, especially Jerusalem, and was calling his fellow Israelites back, in a sense, to their ancestors' wilderness wanderings experience of radical trust in God. He was preparing them, he said, for the coming of the Messiah, who would "gather His wheat into the barn," but who would also "burn up the chaff with unquenchable fire" (v. 12). This fiery wilderness prophet had a fire-and-brimstone message of repentance from sin, preparing the children of Abraham for the soon coming of God's kingdom.

And Jesus came to be baptized. The Holy One, who "knew no sin" (2 Cor. 5:21; cf. 1 Pet. 2:22), willingly went down to the Jordan to receive this baptism of repentance from sin, administered by the mountain prophet. In this act we see Jesus' act of identification with sinners, and it is no coincidence that this marked the official beginning of His ministry—a ministry that, after all, would be characterized by an identification with the sinners, the outcasts, the personae non gratae of first-century Jewish society. We can draw a straight line between Jesus' act of identification with sinners at His baptism, all the way through His ministry to His crucifixion between two thieves. For it is through His identification with us in compassionate, empathic love that Jesus seeks and saves the lost.

In baptism, the new Christian signifies that this same Jesus has indeed found him or her. Just as Jesus was baptized in identification with us in our *sin and lostness,* so also our baptism unites us with Him in His Spirit-anointed *death and resurrection.* His identification with sinners led Him ultimately to the Cross, where indeed we have discovered grace and forgiveness for our sin, and enablement to die to its power as we in turn identify with Him. The rite of baptism, then, involves our immersion into the critical moments of Jesus' own story, and making that story our own through symbolic action—an action that itself is baptized in the Holy Spirit of God.

If baptism is the sacrament of initiation into Christian life, then *the Lord's Supper,* or *Communion,* is the sacrament of sustenance and nurture of Christian life. Though some Christian denominations have restricted its *communicants* to those who are officially members of the denomination, churches in the Wesleyan tradition generally have maintained what is called an "open Communion." This means that such Communion observances are open even to those who are not official members, and the only requirement is true repentance and a sincere intention to love and follow Christ. But while this supper is normally considered a sacrament of sustenance for the person who is already a Christian (and hence, at least in principle, already baptized), Wesley, who encouraged his Methodists to participate in Communion as often as possible, recognized that Communion could also serve as a "converting ordinance," or the occasion of a person's conversion. If Wesley was correct, then it is generally unwise for those who administer the supper to make decisions about who is eligible to partake therein and who is not. One might, in fact, point to Jesus' radically open table fellowship during His ministry—another obvious indication of His identification with sinners—as evidence that His table probably is yet open to those who come to Him recognizing their need of forgiveness and grace.

Even allowing that Jesus' unorthodox table fellowship with prostitutes, tax collectors, and the like might shed new light on Communion, there is no question that it is His final meal with His disciples that should come to mind first in our reflections upon this sacrament. Of course, this powerful reenactment of Jesus' last supper in company with His closest friends bears an intimate connection with the Jewish Passover meal, since it was that meal that Jesus was celebrating (Luke 22). Perhaps this connection should give us a clue as to an important dynamic in the Lord's Supper: for Jews throughout their history, to eat the Passover is not simply to recall casually the historical events of God's deliverance of their ancestors from Egypt, but rather it is to *relive the events, to really be there again,* experiencing as a member of this great people of Israel the Exodus from Egypt. So also, there should be something about Christian observance of the Lord's Supper that is more than simple remembrance, but in some unspeakably profound way is a reliving of Jesus' passion, death, and resurrection, especially as the sacrament is enlivened by the presence of the divine Spirit who anointed Jesus. With this understanding of the sacrament, the old black spiritual, "Were You There When They Crucified My Lord?" could be answered only with a humble "Yes"—and a word of thanksgiving for the love revealed in the Cross. In fact, many Christian traditions call this sacrament the *Eucharist,* which comes from the Greek word for giving thanks.

As powerful as such a reliving of, and giving thanks for, Jesus' passion and death can be, the sacrament of Communion embodies more. In fact, there is a sense in which, every time Christians kneel together to break the bread and drink the wine, they are enacting the whole gospel story. This is probably best illustrated in Luke's Gospel.

First, Jesus' last supper with His disciples includes the element of the *past,* with its *remembrance.* Jesus breaks the bread and identifies it with His body, soon to be given for them on the Cross; He passes the cup and identifies it with a new covenant about to be sealed in His blood (22:19-20). What was in the near future for His disciples is in the past for us, and in partaking of the bread and wine together we "proclaim the Lord's death" (1 Cor. 11:26). It is a proclamation not in words but in the physical elements of bread and wine, and in the physical acts of kneeling, eating, drinking, and praying. We eat and drink "in remembrance of" Him.

But, like Passover, the Lord's Supper is not simply a recollection of past events or a fitting memorial to a dead hero. For it also includes the element of the *present,* with its *communion* (lit., "union with"). Here we encounter the living Lord at His table, and we sit at that table with his multitude of disciples down through the centuries. At this table, Luke reminds us, Jesus is a servant, pouring out His life for us. "For who is greater, the one who reclines at the table, or the one who serves? Is it not the one who reclines at the table? But I am among you as the one who serves" (22:27).

I am among you, says Jesus, assuring us of His continued presence at His table. But it is not simply that He is among us as we gather for Communion; He is among us *as the One who serves.* Jesus is no less a servant in His resurrection glory than He was at His last supper; hence, to come to Christ's table today is to come to be served by Him, and to participate willingly in His life of servanthood. It is not enough that Jesus is among us as one who serves; if we take within us His body and blood in the sacramental elements, we are also saying something about how we, the Body of Christ, intend to live.

Surely Luke drives this home a little later with a Resurrection narrative unique to his Gospel. It is the story of the two grieving disciples on the road to Emmaus, who finally recognize Jesus "in the breaking of the bread" (24:35), perceiving the Lord in the moment He breaks the bread and begins to distribute it to them. Perhaps they noticed the wounds in His hands for the first time, or perhaps there was something uniquely characteristic about the careful way the Stranger handled the bread that reminded them of Jesus. In either case, the point is that in bread that is *broken and shared,* the resurrected Jesus is glimpsed! Augustine suggested that when Christians take into their hands the morsel of broken bread at the Lord's table, they are committing themselves like their Lord to be broken in servanthood and love, the Body of Christ broken anew in and for the world. And when the

Body is broken, Christ's presence in the Church, and indeed in the world, as "one who serves" can be most readily perceived.

But even as the Lord's Supper recalls Jesus' past suffering and His present presence among us as a servant, so it also points to the *future*, with its *anticipation*.

> And He said to them, "I have earnestly desired to eat this Passover with you before I suffer; for I say to you, I shall never again eat it until it is fulfilled in the kingdom of God." And when He had taken a cup and given thanks, He said, "Take this and share it among yourselves; for I say to you, I will not drink of the fruit of the vine from now on until the kingdom of God comes" (*Luke 22:15-18*).

Here we sense the deep comradery between Jesus and His disciples, and the profound meaningfulness of this moment for Jesus. As He anticipates the "exodus" (Gr., **exodos**, departure, Luke 9:31) He is about to accomplish with His death and resurrection, He looks even beyond these things to the glorious fulfillment of God's intentions for creation. It is a poignant moment, in which Jesus vows never again to celebrate the Passover until the fulfillment of God's kingdom brings to fruition the salvation foretasted in the Exodus. To sit at Christ's table in communion today is to anticipate longingly the messianic banquet, "a lavish banquet for all peoples" in which God "will swallow up death for all time" and "will wipe tears away from all faces" (Isa. 25:6, 8). No wonder Paul writes that, in this sacred meal, we "proclaim the Lord's death *until He comes*" (1 Cor. 11:26, italics added). We remember Christ's broken body and shed blood on the Cross, we experience Christ's risen presence among us as a servant among servants, and we look forward to Christ's coming again in the glorious *telos* of God's purposes, for which all of creation awaits anxiously, groaning and suffering "the pains of childbirth together until now" (Rom. 8:19, 22). To echo the sentiments of the first-century Church, *"Even so, come, Lord Jesus"* (Rev. 22:20, KJV, italics added).

23

Salvation in Christ

It is the central theme of the Christian story, the heart of the Church's preaching and sacraments, that Jesus is the Savior of the world. The good news we proclaim is that God, in His matchless love, has taken the initiative in the person of Christ to redeem fallen humanity enchained in sin, to reconcile us to himself, to restore us in the divine image. This is through and through the work of God, who "was in Christ reconciling the world to Himself, not counting their trespasses against them" (2 Cor. 5:19).

The Gospels are so bursting full of stories that put vibrance and color into the Christian doctrine of Jesus as the Savior of the world, it seems thoroughly arbitrary to narrow the richness and variety of those narratives down to one. But there is one, recorded in all three Synoptic Gospels, that is particularly revealing of the saving power of Jesus in the face of the destructive, demonic forces that distort and pervert human life. It is the "horror story" of Jesus' encounter with the demoniac in the graveyard.

What is so striking about this story is that it demonstrates how far Jesus was, and is, willing to go in order to redeem and restore human life. In order to appreciate this point, we must get the full picture of what this encounter entailed:

● First, Jesus and His disciples had sailed across the Sea of Galilee and disembarked in "the country of the Gerasenes" (Mark 5:1), which was *Gentile country*. Perhaps the violent storm that their boat had weathered, before Jesus brought peace to the sea, had blown them off course. In any case, any Jewish reader of the Gospel would have already begun to feel uneasy about this Jewish presence in the territory of unclean Gentiles.

● Next, we are told that a man "from the tombs," who in fact "had his dwelling among the tombs," confronted Jesus and His disciples (5:2, 3). According to Jewish priestly law, touching a corpse rendered a person ceremonially unclean for a week (Num. 19:11).

The uncleanness of a dead body lent a kind of generalized aura of uncleanness to cemeteries, so that on top of the desperate man being Gentile, he had the disgrace of living among the dead, having been rejected and exiled from human community.

● Luke adds that the man "had not put on any clothing for a long time" (8:27), thus adding to the man's condition of shame and indignity. Mark tells us also that the man cut and gashed his own naked, bruised, and vulnerable body with the stones of the graveyard (5:5), which was also an unclean act according to priestly regulations (Lev. 19:28), not to mention horribly self-destructive.

● As one level of uncleanness piles up after another, Mark also reports that the man was possessed (and oppressed!) by an "unclean spirit" (5:2) or demon. The "uncleanness" of the story now reaches cosmic and hellish proportions!

● If all this is not enough, we learn subsequently that this naked, self-abusing man with an unclean spirit living in the tombs was near a herd of pigs—unclean animals, according to Jewish law.

The entire situation reeked with what would have been an unbearable stench of uncleanness for most observant Jews of first-century Palestine. This truly was a "horror story" for these Israelites. But into this setting, Jesus strode as the living Lord of love, determined to bring redemption to this ruined, seemingly hopeless life. Jesus brings the salvation of God! Rather than treating the man like the rest of his society had, depriving him of human identity and dehumanizing him by exile and chains, Jesus confronted this nameless victim as a person of dignity, asking his name (Mark 5:9). And after He exorcised the demons that had plagued the man, those who knew him saw him "sitting down, clothed and in his right mind . . . and they became frightened" (v. 15). In fact, the mighty deliverance Jesus brought to this miserable victim of hell's destructive forces so unsettled the people of the nearby city that they begged Him to leave (v. 17).

What we see in such a story as this is that there is no situation, no matter how bleak and apparently hopeless, into which Jesus is unwilling or unable to enter in order to bring divine healing and deliverance. All of His upbringing in Jewish law would have been screaming at Him to get out of there, and fast!—but compassion and love, the driving forces of God's offer of salvation to us, said otherwise. Jesus encountered this lonely, frightened, demon-haunted Gentile—an "outsider" if ever there was one—and restored him to physical, spiritual, and social well-being (vv. 15, 19). Though in response to his deliverance the man expressed a desire to accompany his Deliverer (v. 18), Jesus refused, telling this one who had been pushed out of family and society, *"Go home to your people* and report to them what great things the Lord has done for you, and how He had mercy on you" (v. 19, italics added).

Indeed, divine mercy is the very root and cause of his deliverance, and of our salvation, in Jesus Christ. It is mercy freely offered, but never unilaterally forced upon us. The same compassionate mercy that moved Jesus through a Gentile graveyard would finally take Him to a Roman cross, but it will never overrule any person's capacity to refuse God's grace. God is committed to reconciliation with us, but reconciliation can occur only within the context of authentic relationship between two parties. Hence, for all the mighty, salvific power evidenced in Jesus' ministry of preaching, healing, exorcising, dying, and being raised to new life, the reconciling work of God nevertheless can fail— in the sense that any person can reject the atonement accomplished in Christ.

The Arminian-Wesleyan tradition's understanding of *soteriology* (Gr., **sōtēria** = salvation), however, insists that no one *has* to reject God's offer of salvation. According to the Scriptures, God does not desire "that any should perish, but that all should come to repentance" (2 Pet. 3:9, KJV). The fact is, however, that many do not come to repentance, providing a most sobering piece of evidence that not everything that God wills comes to fruition. It is no less the case, though, that the Arminian-Wesleyan tradition insists that God does desire all people to be reconciled to himself. The atoning work of God in Christ is, therefore, *unlimited*, meaning not that it has unlimited power (for its power is limited by our response to God), but that it is unlimited in its extent (for it is for all people). Christ lived, died, and lives for all. And while the grace of God does not overwhelm the human will, certainly God is doggedly persistent. This is illustrated by Jesus' refusal to leave the man in his demonic oppression, despite his pleas that Jesus not "torment" him (Mark 5:7).

If God's atoning work is limited in its effectiveness by the nature of human response, it is important to highlight that even our response is enkindled and enabled by prevenient grace, or the presence of God's Holy Spirit stirring deep within us, creating a thirst for our own redemption. Hence, God has made the first move toward us sinners in that Christ died for us, as Paul teaches (Rom. 5:8); further, God even makes the next move by evoking within us a sense of our need. This prevenient grace is the active presence of God within our lives, ever knocking, ever attempting to break through the walls of the self curved in upon itself, ever enlisting our response. We have already encountered this doctrine in chapter 9 with the tragic story of Cain. But contrary to the classic Calvinist-Reformed position, the Arminian-Wesleyan understanding of this grace is that it can be resisted, as in fact it was by Cain. God desires the deepest response of our hearts, and thus wills not to save us against our wills. Prevenient grace simply makes it possible for us to respond at all, one way or the other.

When any person responds positively to the grace offered by God through Christ in the Holy Spirit, such a response is called *conversion* (Fr., **com** = together; **vertere** = to turn). What is involved in this response? Generally, Christian tradition has highlighted two different but tightly related components of the proper response to the gospel, a response enabled and empowered by grace: *faith* and *repentance*.

Faith, in turn, can be seen to have two dimensions. The first might be called faith as *assent,* or the personal belief and affirmation that God truly has acted for our redemption in Christ. "As such," writes Gabriel Fackre, "it entails an affirmation about the way things are, a belief, a Yes! to the telling of the Christian Story about the suffering Love on Calvary that takes away the sins of the world."[1] Important as this intellectual dimension of faith is, it is never truly Christian faith until the second dimension, faith as *trust,* is also evident in one's experience. The New Testament Book of James makes this point well: faith is the profound inner commitment of one's entire life to the God whose Story is told; it is the active entrusting of oneself, "heart, soul, mind, and strength," to love and obey God. If faith as assent confesses, "God was in Christ reconciling the world to Himself" (2 Cor. 5:19), faith as trust says, "I have been crucified with Christ . . . I live by faith in the Son of God, who loved me, and delivered Himself up for me" (Gal. 2:20).

As far as Scripture is concerned, one cannot cleanly separate faith from repentance, since repentance involves the act of turning from sin and self-centeredness toward God and other-centeredness. To believe sincerely in what God has done for us in Christ immediately involves us in a turning, a profound awareness of the call to discipleship and obedience that belief in Jesus implies. Repentance from sin was, in fact, the primary thrust of both John the Baptist's and Jesus' proclamation of the coming kingdom of God (Matt. 3:2; 4:17). Thus, to *believe* in Christ, in the biblical sense, is necessarily also to *repent* from a life of sinning. Such an act of faith/repentance then issues into an ongoing relationship of *obedient discipleship;* thus, faith as obedience says, "I will take up *my* cross and follow Him."

Important as these considerations about the human response to divine grace are, they should never cloud the fundamental Christian conviction that we do not save ourselves. God in His unfathomable mercy saves us. There is a real sense in which we, enslaved to sin and

---

1. Fackre, *The Christian Story,* 201.

spiritually dead (Eph. 2:1-3; Rom. 6:17-21), are every bit as helpless as the Gadarene demoniac. It is only as Jesus the Savior strides mightily and mercifully into our impoverished human situation that we may taste redemption. Titus 3:3-7 states this truth with clarity and power:

> For we also once were foolish ourselves, disobedient, deceived, enslaved to various lusts and pleasures, spending our life in malice and envy, hateful, hating one another.
> But when the kindness of God our Savior and His love for mankind appeared,
> *He saved us, not on the basis of deeds which we have done in righteousness, but according to His mercy,*
> *by the washing of regeneration and renewing by the Holy Spirit,* whom He poured out upon us richly through Jesus Christ our Savior,
> that being justified by His grace *we might be made heirs according to the hope of eternal life (italics added).*

Just as Christian conversion when considered from the side of human response and experience has several components (faith/repentance/obedience), so also from the side of divine mercy and grace. In fact, the Titus passage quoted above reflects the three different dimensions of God's saving activity as it intersects with the human heart in the converting moment, according to Christian tradition: *justification, regeneration,* and *adoption.*

The aspect of conversion known as *justification* is clearly reflected in the words "But when the kindness of God our Savior and His love for mankind appeared, He saved us, not on the basis of deeds which we have done in righteousness, but according to His mercy . . . being justified by His grace." We have already considered the idea of God's justification of us in chapter 19, as we examined what Paul writes about Abraham having been justified or "reckoned righteous" by God on the basis of his belief in God's word. Abraham, Paul argues, found acceptance with God by *his* acceptance of God's promise that he would become the father of many nations. Thus, Abraham was brought into a proper relationship with God because he deemed God to be worthy of trust. A parallel can be drawn between Abraham and ourselves at this point: we too are encountered by divine promises. Paul, in fact, calls Jesus the One in whom all of God's promises find their Amen, their validation. Accordingly, we can look to the life and words of Jesus to discover the nature of God's promises to us—and in the story of Jesus, we hear that God already loves us, that He already offers us forgiveness, that He already has reconciled the world to himself, that divine grace is actively seeking us out. Like Abraham, all we are really asked to do is to believe those promises and live in their light. This is the *jus-*

tification by grace through faith at the heart of Martin Luther's Reformation proclamation: there is nothing we can do to earn, or add to, the offer of grace that God makes to us in Jesus Christ.

This triumphant message of God's surprising grace is undoubtedly the distinctive note of the gospel. God's grace is surprising because so often in schools, the workplace, friendships, and, tragically, even within many families, our worth and standing are evaluated on the basis of performance. God's promise to us in the life, words, death, and resurrection of Jesus, however, is that we are loved and accepted by Him just as we are! If we accept that promise and rest in that grace, we like Abraham are "reckoned righteous." We are justified, or brought into proper relationship to God—a relationship that is grounded in the trustworthiness of the One who promises, but actualized in our believing in the promise. Our tendency, learned from society and family, is all too often to attempt to please God by being pleasing, to gain His favor by being good, to merit His mercy and love by becoming lovable. Our very attempts to become worthy of divine love and grace actually obstruct us from receiving what is already freely offered. The good news is that God loves us and offers us forgiveness *now*—or in the words of a famous sermon on justification by the 20th-century Lutheran theologian Paul Tillich, *Simply accept the fact that you are accepted!*[2]

Regeneration, the second aspect of Christian conversion as viewed from the perspective of God's role and activity, is reflected in the words of the Titus passage, "by the washing of regeneration and renewing by the Holy Spirit, whom He poured out upon us richly through Jesus Christ our Savior." To regenerate literally means "to bring to life again," or "to bring new life to," which is precisely what God's Holy Spirit, the Life-Giver, does in the moment of justification. Thus, while justification is sometimes called a *relative change,* i.e., a change in relationship between God and the person, regeneration is correspondingly called a *real change,* i.e., the beginnings of transformation of one's nature or character by the presence of the Holy Spirit. We are, in the maternal imagery used by Jesus in His conversation with Nicodemus, given rebirth or "born from above" by the Spirit (John 3:3, 7, margin). Paul describes the same reality of transformation begun in our lives by writing that "the love of God has been poured out within our hearts through the Holy Spirit who was given to us" (Rom. 5:5).

Earlier in this book (chap. 17) we described God's Spirit as the very presence of God, creatively bringing order out of chaos and animating all living things (Ps. 104:27-30). Thus, the Spirit is present to every person—and throughout the entire universe, for that matter—as

---

2. Paul Tillich, *The Shaking of the Foundations* (New York: Charles Scribner's Sons, 1948), 162.

creative grace. We have also spoken of God's Spirit present to all people, luring them, wooing them, convicting them of sin, and creating a thirst for redemption. This, of course, is *prevenient grace.* But when a person responds in faith and repentance to God's prevenient grace, she or he is opened up to a new dimension of experience of the Spirit as *transforming grace.* It is one grace, for grace is the active presence of our loving God in our lives, but the character or efficacy of that grace depends upon the nature and extent of the human response.

Since the Spirit who sustains our lives, draws us to faith, and transforms our hearts is the Spirit who was decisively revealed in the person of Jesus, the "real change" that begins in this moment is in the direction of Christlikeness. Obviously, we are not entirely transformed in the moment of conversion in such a way that there is no need for further transformation and growth; this is simply the beginning of the process whereby we are being "conformed to the image of His Son" (Rom. 8:29), a process that will not be completed until we see Jesus (1 John 3:2). This lifelong process of becoming increasingly Christlike in thought, word, and deed is sanctification. Hence, this aspect of conversion called regeneration is sometimes also identified as *initial sanctification,* since it is the initial and initiating point at which we embark on the path of being made holy. As we have already seen, for Wesley this holiness is, in essence, Christlikeness—which, in turn, is essentially love for God and neighbor. In this light, regeneration can be understood as the moment in which we are placed upon the path of love. Paul's description of regeneration, already cited, as the outpouring of the love of God in our hearts can therefore be interpreted as referring both to our love *for God* and God's love *for others* working in and through us (cf. Gal. 5:22).

The third and final dimension of conversion as viewed from the perspective of God's doing is called *adoption* and is reflected in the words of the letter to Titus "that . . . we might be made heirs according to the hope of eternal life." To be an heir is to be a rightful inheritor in the will of a parent, a member of the family. Paul states that "all who are being led by the Spirit of God, these are sons of God," and that we "have received a spirit of adoption as sons" (Rom. 8:14, 15). To be adopted into the family of God at the moment of conversion gives us the freedom to approach God with boldness and honesty and to cry out with Jesus, "Abba! Father!" (v. 15; Gal. 4:6). Of course, becoming a child of the Father also means we enter into a family with countless brothers and sisters and Jesus as our Elder Brother (Heb. 2:10-13). It is He who is the Heir of the Father's glory and power, but we by faith in Him are "heirs also, heirs of God and fellow heirs with Christ, if indeed we suffer with Him in order that we may also be glorified with Him" (Rom. 8:17). Paul's words about suffering with Christ are a sobering reminder that being adopted into God's family, becoming Christ's "little brother or sister" and fellow heir of life eternal, may exact its costs in a world alienated from God.

On the more positive side, the imagery of adoption reminds us that Christian conversion is always conversion into a community of faith. We are brought into a Christian family that precedes us and surrounds us with love and encouragement, and that celebrates the great Story of God's redemption each Lord's day. God's Spirit, who witnesses to our adoption, crying out "Abba!" within our hearts (Rom. 8:15; Gal. 4:6), is the same Spirit in whom all believers share together in the Church (1 Cor. 12:7, 13). The reality of **koinōnia**, or mutual sharing in God's own outpoured Spirit, should press us to an awareness of our need for one another; we are placed into the Body of Christ to encourage each other and to enable each to tell and live the Story. Thus we sing to our fellow members in the family, brothers and sisters in the company of the resurrected Christ,

> *Tell me the story slowly, That I may take it in—*
> *That wonderful redemption, God's remedy for sin.*
> *Tell me the story often, For I forget so soon.*
> *The early dew of morning Has passed away at noon.*
>
> —KATHERINE HANKEY

Technically speaking, the Gerasene demoniac did not undergo Christian conversion. He did, however, meet Jesus—and the narrative of that encounter does provide us with a portrait of the many-faceted miracle of the saving moment as we have discussed it in this chapter:

● Jesus' willingness to march unwaveringly through the death and decay of the tombs to meet the possessed and oppressed man, and there to ask his name, is a portrait of God's unconditional love accepting us as we are, or *justification*.

● Jesus' transformation of this ravaged, anguished man into a man of confidence and calm, "sitting down, clothed and in his right mind" (Mark 5:15), is a portrait of the radical change in heart and character offered us in *regeneration*.

● Jesus' restoration of the man to the family and society that had exiled him in their fears, that he now might once again enter into human relationships of intimacy and caring rather than continuing in the horror and loneliness of the tombs, is a picture of that dimension of conversion called *adoption*.

There is a final point. This man, redeemed from the destructive powers of hell, "began to proclaim . . . what great things Jesus had done for him" (5:20). May we go and do likewise!

24

Scriptural Holiness

John and Charles Wesley believed it was the divine calling of the Methodists to "spread scriptural holiness throughout the land" of England and beyond. So too, Christians of the Wesleyan tradition—particularly those of the Holiness Movement, whose immediate historical roots are in 19th-century American revivalism—continue to view holiness, or the doctrine of entire sanctification, as deserving primary emphasis.[1] They believe their function in the larger, more comprehensive Body of Christ is to bear witness, both by word and by life, to the explicit call toward "holiness of heart and life" in the Story of God.

There is no mistaking it: throughout the Bible the expectation that God's people can and should be holy is an explicit theme. That divine call is rooted in the recognition that God is holy and seeks a people who will represent Him in holiness.

The critical question, then, is What is holiness? What do the Scriptures mean by this term? In the Hebrew Scriptures, holiness (**kadosh**) refers first of all to the very *Godness* of God, to His awesome glory, His unspeakable otherness, His unfathomable majesty and mystery that may simply overwhelm human beings. Think of the prophet Isaiah's experience in the Temple, in which he "saw the Lord . . . high and exalted" (6:1, NIV). In the Hebrew tradition, it was believed to be impossible to "see" God because the experience would be so overwhelming as to destroy the beholder. Hence, for Isaiah simply to make such a claim was revolutionary and signaled the strangeness of the event. Isaiah reports having heard seraphim (what we might call angels) crying out, "Holy, Holy, Holy, is the Lord of hosts, the whole earth is full of His glory" (v. 3). This encounter with the Holy reduced Isaiah to utter terror: "Woe is me, for I am undone, for I am a man of

---

1. Denominations within the Holiness Movement include the Church of the Nazarene, the Salvation Army, the Free Methodist Church, the Wesleyan Church, the Church of God (Anderson, Ind.), and others.

unclean lips, and I live among a people of unclean lips; for my eyes have seen the King, the Lord of hosts" (v. 5). We find similar responses in the Israelites' fear of the manifestation of divine glory and holiness at Mount Sinai (Exod. 20:18-21), in Job's final exclamation of utter humility in response to the Voice in the whirlwind (42:1-6), and in the disciples' falling on their faces when God speaks from the cloud of glory in the Transfiguration accounts (e.g., Matt. 17:1-8).

In this first sense of the word, then, God is holy because God is wholly Other, different, mysterious, unique. "Who is like Thee among the gods, O Lord?" sang Moses and the Israelites after their deliverance from the Egyptians in the Exodus. "Who is like Thee, majestic in holiness, awesome in praises, working wonders?" (Exod. 15:11).

On this basis, just as He is holy because God is in a class by himself, separated from everything else in reality, so also things or objects can be described as holy, such as the ground (Exod. 3:5) or the Sabbath (Gen. 2:3). These are holy because they are uniquely associated with the holy God; His presence, blessing, or name *sets them apart* (i.e., sanctifies them) for His own purposes. In the same way, the Israelites were also required to be holy, to be God's own people and possession. Leviticus 19, part of a longer passage (chaps. 17—26) sometimes called the Holiness Code by biblical scholars, begins with the command, "You shall be holy, for I, the Lord your God am holy." Israel had been set apart by association with Yahweh, who had bound himself to this people in the Exodus and in the gift of Torah. It is important to note that, in this biblical passage, not only does the concern for holiness deal with what are sometimes called *ceremonial* practices that set the Israelites apart from other nations, such as sacrifices (v. 5) and keeping different kinds of animals, seed, and clothing material separate from one another (a sign of "setting apart" or sanctification); but also it deals with what are sometimes called *moral* practices that set the Israelites apart by virtue of the quality of their relationships, such as feeding the poor and the alien (vv. 9-10), respecting the handicapped (v. 14), and practicing impartial justice (v. 15). This Holiness Code, in fact, not only contains the well-known command to "love your neighbor as yourself" (v. 18) but also commands the Israelites to love the stranger or alien "as yourself, for you were aliens in Egypt" (v. 34, NIV). The people were to nurture the memory of their own alienation, their own oppression and slavery, as the basis for an empathy with the suffering and poverty of others. And all this was said to represent, to *re-present* on the human level, the holiness of Yahweh. The chapter ends with words that draw these themes together: "Do not use dishonest standards when measuring length, weight or quantity. Use honest scales and honest weights, an honest dry measure [margin] and an honest liquid measure [margin]. I am the Lord your God, who brought you out of Egypt. Keep all my decrees and all my laws and follow them. I am the Lord" (vv. 35-37, NIV).

This gift of the Torah, then, was to sanctify the people Israel, to set them apart as God's unique people through both ceremonial and ethical practice. It should be added, though, that traditional Jews, from biblical times even into the present, tend to reject any such distinction between the ceremonial and ethical laws, since all the Mosaic laws are understood to be rooted in divine command. In any event, it is obvious that an integral aspect of representing the holiness of God was a concern for social justice, an aspect of the Torah that the prophets would subsequently highlight.

Just as Moses received God's gift of the Torah on the mount, so in Matthew's Gospel, where a narrative theology of Jesus as the new Moses is developed (see chap. 16 of this book), we find Jesus on a mountainside giving to His disciples the word of life (5:1). Today we call it the Sermon on the Mount, and one of the striking parallels in this sermon to Leviticus 19 is Jesus' injunction, "Therefore you are to be perfect, as your heavenly Father is perfect" (v. 48). We will return to this a little later.

Within the biblical notion of holiness, then, two different emphases or aspects begin to take shape: first, a *ceremonial* holiness (typical of priestly ritual) intended to mirror God's utter difference and distinction from the created order, whereby objects and persons become holy as they are set apart or separated from simply a secular purpose to a sacred use, in association with God; and second, an *ethical* holiness (typical of the message of the prophets) intended to mirror God's own holy love and concern for all people.

It is safe to say that Jesus shared with the Hebrew prophets before Him a more profound concern for justice, love, and mercy than for the holiness associated with ritual practices like Sabbath observance, tithing, and hand washing, though He certainly did not reject the latter category entirely. His attitude toward such matters is perhaps best summed up in His answer to those who criticized His grain-picking disciples, "The Sabbath was made for man, and not man for the Sabbath" (Mark 2:27), implying that concern for human wholeness and wellness supersedes any law. Many Pharisees of the time also taught that human life was more valuable than any injunction of the Torah, but Jesus appears to have gone beyond them by performing miracles of healing non-life-threatening ailments on the Sabbath—labors that could just as easily have waited till the next day (Mark 3:1-5).

While Jesus stood in the ethical tradition of the prophets, there is a sense in which the gospel brings together both the ceremonial and ethical streams in the Christian concept of sanctification: human beings (Christians, specifically) are called upon to consecrate themselves, to offer themselves as living sacrifices to God (Rom. 12:1), but such a consecration or offering immediately leads to ethical considerations that arise out of the command to "clothe yourselves with the Lord Jesus Christ" (12:2—13:14, NIV). This means that our part is to consecrate ourselves, to set ourselves apart, even to sanctify ourselves (2 Cor. 6:14—7:1). It is God the Holy Spirit's part to begin the transforming work of divine love in our character and choices. Sanctification is the overall work of God, the process whereby we are being made increasingly in the likeness of Jesus (Col. 3:10)—but God respects the person too much to re-create us without our willing participation.

It is the conviction of Wesleyan Christians in the holiness tradition that, as we willingly offer our lives to God's sanctifying presence, it is possible by the transforming power of God to become "perfected in love," a favorite phrase of John Wesley, found in his favorite book of the Bible (1 John 4:16-18). If Jesus not only taught but also wrought love for God and neighbor, then to be re-created by the Spirit is to be increasingly like Jesus, which is to be increasingly a lover of God and people. This takes us back to *relationships* as the real arena of the sanctified life, the life set apart for God: do we express God, do we re-present Him, in our relationships to those around us? Remember that Leviticus 19, the Holiness Code of Moses, included a great deal about how being holy as God is holy involved the Jews' everyday relationships and practices. And if we interpret Jesus' Sermon on the Mount as *his* holiness code, the same truth emerges: Jesus, who challenges His disciples to be "perfect, as your heavenly Father is perfect," does not leave us in the dark about the perfection He has in mind. He is talking about relationships with people.

> You have heard that it was said, "Love your neighbor and hate your enemy." But I tell you: Love your enemies and pray for those who persecute you, *that you may be sons of your Father in heaven.* He causes his sun to rise on the evil and the good, and sends rain on the righteous and the unrighteous. If you love those who love you, what reward will you get? Are not even the tax collectors doing that? And if you greet only your brothers, what are you doing more than others? Do not even pagans do that? *Be perfect, therefore, as your heavenly Father is perfect (Matt. 5:43-48, NIV, italics added).*

This is the way in which is it possible, according to the Scriptures, to be holy, to be perfect, to be children of a holy God: we can be perfect in love, or perfected in love by virtue of the empowering of divine love, for "God is love" (1 John 4:8, 16). But more must be said, yet, about the possibility of such a quality of life and relationships.

To speak of sanctification as a life filled with love for God and neighbor, as we are here, is to speak in *relational* terms. Within this framework of understanding, sin is not some thing or substance God uproots and takes out of us; rather, sin is *lovelessness,* a lack or privation of authentic, loving relationship to God. When God begins to salvage us through enabling our response of faith to God's grace given freely through Jesus Christ, we are then brought into relationship with God (reconciliation). And we are at that point sanctified, set apart by God in Christ Jesus. We are, in New Testament terms, already saints! We are brought into a new relationship with God (justified) and given His Spirit (regenerated), and that same Spirit bears witness that we are now God's children (adopted).

People in the Wesleyan-holiness movement would do well to recall Wesley's advice that, while recommending entire sanctification to one's hearers, one ought not to belittle or ignore regeneration, in which the process of sanctification is already begun (and hence sometimes called *initial sanctification,* as noted earlier). It has been suggested that what occurs in entire sanctification (not as opposed to, but as a furtherance of, initial sanctification) is that we begin truly to recognize the implications of our having been set apart by God in our conversion to Christ. In this recognition of the deeper implications of relationship to God and others, we actively and willingly and lovingly entrust our redeemed selves to God.

The "secondness" ("a second definite work of grace" is an important phrase in the holiness tradition) of sanctification is this deeper relationship to God that is based upon our response to His love—a response of entire consecration, a response of offering our deepest selves as a living sacrifice. *So long as a person continues,* by the gracious empowering of God's Spirit, in that relationship, he or she is entirely sanctified—for that commitment is essentially one of love of one's entire being for God, and love of one's neighbor expressed in concrete acts of commitment to the other's well-being. And that orientation of active loving, John Wesley argued, excludes sin by definition—if *sin* is understood to be the absence or rejection of that deeper relationship of love, and sins are understood to be attitudes and actions (or nonactions) that manifest that lovelessness. In his *Plain Account of Christian Perfection,* Wesley put it this way: "Scripture perfection is, pure love filling the heart, and governing all the words and actions. . . . But if the love of God fill all the heart, there can be no sin therein. . . . [It is] love filling the heart, expelling pride, anger, desire, self-will; rejoicing evermore, praying without ceasing, and in everything giving thanks."[2]

---

2. Wesley, *Plain Account,* 60, 45, 84.

When, by the grace of God, we do live in such a relationship of love to God and others, we are *perfect* (Gr., **teleios**, aim or purpose) in the sense that we are being what we are created to be. We are perfect in *intention,* for the underlying motivation of our lives will be to love God and neighbor. We are also perfect in *direction,* for our lives will be aimed toward becoming increasingly Christlike, which, as Wesley pointed out, is to be increasingly a person of love. This is the sanctified life, the life set apart for loving God and others. When we are in this open, growing, deepening relationship to God through the gracious presence of His transforming Spirit in our lives, the "bent to sinning" (Charles Wesley) is necessarily gone—because the "bent to sinning" means precisely the fundamental bending inward of ourselves toward ourselves (lovelessness). It is important to remember, however, that since this understanding of sanctification is framed in relational terms, there is no absolute guarantee that the "bent to sinning," or carnal nature, cannot return. After all, it is not a *thing* that is taken out of us in such a way that it cannot return. Since with the word *love* we are referring to a relationship to God in which we seek nothing but His will (and with *sin* the rejection or perversion of that relationship), it is a relationship out of which it is possible to fall. Yet surely the God who "gives us the victory through our Lord Jesus Christ" (1 Cor. 15:57) offers us all the grace and help necessary to remain in a sanctified relationship to God and others.

At the center of the issue of the doctrine of entire sanctification is what the Bible calls the heart, or the deepest self. The self never is destroyed, nor is it "cleansed" in such a way that some thing or blot is removed, never to return. The words *love* and *sin,* as here used, describe the basic qualities of relationship to God and neighbor in which we may live. Hence, we are talking about relationship—and relationship by definition means that oneself is always involved. Being "filled with the Holy Spirit" does not remove or negate one's selfhood, either, though sometimes it is mistakenly described as being "controlled" by the Spirit in ways that veer dangerously close to suggesting that we become a God-operated robot or a puppet on His string. Such images of God are obviously in direct contradiction to the emphasis in this book on God's desire for covenantal partnership, and with the Arminian-Wesleyan understanding of synergism. In this connection, it is significant that Paul's list of the fruit of the Spirit includes "self-control" (Gal. 5:23), and that Timothy is told that God's gift to us is not "a spirit of timidity, but a spirit of power, of love and of self-discipline" (2 Tim. 1:7, NIV).

God is creating the unique selves that we are to become, and His intention, according to the Scriptures, is to redeem our selves and call us to our highest potential. But what is that? Keep in mind that human beings are created in God's image, and further that God is love; the implication, then, is that the human being's primary intention ought to be to *love*. That was indeed embodied for us, narrated for us, in the words and acts of Jesus, who said to His followers, "This is My commandment, that you love one another, just as I have loved you. . . . The world will know that you are my disciples, if you have love for one another" (John 15:12; 13:35). Jesus' own life makes it obvious that the love He means is not a flowery, romantic idealism; it consists in laying down our lives and thus is best exemplified in Jesus' self-giving on the Cross (15:13; 1 John 3:16-17). Thus, the biblical idea of love is not emotionalism, but the everyday, every-moment commitment to laying down our lives for others, whether in terms of time, interests, money, or our very selves.

This, then, is the Christian ideal, God's calling upon every Christian life, as envisioned by John Wesley as he read the Scriptures: that it is possible *in this moment* and in each passing moment, by the graciously transformative power of God's Holy Spirit, to love God with all our heart, soul, mind, and strength, and to love our neighbor as ourselves. To live in this way is to be delivered from sin (1 John 1:6—2:1, 7; 3:11; 4:19-21). It is to be loved by God, and to know it, and then to return that love by giving oneself to God and neighbor as God has given himself to us in Christ. Earlier in the book I quoted a poem John Wesley once wrote in his journal. It seems appropriate to quote it again, this time a closing for these reflections upon scriptural holiness:

> *O grant that nothing in my soul*
> *May dwell, but Thy pure love alone!*
> *O may Thy love possess me whole.*
> *My joy, my treasure, and my crown.*
> *Strange flames far from my heart remove!*
> *My every act, word, thought, be love.*

25

The Praxis of
Christian Existence

The word *praxis* has become widely used in contemporary philosophy and theology to refer to a very specific understanding of the relationship between our ideas and our actions. In short, this view calls into question the traditional understanding of the relationship between human thinking and doing. Although people in Western civilization have generally believed that ideas and actions are inseparable, most usually it has been assumed that ideas provide the foundation and rationale for actions and practices. On the other hand, thinkers who utilize the term *praxis* tend to believe that the relationship works both ways, so that quite often it is our actions (and nonactions) that give rise to, or even create, our ideas. Praxis, then, generally suggests a kind of intentional action that generates reflection, and a mode of reflection that remains closely attentive to human action in the world, especially in response to marginalized peoples who are politically and economically oppressed.

To title this chapter "The Praxis of Christian Existence," then, is to seek to think carefully and intentionally about what kind of life, as lived by a Christian, is most conducive to generating good theology. It is to ask, What kinds of actions and attitudes most clearly and decisively characterize the committed Christian life in this world? What sort of life helps us best understand the nature of the relationship between God and human beings, and what it is that God desires and requires?

For the Christian, the most obvious answer to such questions involves an appeal to a story: the story told in the Gospels, the story of Jesus. It is the story of this Jew, His life and ministry, His death and resurrection, that has generated and sustained the ongoing tasks of Christian thought and practice for nearly two millennia. This is the one through whom "grace and truth came," for "no one has ever seen God, but God the One and Only, who is at the Father's side, has made him known" (John 1:17-18, NIV). This same Jesus made it clear that the revelation of God the Father occurred through His life precisely in His praxis: "The one who sent me is with me; he has not left me alone, for *I always do what pleases him*" (8:29, NIV, italics added). It is precisely because, and insofar as, Jesus "went about *doing good*" that we comprehend that "God was with him" in a uniquely powerful and revelatory way (Acts 10:38, italics added). In the story of Jesus, the true nature of Christian praxis is offered to us.

But how do we get a handle on that story? How might we characterize it? If you were asked, "What is it that we learn about God and human beings by looking at Jesus?" how would you reply?

Each of the Synoptic Gospels presents a variation on that question. In Matthew the question is "Which is the greatest commandment in the Law?" (22:36). In Mark the question is similarly posed: "Of all the commandments, which is the most important?" (12:28). In Luke, it is "What must I do to inherit eternal life?" (10:25, all NIV). In every case, the question posed to Jesus is a question about what human beings are meant to be and do. And here, perhaps more than anywhere else, we learn from Jesus—in His life and words, His *praxis*—what it means to be truly Christian, truly human, truly God's.

Of the three similar (and perhaps parallel) passages, Luke's is the most compelling and interesting, if for no other reason than that it presents Jesus as a "narrative theologian" at His best. In other words, as we seek to outline the nature of Christian praxis, we are drawn to the story *of* Jesus, and thereby drawn to a story *by* Jesus. It is the story of a compassionate Samaritan.

Part of the power of this story, often forgotten or ignored by modern readers, is its setting within a larger story Luke is telling. The conversation in which Jesus is engaged when He weaves this parable is as much a part of Luke's narrative as the parable itself. It is, therefore, critical to keep in mind that the conversation begins with the question of a Jewish theologian, "Teacher, what must I do to inherit eternal life?" The question lends the entire conversation that ensues a kind of eschatological significance; the implication is that human existence in the here and now is somehow a prelude to that which is to come.

Jesus, recognizing that the theologian is trying to entrap Him in theological niceties, puts the ball back into His court: "You're the expert in the Law. What do *you* see there?" (Jesus' tendency to answer questions with questions not only is an excellent teaching device but was also a common practice among Jewish rabbis and remains so today. I once asked a Jewish rabbi who was a teacher of mine, "Why do Jews so often answer a question with another question?" He replied, "And why not?")

The theologian replied with two commandments from Moses, the dual command of love for God and neighbor. In Matthew's and Mark's Gospels, this answer is found upon Jesus' lips. The fact that in Luke it is the theologian who offers this summary of God's Torah suggests that this answer was in fact floating about in Jewish religious discussion; rabbinic literature of roughly the same period does indeed bear this out. The point here is that Jesus happily recognized that the Mosaic law contained the very heart of the matter of being human before God; eternal life is in fact a matter of *love*—love for God and others.

"You have answered correctly," Jesus replies. *"Do this, and you will live"* (10:28, italics added).

Luke then tells us that the theologian wanted to "justify himself." What does that mean? It might mean that he felt silly, because Jesus had cut the discussion short with such an easy and obvious answer when the expert had wanted to throw his theological weight around. In this interpretation he wanted to "justify himself" as a theologian and so endeavored to keep the discussion alive with the follow-up question, "And who is my neighbor?" (v. 29). Or it is possible that this theologian had seen the freedom of Jesus' love for others and somehow wanted to justify the narrowness of his own love by giving "neighbor" a tight definition.

Whatever the motives behind the question, Jesus, as usual, refuses to be drawn into a theoretical discussion intended to make theologians feel better about themselves! Instead of engaging in abstract definitions and argumentation about the concept of neighborship, Jesus simply *tells a story:*

> A certain man was going down from Jerusalem to Jericho; and he fell among robbers, and they stripped him and beat him, and went off leaving him half dead. And by chance a certain priest was going down on that road, and when he saw him, he passed by on the other side. And likewise a Levite also, when he came to the place and saw him, passed by on the other side. But a certain Samaritan . . .

At that moment the mouths of Jesus' listeners plummet wide open in a collective gasp. "Did He say what I thought He said? *Samaritan?"*

Jesus, the Master Weaver of stories, thoroughly shocks those gathered around Him as He utters that simple word. Not unlike the style of many Jewish teacher-storytellers, Jesus seems to be setting up a typical tripartite structure in which the third character to stroll down the path of the parable, following two negative examples, would be the hero. The first two characters, the priest and the Levite, represent the Temple religious establishment; it appears, then, that this rural

Galilean Storyteller is about to take a jab at the organized holiness power structure represented by the Jerusalem Temple and its servants. In that case, perhaps His listeners expect the third character to be a Jewish layperson, maybe even a Galilean Jew like himself and His disciples. Instead, Jesus says,

But a certain Samaritan . . .

We must strive to appreciate the shock value of Jesus' mentioning a Samaritan as the heroic third character of the parable. Unfortunately, the centuries of retelling this story has turned the good Samaritan into a cliché, and the shock value is gone. But for first-century Jewish society, Samaritans were, bluntly speaking, dirt. They were considered racially inferior, half-breeds, for having been the product of Jewish intermarriages. They were also considered religiously inferior, as heretics who had synthesized the teachings of Moses (they accepted the Pentateuch, or the first five books of the Bible) with foreign ideas. The Gospel of John, in setting the scene for Jesus' conversation with the Samaritan woman at the well, describes the first-century sociological situation well when it states, "Jews have no dealings with Samaritans" (4:9). In fact, in that very conversation at the well, Jesus reflects Jewish religious attitudes of that time when He says to the woman, "You [Samaritans] worship that which you do not know; we [Jews] worship that which we know, for salvation is from the Jews" (v. 22).

It is worth mentioning, too, that the animosity between Jew and Samaritan was not simply a generalized attitude rooted in racial and religious prejudice. For Jews, there was a particular historical event, roughly 30 years in the past by the time Jesus would have spun this yarn, that was still an open wound on the Jewish psyche. During one Passover season, probably during the early childhood of Jesus, Samaritan vandals had sneaked into the Jerusalem Temple under cover of night and scattered the bones of a human skeleton on the floor of the Temple precinct. This act of desecration was a graphic symbol of the Samaritan rejection of the Jerusalem Temple as God's accepted locale for worship and sacrifice, in favor of the Samaritan site on Mount Gerizim to the north. It was an act not to be easily forgotten by the Jewish people, and undoubtedly Jesus had grown up hearing stories about those filthy, blasphemous heretics, the Samaritans.

There is one last detail to heighten further our sense of the shock value of Jesus' parable. This parable is unique to Luke's Gospel, and probably it is no coincidence that there is another passage, critical to appreciating this one, that is also unique to Luke: the account of the rejection of Jesus and His disciples when they attempt to stop in a Samaritan village for the night. Why are they rejected? "Because He was journeying with His face toward Jerusalem" (9:53). The disciples respond to this slap in the face with the suggestion that they "command fire to come down from heaven and consume [the Samaritans]" (v. 54). Jesus, however, immediately rejects this suggestion of vengeance.

Keep in mind that Luke places the story of the Samaritans' rejection of Jesus and His disciples not much prior to Jesus' parable of the compassionate Samaritan. It is not hard to imagine His disciples still feeling the pain and humiliation of rejection; thus, when Jesus utters those explosive words, "a certain Samaritan," He is virtually rubbing salt in those wounds. It is almost possible to hear them mumbling among themselves in embarrassment and anger:

How can Jesus speak like that about a Samaritan?
Doesn't He realize that Samaritans are dirty, half-breed heretics?
Doesn't He remember how they kicked us out of town just the other day?
Doesn't He see that people aren't going to stand for this kind of talk?

It is crucial to recognize that, in the very telling of this parable, Jesus was actively *loving* his neighbor. Indeed, He was actively loving His enemy, as defined by contemporary Jewish society. By telling a story that put a "half-breed heretic" Samaritan into a favorable light—indeed, that made a Samaritan the model of love for neighbor, and in fact the model of what it means to *truly live* (10:28), and to inherit eternal life (v. 25)—Jesus was challenging accepted Jewish theological and social prejudices. He made even the telling of a story a powerful moment of *praxis,* a moment in which the *story* of neighborly love actually becomes an event or an *expression* of neighborly love. It does not matter whether a Samaritan ever had, or ever would, actually stop to help a beaten and helpless Jew. What matters is that Jesus forced His listeners to reconsider the entire relationship between Jew and Samaritan, and between Samaritan and God.

It is also important to note that, at the conclusion of the story, Jesus directs another question back to the theologian. Jesus' question, however, is the very one the theologian had asked ("And who is my neighbor?") turned inside out and on its head. So Jesus asks this question, "Which of these three do you think *proved to **be a neighbor** to the man who fell into the robbers' hands?*" (10:36, italics and boldface added). The question is no longer a theoretical one concerning the proper definition of neighbor (since if I can define neighbor tightly enough, I also can easily recognize who is not my neighbor, and hence whom I need not love). Now the question is about what it takes to *be* a neighbor. The movement of thought is away from abstraction and toward a personal, "neighborly" commitment and openness to every fellow human being. To freely render Jesus' point, "Do not theorize on who is your neighbor and who is not, or who is deserving of your help and compassion. Your neighbor is every person with whom you come into contact—and *you* are to be a neighbor to all, without exception." By the time Jesus is done with His parable, "neighbor" does not so much describe some other person as much as it describes a certain attitude or orientation that we are challenged to adopt and put into practice. For after the theologian admitted that the neighbor was "the one who showed mercy toward [the victim]" (10:37; apparently he could not bring himself to come right out and say "Samaritan"), Jesus again turned the parable toward praxis: *"Go and do the same"* (10:37, italics added).

"What shall I *do* to inherit eternal life?" *"Do* this, and you will live." *"Go and do* the same." These critical remarks within the conversation between the Jewish theologian and Jesus make it clear that the issue of eternal life really does center on *doing,* on *praxis,* on love. For it is in loving God with all we are and have, and loving others as people like ourselves, that we truly are living a quality of life called *eternal*—for in fact, very often in the New Testament "eternal life" is first of all a quality of divine life before it is a quantity of life (i.e., everlasting). Eternal life begins here, begins now, in a life wholly given to love. It is such a life that characterizes following Jesus, and that characterizes what Wesley meant by "perfection." No wonder Wesley, in commenting upon this parable, wrote,

> He, and he alone, shall live for ever, who thus loves God and his neighbour in the present life. . . . Let us go and do likewise, regarding every man as our neighbour who needs our assistance. Let us renounce that bigotry and party-zeal which would contract our hearts into an insensibility for all the human race, but a small number whose sentiments and practices are so much our own, that our love to them is but self-love reflected. With an honest openness of mind, let us always remember the kindred between man and man; and cultivate that happy instinct whereby, in the original constitution of our nature, God has strongly bound us to each other.[1]

---

1. Wesley, *Notes upon the New Testament,* 240-42.

PART VII

THE END OF GOD'S STORY: THE DOCTRINE OF LAST THINGS

The doctrine of *eschatology* (Gr., **eschaton,** last or end) has to do with the events or expectations that are associated in Christian tradition with the end of God's Story. How do we expect that it will all come out, and why?

As we begin to probe the issues surrounding the end of the Story, we should keep in mind that the word *end* has two differing, if related, meanings, both of which are important to Christian eschatology. The first and more common meaning of end is the temporal conclusion of some process. For example, you are nearing the end of this book, and the end of a basketball game arrives when the clock shows :00 and the final buzzer sounds. The other meaning of end refers to the goal or purpose of some action. In this case, my end in writing this book is to offer an introduction to the discipline and art of theology through narrative thinking, while the end that basketball players have in mind generally is to win the game—although more noble ends such as building character, teamwork, and sportsmanship are often given lip service.

People seem usually to have in mind the first meaning of end when they speak about "the end times" of eschatology. In this case, eschatology is thought to address some timetable of end-time events that mark the ticking down of creation's clock to the finale of the world as we know it, as when the final trumpet sounds. The end of this age, then, is marked by the second coming of Christ, the general resurrection of the dead, and the final Judgment. Or, the end understood as a temporal stopping point can also be applied to our individual lives, as when we die.

It appears unavoidable that this meaning of end certainly must play a part in what we mean by the end of God's Story. Everything finite comes to a conclusion sooner or later; quite apart from the Chris-

206 / The Story of God

tian expectation about the world's end, cosmologists and physicists tell us that, even if human life on this planet manages to survive nuclear and environmental threats, overpopulation or mass famine, eventually the medium-sized star we call "the sun" will burn itself out, and life on this planet will come to a chilling end. And if human beings were someday to develop the space-travel technology to send a colony of people to some habitable planet in the far reaches of our galaxy—thus escaping the sun's demise—astronomers generally believe that eventually the entire universe will either become too cold for life or else will finally collapse in upon itself in one unimaginably hot fireball. Either way, the universe as we know it comes to an end, and all human life with it. In New Testament terms, we are approaching "the day of God, on account of which the heavens will be destroyed by burning, and the elements will melt with intense heat!" (2 Pet. 3:12). Another New Testament author strings together quotations from the Hebrew Bible to make the same point in more poetic language:

> In the beginning, O Lord, you laid the foundations of the earth,
>   and the heavens are the work of your hands.
> They will perish, but you remain;
>   they will all wear out like a garment.
> You will roll them up like a robe;
>   like a garment they will be changed.
> But you remain the same,
>   and your years will never end.
>
> (Heb. 1:10-12, NIV)

In this first sense of the word, then, eschatology's end times remind us that our individual lives, as well as the life of our universe as a whole, is finite and limited. All existence as we know it will come to an end.

The second meaning of end times in eschatology, however, is probably the more significant. Here we speak of God's end or goal for His creation, the universe. Eschatology in this vein attempts to speak about what we believe to be God's intentions for the created order, or where the universe will "end up" as it is brought to its end by His providential leadings. The Book of Revelation provides a compelling vision of God's end for creation:

> And I saw a new heaven and a new earth; for the first heaven and the first earth passed away, and there is no longer any sea. . . . And I heard a loud voice from the throne, saying, "Behold, the tabernacle of God is among men, and He shall dwell among them, and they shall be His people, and God Himself shall be among them, and He shall wipe away every tear from their eyes; and there shall no longer be any death; there shall no longer be any mourning, or cry-

ing, or pain; the first things have passed away." And He who sits on the throne said, "Behold, I am making all things new." And He said, "Write, for these words are faithful and true" (21:1, 3-5).

The end time in this second sense, then, is rooted in the biblical conviction that God the Creator will re-create the universe, that God the Redeemer is faithful to bring about a redeemed and renewed creation immersed in the joy and fellowship of God. Christian eschatology proclaims that God is able to bring about His purposes for creation—and that He will do so! Every story comes to an end, and the end of God's Story, in terms of both its temporal end and its purposive end, is *shalom*: "the healing of the nations" (Rev. 22:2).

26

What Do You Expect? A Lesson from John the Baptist

When eschatology becomes the focus of people's attention, it is not unusual for a great deal of speculation and argument to occupy center stage. We often find it intriguing to debate fine points about pre- or post-millennialism, or pre-, post-, or mid-tribulationism, or the Rapture, or the Great White Throne Judgment, or the Antichrist, or heaven and hell, or, most frightening, all of the above at the same time. The doctrines of eschatology will always generate plenty of controversy and excitement, because they have to do with our expectations about unknown, future events. For this reason, it may be profitable for us to begin our reflections about eschatological matters by considering a bit of narrative theology from Matthew's Gospel. The passage begins this way:

> Now when John in prison heard of the works of Christ, he sent word by his disciples, and said to Him, "Are You the Expected One, or shall we look for someone else?" (11:2-3).

In order to understand John's question, perhaps we should attempt to sit down with him in his prison cell. Feel the damp darkness that surrounds him, the tepid water that comes up to his ankles, the strong steel shackles that cut into his skin and hold him prisoner. See the rats that scamper in and out of his cell, providing his only company. Imagine the darkness of his spirit as he languishes in his cell, the discouragement that arises from deep within, threatening to choke him. John, the one called Baptizer, is wasting away in Herod's dungeon.

John is thinking. He is thinking about all that has happened to him since the word of God came to him in the wilderness. Like the prophets of old, it seems speaking God's word has only gotten him into trouble. And he is confused. Nothing is making any sense, and in the darkness of his cell, the darkness of his doubt, he questions his own message. He remembers how, in the beginning, it had all seemed so clear. He had come preaching with the fire of a grizzled mountain man, "Repent! For the kingdom of heaven is at hand!" (Matt. 3:2). He had insisted that baptism was not only for Gentiles who desired to convert to Judaism, but a sign of repentance for Jews as well—a radical and revolutionary message. To those who were counting on their Jewish heritage for right standing with God, he boomed, "Don't think you can say to yourselves, 'We have Abraham for our father,' for God is able from these stones to raise up children to Abraham!" (v. 9).

He had insisted that those who would repent, or turn from their sins, be baptized as a sign of their repentance. He had warned that One was soon coming who would "clear [the] threshing floor" and would "burn up the chaff with unquenchable *fire*" (v. 12, italics added).

And then, *He* came. He came down to the banks of the Jordan and asked for baptism.

"What, *me* baptize *You?*" John had asked in shock and bewilderment. His was a baptism of repentance from sin! What need did the Holy and Righteous One to be baptized with these sinners? If anything, John remembered saying, he should be baptized by Jesus! Yet Jesus had insisted that it must be done that way. John had finally acquiesced, but somehow it simply had made no sense then—nor does it now, as he sits in that dark cell.

His mind begins to replay the events that have landed him in this hellish place. His preaching of repentance and righteousness was no respecter of persons; he had gone after even Herod the king for living in adultery. He had stuck out his neck for righteousness' sake, and now he sits here in the darkness, wishing to see the light of day once more.

Finally, though, it is not his immediate circumstances that trouble him now. He realizes that those who stand for righteousness often suffer hardship at the world's hands. After all, had not the great prophet Isaiah been sawn in half? No, his suffering, bleak as it is, is not what plagues him most. It is the reports of Jesus' ministry that are filtering down into Herod's dungeon—these are what trouble him. "When John in prison heard of the works of Christ . . ."

Yes, it was those *deeds of Jesus* that had moved him to send a couple of his disciples to Jesus. They were to ask Him, "Jesus, what in the world are You doing?"

Are You really the One I said You were? I went out on a limb and pointed to You as the Messiah, the Anointed One, Israel's Redeemer. But now I really want to know, *who are You?* I spoke of One who would baptize the world in the fire of judgment, who would separate the godly from the sinners like wheat from the chaff, who would cleanse this world from sin and burn the ungodly in unquenchable fire!

Tell me, are You the Coming One . . . or do we look for another?

*   *   *

Jesus was not performing according to John's expectations. John was perplexed, discouraged, in the dark. And only an hour ago his messengers had returned with a reply from Jesus. Probably, John had hoped to hear something like this:

"My armies are growing, John. Caesarea, the headquarters of the Roman government, is about to fall. A group of underground resistance fighters will soon spring you from jail. Sinners are being destroyed, and the judgment and wrath are about to begin."

But no. John is still mulling over that mysterious reply from Jesus, brought to him by his disciples:

"Go and report to John what you hear and see: the blind receive sight and the lame walk, the lepers are cleansed and the deaf hear, and the dead are raised up, and the poor have the gospel preached to them" (Matt. 11:4-5).

"Couldn't Jesus just give me a straight answer to my question?" John asks. "I mean, He replies with His actions—*the very actions that raised my question in the first place!* He's not what I expected, and now He rubs it in good while I sit in this prison . . .

the blind see . . .
   the lame walk . . .
      lepers are healed and the deaf hear . . .
      the dead are raised up, and the poor hear the Good News.

"The Good News? What about judgment? What about the unquenchable fire of God's angry wrath? What about . . . ?" And then John remembers Jesus' brief postscript:

"And blessed is he who keeps from stumbling over Me" (v. 6).

"Jesus, what do You mean by *that?*"

*   *   *

As we sit here in this prison cell with John, perhaps we can understand his feelings. He sits in misery—for doing what is right. And God is not acting in the way John expects. He expects a vengeful, mighty Messiah who forces compliance by brute power, who destroys the opposition and casts His enemies into hellfire. Instead, he's hearing reports of a gentle, humble healer who loves tax collectors and welcomes prostitutes. John is a wilderness ascetic, wearing a coarse camel hair garment and eating grasshoppers; Jesus, on the other hand, is called "a gluttonous man and a drunkard, a friend of tax-gatherers and sinners!" (Matt. 11:19). Where's the might, where's the judgment, where's the vengeance in all this?

"God, what are You doing?"

Surely there is a very simple lesson here for us. John the Baptizer, like most of his contemporaries, expected a messiah who would be a mighty military deliverer. Though he was considered by Jesus to be "a prophet . . . and . . . more than a prophet" (Matt. 11:9), John did not understand how Jesus could possibly be the Fulfillment of Jewish eschatological hopes. And it seems that, indeed, Jesus did not fulfill those hopes—and perhaps that is just the point.

What do *you* expect? What kinds of sermons or lectures have we heard that have created certain expectations, or set certain dates for certain eschatological events, only to see those expectations go unfulfilled? The basic lesson from John the Baptist would be, then, that God is free and God is unpredictable. He is not restricted by, nor under any obligation to fulfill, any particular eschatological scenario that may be laid out for Him by the finely tuned eschatological charts drawn up by so-called prophecy experts. This was a lesson that John Wesley seemed to have learned, for he demonstrated little interest in the popular prophecies of his own era. A typical example of his attitude is found in a letter in which Wesley comments on the prediction of a Bible scholar named Johann Bengel that "the milennial reign of Christ would begin in the year 1836. I have no opinion at all upon the head: I can determine nothing at all about it. These calculations are far above, out of my sight. I have only one thing to do, to save my soul, and those that hear me."[1]

The one affirmation we can make, on the basis of this Matthean narrative, is that God's labor in history toward eschatological fulfillment has to do with healing, restoration, life, good news—for that is what He has revealed about himself in Jesus. God has revealed himself in Jesus—and eschatology must be shaped by that revelation. In other words, Christian eschatology at its best affirms that the ultimate fulfillment of God's purposes has already been glimpsed in the loving and merciful ministry of Jesus. That means, therefore, that our expectations and speculations about end-time events must never be allowed to run free of the revelation of God's heart in the person of Jesus, the "gentle and humble in heart" (Matt. 11:29). If "Jesus Christ is the same yesterday and today, yes and forever" (Heb. 13:8), then the Second-Coming One will not, indeed cannot, be essentially unlike the One who has already come.

"Even so, come, Lord Jesus" (Rev. 22:20, KJV)—even if the manner of Your coming surprises us.

---

1. Wesley, *Works* 12:319.

27

The Coming of the Kingdom

The confusion John experienced in his prison cell can surely be traced to a considerable extent to the fact that both he and Jesus seemed to be preaching the same message. The Gospel of Matthew, in fact, characterizes the preaching of John the Baptist and Jesus with identical words: "Repent, for the kingdom of heaven is at hand" (3:2; 4:17).[1]

Since this was the message proclaimed by both Jesus and John, it is crucial for us to understand as fully as we can what that message meant to those who heard it. When first-century Jews heard that God's kingdom was near, what images or hopes did this evoke in their minds? Or what did it mean to Jesus' disciples when He instructed them to pray for the coming of God's kingdom?

It is noteworthy, and a bit surprising, that the phrase "kingdom of God," which is predominant in the Synoptic Gospels, rarely appears, if ever, in the Hebrew Scriptures. The *concept* of God's kingdom or reign is, nonetheless, strongly present. When God called the Jewish people to partnership with himself in the covenant at Sinai, He summarized the purpose of the covenant with the prefatory proviso, "Now then, if you will indeed obey My voice and keep My covenant, then you shall be My own possession among all the peoples, for all the earth is Mine; and you shall be to Me a kingdom of priests and a holy nation" (Exod. 19:5-6). Israel was called out from among the nations to be a nation of representatives for God—a kingdom of priests with the obvious impli-

---

1. Matthew tends to use the phrase "kingdom of heaven," while the other Gospels often use "kingdom of God" instead. Occasionally someone attempts to build some theological scheme on a supposed difference between the "kingdom of God" and the "kingdom of heaven," but since the phrases often appear in precisely parallel passages, such attempts are ill-founded and futile. More to the point, Matthew is the most distinctively Jewish of our four Gospels, and Jews in Jesus' time often used the word "heaven" in the place of "God" out of sheer reverence for the divine name and majesty. One is left to wonder whether Matthew used "kingdom of heaven" out of his own Jewish sense of reverence, or whether he used it out of deference to his primarily Jewish audience—or if indeed Jesus himself, a first-century Jew, after all, actually utilized the phrase at least on occasion.

cation that it would be God who would reign in this kingdom. God is no less the Ruler of all creation and its peoples when establishing this particular covenantal kingdom; the text, in fact, makes it clear that Israel's task of representing God has as its goal to be a priesthood to all peoples, *"for all the earth is Mine."*

The concept of God as the King of Israel (and again, to be sure, of all creation) is strongly implied also in the story of Israel's clamoring for a king, and the prophet Samuel's response to that desire (see chap. 14). Samuel insisted that God was to be their King, but God, the story says, gave in to their request. The royal career of God's first choice, Saul, ended in failure, shame, and finally suicide; but he was followed by the greatest king in Israel's history and memory: David. When in subsequent generations Israel's fortunes began to fade, when in fact destruction and exile became Israel's lot, the memory of David's glory remained as a ray of hope. The prophets of Israel began to look forward to a future fulfillment of God's reign in which, more often than not, the fond (and romanticized) memories of David's kingship provided the model and ideal. For example, Jeremiah prophesied,

> "Behold, the days are coming," declares the Lord,
> "When I shall raise up for David a righteous Branch;
> And He will reign as king and act wisely
> And do justice and righteousness in the land.
> In His days Judah will be saved,
> And Israel will dwell securely;
> And this is His name by which He will be called,
> 'The Lord our righteousness'"
>
> (23:5-6)

Or, in Isaiah's vision of the future,

> Then a shoot will spring from the stem of Jesse [David's father],
> And a branch from his roots will bear fruit.
> And the Spirit of the Lord will rest on Him,
> The spirit of wisdom and understanding,
> The spirit of counsel and strength . . .
> He will not judge by what His eyes see,
> Nor make a decision by what His ears hear;
> But with righteousness He will judge the poor,
> And decide with fairness for the afflicted of the earth . . .
> Also righteousness will be the belt about His loins,
> And faithfulness the belt about His waist.
>
> (11:1-5)

It should not surprise us, then, that Israel's hope for redemption had a distinctively political tone; their deliverer was to be a righteous king whose glory would surpass even that of David. This is why the anticipated Messiah was called "the son of David." It was not primarily a matter of genealogy, though that was not unimportant. Rather, "son of David" meant first of all the one who would come in the spirit of David, under divine anointing, to restore God's rule over Israel and even over all the earth. The deliverer would be *another David.* This is why Matthew was careful to identify Jesus as the Son of David in the opening of his Gospel, and why on several occasions the Gospels tell us that people addressed Jesus as "the Son of David." There is every reason to believe that the people who greeted Jesus in His royal triumphal entry into Jerusalem believed that He was about to overthrow pagan occupation and rule of the land of Israel and replace it with divine rule:

> Hosanna!
> Blessed is He who comes in the name of the Lord;
> Blessed is the coming kingdom of our father David;
> Hosanna in the highest!
>
> *(Mark 11:9-10)*

We know that those eschatological hopes were dashed less than a week later when this hoped-for Messiah, rather than having conquered the Romans, was himself crucified on a Roman cross as so many other Jewish insurrectionists had been and would be. The disappointed sentiments of the pair of disciples on the Emmaus road undoubtedly were common: "We were hoping that it was He who was going to redeem Israel" (Luke 24:21). There is, clearly, a radical disparity between common Jewish expectations of divine intervention and rule and what Jesus actually delivered. And yet Jesus insisted that the kingdom of God was near at hand! If He did not necessarily mean by "kingdom of God" what most of his fellow Jews meant by the phrase, what *did* He mean? I would suggest three spheres of His ministry that shed light on His intended meaning of "kingdom of God":

First, in His *teachings,* especially His *parables,* the kingdom of God is revealed. Recall how often Jesus' parables open with, "The kingdom of heaven is like . . ." Jesus' images for God's kingdom are drawn from a vast fund of experience in everyday life: divine rule is like a mustard seed that starts out tiny and eventually grows into a great tree; it is like a woman working a bit of leaven into a lump of dough until the lump is thoroughly leavened; it is like a king who forgives vast debts but who in turn expects such graciousness to be extended by his subjects to one another; it is like a shepherd who lovingly seeks out the one stray lamb; it is like a woman who rejoices at having discovered a lost coin while cleaning the house. These, of course, are but a sampling of Jesus' kingdom images in His parables, but they and many others of His tales share a dominant theme: there is much that is unexpected and surprising in God's kingdom. It is a realm in which those hired at the eleventh hour may indeed receive equal wages as those who worked all day, a realm in which the vagabonds of "the highways and byways" are invited to the royal table in place of the rich and influential, a realm in which the poor have a special place and inheritance, a realm in which the hungry are fed and those who weep will laugh for joy, where all the economic and political structures of this world will be upended and inverted (Luke 6:20-26). Jesus shared in His Jewish contemporaries' expectations of an impending reign of God, but there was plenty in His parables to suggest that the element of profound surprise, the element of God's delightful unpredictability, made it impossible for human imagination fully to understand the nature of God's coming rule.

Second, we see the coming of the Kingdom in Jesus' *healings* and *exorcisms.* Jesus was known as One whose teaching, delivered with a sense of inner authority, was ratified by His mighty works. After one exorcism early in His ministry, Luke reports that "amazement came upon them all, and they began discussing with one another saying, 'What is this message? For with authority and power He commands the unclean spirits, and they come out'" (4:36). His defeat of demons was a powerful sign of the approach of God's kingdom, overcoming the powers of darkness and oppression. We have already seen in chapter 17 that Jesus, in defending His ministry of exorcism against the Pharisees' accusation that He "casts out demons only by Beelzebul the ruler of the demons," responded that He cast out demons by the Spirit of God—and, in His words, "If I cast out demons by the Spirit of God, *then the kingdom of God has come upon you*" (Matt. 12:24, 28, italics added).

Similarly, Jesus' ministry of healing, often done in the context of His proclamation of God's kingdom (cf. Mark 2:1-12), can be understood as a manifestation of God's future kingdom as it invaded first-century Galilee in the person of Jesus. If indeed God's rule will be one of *shalom,* that is, of peace and well-being in every dimension of earthly existence, including physical, emotional, relational, political, and ecological, then Jesus' acts of healing were like invasions from the future, a foretaste of the "healing of the nations" that God has in store (Rev. 22:2).

Third, Jesus expresses and reveals the kingdom of God in His *love* and *humility,* particularly as He extends himself to the *downtrodden, outcast,* and *marginalized* of society. For Jesus, God's kingdom is a kingdom of love—love for neighbor, yes, but more amazingly (and thus more in line with the nature of divine rule), love for enemy. It was a love that was to encompass the Romans who oppressed them, the Samaritans who despised them, and the tax gatherers who cheated them. So free and radical with His love was Jesus that at least a handful of prostitutes were liberated by His reconciling love from their enslavement in their degrading, dehumanizing profession. While the Pharisees tended to define themselves particularly by the company they would keep at a dinner table, Jesus was the honored Guest (and sometimes the Host) of dinner gatherings whose participants it would be kind to describe as a motley crew. Tax collectors, prostitutes, and other assorted sordid sinners were all welcome at His table. Jesus' "table fellowship," as it is referred to by modern biblical scholars, was undoubtedly for Him (and for those who got the point) a sign and symbol of the coming messianic feast in God's kingdom—a feast in which, in Jesus' own words, "Many shall come from east and west [i.e., non-Jews], and recline at the table with Abraham, and Isaac, and Jacob, in the kingdom of heaven" (Matt. 8:11). Jesus' festive dinners with outcasts and sinners was an enactment of the prophet Isaiah's vision of "a lavish banquet for all peoples" to be prepared by God, "a banquet of aged wine, choice pieces with marrow," in which God will "swallow up death for all time, and the Lord God will wipe tears away from all faces" (Isa. 25:6, 8). Jesus' table fellowship, for which He was roundly criticized by the Pharisees, was a foretaste of this feast in God's coming kingdom.

There was another marginalized and oft-forgotten group of people to whom Jesus' love and welcome were particularly extended: children. Recall that when Jesus' disciples attempted to prohibit a crowd of parents who wanted Him to bless their children, He scolded the men, welcomed the children, and told all the adults present that "of such is the kingdom of heaven" (Matt. 19:14, KJV). And of course, when His disciples debated over which of them was "greatest in the kingdom of heaven," Matthew's Gospel offers us this memory of the Lord of love:

> And He called a child to Himself and set him before them, and said, "Truly I say to you, unless you are converted and become like children, you shall not enter the kingdom of heaven. Whoever then humbles himself as this child, he is the greatest in the kingdom of heaven. And whoever receives one such child in My name receives Me" (18:1, 2-5).

It is remarkable that Jesus characterized God's reign as having the nature of a child's humility, and so identified himself with children as to teach that receiving a child in His name was in fact receiving Him. If God's kingdom is about love for God and neighbor (Mark 12:28-34), indeed for enemy; if God's kingdom is about extravagant, reconciling love lavished upon sinners; if God's kingdom is about the vulnerability and humility of a child: *then this King and His kingdom are like none on earth!* This is important because it chastens our tendency to think of God along the lines of an earthly king sitting on a royal throne, surrounded by wealth and power, and essentially untouched by the struggles and suffering of his subjects. It challenges our notions of divine power when they are rooted in the experience of worldly potentates, who all too often have enforced their wishes unilaterally upon powerless peons. God's reign, as revealed in Jesus' words and works, is a quiet, humble, loving, reconciling reign. God's rule is not inflicted upon us; rather, we are invited to partake. Perhaps the nature of the divine Kingdom is best exemplified in Jesus' words, "Come to Me, all who are weary and heavy-laden, and I will give you rest. Take My yoke upon you, and learn from Me, for I am gentle and humble in heart; and you shall find rest for your souls. For My yoke is easy, and My load is light" (11:28-30).

No wonder John the Baptist felt confused! He preached the coming of a kingdom that would blaze forth in wrath, fire, and judgment (Matt. 3:7, 10-12), while Jesus offered forgiveness, healing, and grace. And Christian faith confesses that indeed in Jesus the kingdom of God is come. Jesus, in His teaching, mighty works, and humble love, embodies the actual reign of God. He is the Prince, heaven's Vanguard, the One who establishes a beachhead for the kingdom of heaven on earth. Thus, when a group of Pharisees quizzed Him concerning the date for the arrival of God's kingdom, Jesus responded, "The kingdom of God is not coming with signs to be observed; nor will they say, 'Look, here it is!' or, 'There it is!' For behold, the kingdom of God is in your midst" (Luke 17:20-21). Modern biblical scholarship is virtually unanimous in understanding Jesus to be referring to himself in this statement, revealing that He is the Representative of the Kingdom, the One in and by whom the kingdom of God was in their midst.

But if the Kingdom was truly *present* in Jesus' ministry, there is nonetheless also a *future* dimension to God's rule. In Luke's Gospel, we find a poignant portrait of Jesus' own anticipation of the future fulfillment of all creation, set within the narrative of His last meal with His disciples. As He eats and drinks with His friends, he vows not to partake again "until it is fulfilled in the kingdom of God," or "until the kingdom of God comes" (22:16, 18). Later that night, Jesus once more speaks of God's rule as being diametrically opposed to political powerhouses who "lord it" over others, indeed as being of the nature of servanthood. (In other words, God is a servant.) This is the dimension of the Kingdom that is realizable in our lives today, through the enabling presence of Christ the Servant among us (v. 27). But Jesus then looks around the table and envisions once more a future dimension of the

Kingdom: "And you are those who have stood by Me in My trials; and just as My Father has granted Me a kingdom, I grant you that you may eat and drink at My table in My kingdom, and you will sit on thrones judging the twelve tribes of Israel" (vv. 28-30).

It is such promises as those that keep us from spiritualizing the concept of God's kingdom entirely, or of believing that in His first coming Jesus has already established God's rule in a definitive or final fashion. We find, here, a tension between the traditional Jewish eschatological hope of political redemption by a son of David, and the Christian affirmation that in Jesus the kingdom has come. But it is a tension that the New Testament does in fact maintain. It is no wonder that following Jesus' resurrection, the disciples assumed that the political redemption they had hoped for was now imminent. "And so when they had come together, they were asking Him, saying, 'Lord, is it at this time You are restoring the kingdom to Israel?'" (Acts 1:6). Had Jesus desired to dispel such a notion, this would have been a golden opportunity. Instead, Jesus replied, "It is not for you to know times or epochs which the Father has fixed by His own authority; *but you shall receive power when the Holy Spirit has come upon you*" (vv. 7-8a, italics added). Jesus did not deny the Jewish hope that John the Baptist had envisioned, in which God's rule would decisively usher in an age of righteous judgment; Jesus did, however, turn their attention away from the future Kingdom and toward the present rule of God in human lives through the power of the Spirit.

So it is that the kingdom of God is both present and future, holding us in the tension of "already/not yet." The rule of God is already here by the coming of Jesus and in His continued presence through the gift of the Holy Spirit (Rom. 14:17); it is not yet in the sense that we await the fulfillment of that Kingdom in the messianic banquet and the healing of the nations.

It is because we yet await the coming of God's kingdom in its fullness that we ought not to identify the kingdom of God with the Church of Jesus Christ. Since the time of Augustine, there has been a tendency, particularly in Roman Catholicism, to do just that: to think of God's reign virtually solely in terms of the present power and influence of the Church in history. The general Protestant reaction has tended toward identifying the kingdom of God not with visible institutions but with an invisible reign of God in the hearts of believers. Neither idea, however, does full justice to the biblical hope that the Kingdom's fulfillment involves a *future* fulfillment of *all* of God's creation, so that the rule of God is much bigger, much more comprehensive and universal in scope, than the Church. All Christians are, nonetheless, called to be citizens of that Kingdom now and to struggle and pray for its soon coming; in the words of Paul Tillich, "They feel—or should feel—that they are fighting agents of the Kingdom of God, leading forces in the drive toward the fulfilment of history."[2]

This certainly should drive home the important theological idea that eschatology is not simply about what we are waiting for God to do; eschatology is about His vision of *shalom* for all creation, a vision He shares with us and, at least to some extent, entrusts to us. If eschatological reflection should ever encourage us to sit on our hands and wait for deliverance, it is counterproductive to God's commitment to covenantal partnership with us. It is true that His reign is a reality that only He can enact, and yet we have seen repeatedly that God's apparently preferred mode of action is to enlist and enable our own active response to His initiatives. It is incumbent upon us to understand the concept of God's kingdom not as an "opiate for the masses," as Karl Marx believed about religion, but as a goad to our praying and acting for human societies that ever more nearly approximate the model of the Kingdom as we have glimpsed it in Jesus. For in the words of contemporary theologian Jurgen Moltmann, "We are construction workers and not only interpreters of [God's] future."[3]

2. Paul Tillich, *Systematic Theology*, 3 vols. (Chicago: University of Chicago Press, 1951-63), 3:376.

3. Jurgen Moltmann, *Religion, Revolution, and the Future* (New York: Charles Scribner's Sons, 1969), 34.

28

Death, Resurrection, and Immortality

We all die. This is a fact that, while not particularly inviting, is inescapable for each of us. Death, from the perspective of the living, signals the end of the story of our lives, the final period on the final page of the story we are.

Eschatology, we have noted, has to do with end times and end events. It is therefore no surprise that the meaning of our deaths, and questions concerning the possibility of our enduring beyond death, are typically considered eschatological issues. In fact, one of the important considerations of eschatology is precisely the question of our destiny beyond death. Do we, in some fashion or another, continue to live beyond the horizons of this life?

That question has been answered by curious human beings in a variety of ways. The answer least amenable to Christian faith is the idea of *reincarnation* or *transmigration of souls*, which is rooted most typically in the Hindu and Buddhist traditions. This idea recently has gained popularity in the West, particularly with the onslaught of New Age thinking. Essentially, reincarnation is the belief that the soul is an eternal entity that undergoes a virtually infinite number of creaturely incarnations throughout history, perhaps not even always as a human being. From a Christian perspective, this idea tends to devalue the present life, in the sense that the "real" life of the soul is not identified with any of its finite embodiments but rather with its eternal, transcendent journey. One's personal identity and sense of responsibility for *this life*, therefore, tends to be diffused or even lost. Christian Scripture and tradition offer no support to such an idea, precisely because it deemphasizes human answerability before God for one's allotted lifetime here and now. In the words of Heb. 9:27, often marshaled as evidence against reincarnation, "It is appointed for men to die once and after this comes judgment."

Another answer to the question of whether and how human beings survive death has been offered by the classical Greek philosophical tradition. Here we encounter the idea of *the immortality of the soul,* probably best represented in the writings of Socrates and Plato. For this tradition of thought, human beings are a dualism of body and soul: the body changes, grows old, wrinkles and finally dies, at which point the essentially unchanging soul is liberated. Thus, in this tradition the body is little more than a prison of the soul. For Socrates and Plato, belief in the soul's immortality implied the preexistence of the soul as well, since if the soul truly is immortal, it must be immortal in both temporal "directions," the past as well as the future. Very few Christian theologians, however, have accepted the idea of the soul's preexistence; the most notable of them, the imaginative third-century thinker Origen (185-254), was repeatedly condemned as a heretic by official church councils. The more dominant idea that developed in Christian tradition was a kind of hybrid doctrine of immortality: God creates the soul at the moment of conception, but once created, the soul is eternal. This understanding of the human soul and immortality, called *creationism,* has exercised considerable influence in the history of Christian faith and practice.

Modern biblical scholarship has challenged the classical Greek dualism of body and spirit as being foreign to the dominant anthropology of Scripture. The ancient Hebrews understood the person to be a psychophysical unity, a body animated by **ruach** or breath from God. In the words of biblical scholar D. S. Russell, "Man is regarded [in Israelite thought] as a unity of personality, not a dichotomy of body and soul or a trichotomy of body, soul and spirit. The body is not . . . the mortal shell of the immortal soul."[1] The Hebrew understanding of the human, therefore, left little room for a body/spirit dualism; when the body died, the **nephesh**, or living self, also ceased to be.

The closest the earlier Hebrews appear to have come to a belief in life after death involved the idea of Sheol, the place of the dead, which was a realm of forgetfulness, darkness, and despair. Into this world, a shadowy resemblance of the once-living person descended, forever cut off from the world of life and personality. "When a cloud vanishes, it is gone, so he who goes down to Sheol does not come up" (Job 7:9). There was no particular concept of divine judgment or retribution associated with Sheol, for it was simply the common assembly ground for all the dead. "It is the same for all. There is one fate for the righteous and for the wicked . . . the dead do not know anything, nor have they any longer a reward, for their memory is forgotten" (Eccles. 9:2, 5). In-

---

1. D. S. Russell, *The Method and Message of Jewish Apocalyptic* (Philadelphia: Westminster Press, 1964), 140.

deed, for the pious Hebrew the worst aspect of Sheol is that it involved utter alienation from God: "The dead do not praise the Lord, nor do any who go down into silence" (Ps. 115:17). For the ancient Israelite, the only way to live on beyond death was through one's children and heritage, or in the continuing corporate life of the people Israel.

Despite scattered individual hopes of continuing fellowship with God after death, the typical Jewish conception of Sheol prevailed into the second century before Christ and was officially represented in Jesus' era by the Sadducees. But other ideas, often assimilated by the Jews from surrounding Greek and Persian cultures and given a new slant to fit Jewish presuppositions, had begun to work their way into Jewish literature and speculation about life beyond death. These ideas ran the gamut from the immortality of the soul, to transmigration, to *resurrection of the body.* This, however, is not to suggest that the resurrection hope was merely borrowed wholesale from other cultures. Russell, in *The Method and Message of Jewish Apocalyptic,* argues that there was an inner logic at work within Judaism that eventually gave rise to belief in resurrection:

> The resurrection belief in Israel grew naturally out of [their] convictions that the fellowship they had enjoyed with God in this life could not be broken even by death; and . . . by reason of their particularly Hebrew conception of personality, it was inevitable that they should interpret such survival ultimately in terms of bodily resurrection.[2]

By the time of Jesus, the resurrection hope had gained fairly widespread acceptance among the Jewish people and was championed especially by the Pharisees. The dispute about resurrection was, in fact, one of the major points of contention between the Pharisees and the Sadducees. It was, however, symptomatic of a deeper, more profound difference.

The Sadducees were the politico-religious sect most closely associated with the Jerusalem Temple and its priestly rites. They tended to be among the wealthy elite, having managed to strike a fairly happy compromise with the Roman government occupying Palestine. As such, they were the political and religious "conservatives" of first-century Judaism, with no interest either in overthrowing Roman rule or in religious innovation. As representatives and upholders of the priestly class associated with Temple rites, they accepted only the Pentateuch (Gr., **penta** = five; **teuchos** = book), or the five books of Moses (Genesis, Exodus, Leviticus, Numbers, and Deuteronomy) as canonical Scripture.

---

2. Ibid., 389.

The Pharisees, on the other hand, were much more deeply interested in a Judaism of study and practice than in a Judaism of ritual and sacrifice. They could thus more readily associate with localized synagogues, as opposed to the centralization of power that the Temple represented. Although the Pharisees acquiesced to Roman rule for the sake of Jewish survival, they neither enjoyed nor sought obvious and outright collaboration. They were the "progressives," accepting the writings of the Jewish prophets, poets, and historians as Scripture along with the Pentateuch. On the basis of this significantly larger body of Scripture from which to draw, the Pharisees differed from the Sadducees by believing in angels and demons, the resurrection of the dead, and final judgment. For the Pharisees and many other Jews, in fact, the twin beliefs in resurrection and final judgment complemented their rejection of Roman oppression; soon enough, God's Messiah would come to usher in the consummation of history, which included the resurrection of all people (and often nations) for reward and punishment. A belief in resurrection as the end point of history implies an overturning of history, a righting of wrongs, the establishment of divine justice. Such beliefs would be considered potentially insurrectionary by any ruling political power, including the Romans in first-century Palestine. Hence, the Sadducees had political as well as religious reasons for rejecting the Pharisaic belief in resurrection.

For all of the criticisms Jesus leveled at the Pharisees, it is clear that He sided with them in their differences with the Sadducees. In Matt. 22:23-33, we read of a group of Sadducees who attempted to test Jesus' theology with their "story problem" of the hardy woman who outlasted seven brothers who all tried unsuccessfully to keep the family name alive. According to Jewish law, under certain circumstances the brothers would have been required in turn to marry the woman, but none succeeded in producing offspring. "In the resurrection therefore whose wife of the seven shall she be?" quizzed the Sadducees. "For they all had her" (v. 28).

But notice first of all the role of the woman in the story. She is nothing more than chattel, property, the possession in question. "Whose wife will she be? *For they all had her."* It is significant that Jesus rejects the very basis of the problem. The woman, first of all, does not "belong" to any one or the other of the brothers. If not in the first-century Palestinian world of male domination and supposed superiority, then at least in the resurrection the woman is equal to man, for all "are like angels in heaven" (v. 30).

Jesus then proceeds to offer His argument for resurrection on the basis of Scripture. In doing so, He is willing to engage the Sadducees on their own turf by appealing to the Pentateuch; He quotes from the Exodus story of God's burning bush encounter with Moses: "I am . . . the God of Abraham, the God of Isaac, and the God of Jacob." It is found in Exod. 3:6, though similar self-designations are sprinkled throughout the five books of Moses, the Scriptures the Sadducees recognized as authoritative. Jesus quotes Scriptures they do believe in order to demonstrate the reality of the resurrection, in which they do not believe. His line of argument may seem distant to us, but it has a fairly characteristic Pharisaic-rabbinic ring to it in terms of its interpretation and application of Scripture. When speaking of Moses, Jesus argues, God did not identify himself as the God of the dead (e.g., "I *was* the God of Abraham"), but of those who live ("I *am* the God of Abraham"). Beyond the surface argument based on a simple grammatical point, however, is the more profoundly theological concern for affirming the covenantal faithfulness of God. If He truly is faithful to the covenant relationships and promises established with Abraham, Isaac, and Jacob, surely that divine faithfulness will reach beyond the grave. The underlying truth of the resurrection is that God values relationship with us sufficiently to sustain our identities even beyond our physical death!

For Christian faith, of course, belief in the resurrection does not hinge particularly on the validity of Jesus' repartee with the Sadducees, but rather on His own resurrection from death. Certainly we affirm with Jesus that God is faithful to covenantal relationship to Abraham, Isaac, and Jacob, but the apostle Paul reminds us that God's faithfulness and promises are decisively fulfilled and confirmed in Christ (2 Cor. 1:18-20). It is because of Christ's own resurrection that we "trust . . . in God who raises the dead" (v. 9).

God who raises the dead! This underscores an important truth about belief in resurrection: it is *the act of God,* so that the Christian hope of life beyond this life's horizons does not depend upon some notion of human immortality per se, but squarely and entirely upon divine grace. "This produces a sense of utter dependence upon God in the hour of death, a feeling that is in accordance with the biblical understanding of the human being as having been formed out of 'the dust of the earth,'" writes the philosopher of religion John Hick. "Only through the sovereign creative love of God can there be a new existence beyond the grave."[3]

To be sure, one could argue that the creationism advocated by Augustine and Aquinas and dominant in much of Christian tradition, while teaching a kind of immortality of the soul, recognizes equally surely that life after death is a divine gift. And if one keeps in mind the

---

3. John Hick, *Philosophy of Religion,* 4th ed. (Englewood Cliffs, N.J.: Prentice Hall, 1990), 122-23.

Christian understanding of the universe as being sustained in being every moment by the gracious creative power of God, one could demonstrate that the doctrine of the immortality of the soul, at least in a Christian context, depends just as entirely and radically upon God as does the doctrine of the resurrection.

Even granting this, there are three critical reasons for upholding *divine resurrection* in preference over *immortality of the soul* as the Christian hope for life beyond death: (1) the good news of the apostles was not that Jesus was an immortal soul, but that God had raised Him from the dead; (2) the Bible in general has little to say about the soul as an immortal entity, speaking usually instead of "soul" as roughly equivalent to *livingness;* and (3) resurrection in the biblical proclamation is a resurrection of *the body,* and thus implies yet another affirmation of the goodness of the material order in a way that "immortality of the soul" simply does not and cannot.

The third point deserves a bit more consideration. Paul assured the Corinthians that God's act of resurrection does not depend upon resuscitating corpses or reconstituting the same atoms and molecules that composed the person at death; the resurrection body, after all, is raised "in glory" and "in power," a "spiritual body" (1 Cor. 15:43, 44). It is, nonetheless, a *body,* underscoring once again that God is the Creator and Sustainer of the material order, and that He affirms its goodness. Human beings are not spirits encased in bodies eagerly anticipating their emancipation. Rather, they are created and in-breathed ("enspirited") bodies whose final destiny before God is to be re-created and restored spiritual bodies.

In Christian faith, the goodness of the body (and by implication, the material order of creation) is celebrated in creation, reaffirmed in the Incarnation, and anticipated in resurrection. Indeed, Paul in his Epistle to the Romans extends the glorious resurrection hope to the entirety of the created order:

> For the anxious longing of the creation waits eagerly for the revealing of the sons of God. For the creation . . . itself also will be set free from its slavery to corruption into the freedom of the glory of the children of God. For we know that the whole creation groans and suffers the pains of childbirth together until now. And not only this, but also we ourselves, having the first fruits of the Spirit, even we ourselves groan within ourselves, waiting eagerly for our adoption as sons, *the redemption of our body (8:19-23, italics added).*[4]

If our bodies are created by God, and redeemed by God through

---

4. For a penetrating analysis of Paul's "body language," see John A. T. Robinson's little book *The Body* (Philadelphia: Westminster Press, 1952).

Christ's incarnation and resurrection, then a Christian sense of obligation to human need must go much deeper than the notion of "a never-dying soul to save." It is the whole person in all of his or her embodiedness that God creates, loves, and cares for, and to whom Jesus directs His disciples' attention as servants (Matt. 25:31-46). But using Paul's imagery of a groaning creation as a basis, we can also argue that God's love and concern for embodied, material creation extends beyond human beings to include the whole universe. This, in turn, leads again to the legitimacy—not to mention validity and even divinely ordained obligation—of developing a Christian ecological awareness and commitment. Surely there *is* "a wideness in God's mercy," a wideness in which the doctrine of bodily resurrection calls us to participate.

29

Human Responsibility and Divine Judgment

The doctrine of resurrection as explored in the previous chapter teaches us that we are all of lasting significance to God, sufficiently important to our Creator that He wills us to exist even beyond our earthly demise. The doctrine of judgment, on the other hand, reminds us that we are not only *significant* to God but also *accountable* to God. To be accountable means that we are required and able to give an account of our lives; we are answerable for our thoughts, deeds, and words, and asked by God to give such an answer.

The doctrines of resurrection and judgment are, in fact, closely related in the history of Christian thought. Their inseparability is powerfully anticipated in Dan. 12:2, one of the clearest statements concerning resurrection in the Hebrew canon: "And many of those who sleep in the dust of the ground will awake, these to everlasting life, but the others to disgrace and everlasting contempt." The apostle Paul writes out of this Jewish tradition of resurrection and judgment when he refers to "the day of wrath and revelation of the righteous judgment of God, who will render to every man according to his deeds: to those who by perseverance in doing good seek for glory and honor and immortality, eternal life; but to those who are selfishly ambitious and do not obey the truth, but obey unrighteousness, wrath and indignation" (Rom. 2:5-8).

Paul goes on in the same passage to touch upon one of the enduring questions raised by the biblical doctrine of a final judgment: if the criterion of judgment is the extent to which a person, in Paul's phrase, "obeys the truth," what of the vast millions of people who have never even heard the truth of biblical revelation? This is an important question, but not the only one. We might also ask: And for those who have heard, what precisely does it mean to "obey the truth"? Does this imply that we are saved by our works? How do divine grace and human faith figure into the meaning of final judgment?

As is the case with other eschatological doctrines, the doctrine of judgment has tended to spawn considerable speculation upon the number and modes of divine judgment. Each differing scenario that has been offered tends to answer such questions as we have already formulated in its own distinctive fashion. Rather than trying to sort through these various possibilities, we shall stay nearer the heart of Wesleyan eschatology if we offer some basic (if general) convictions about the doctrine of judgment rather than entering into the ongoing fray about who gets judged when and under what circumstances. Those basic convictions or principles are three in number:

First, God is a just Judge. This is a conviction that flows out of the basic biblical affirmation that God is love. If He truly is love, then we can be confident that His demand that we be answerable for our lives will be a demand grounded in ultimate justice or fairness. Because only God truly "knows our frame," or of what we are made, and is "mindful that we are but dust" (Ps. 103:14), only He can adequately judge each individual person. In our quest for fairness in our individual relationships with others, as well as in our society's lawcourts, we attempt to take motives into consideration as we judge others' deeds. But in the final analysis, it is only God who is able, in Paul's words, to "judge the secrets of men through Christ Jesus" (Rom. 2:16). In this connection H. Orton Wiley wrote, "He, only, is all-wise and to Him alone are known the innermost secrets of men's lives. He understands not only their actions, but their inward thoughts and hidden motives—even their natures and the possibilities of those natures."[1]

It is both comforting and discomforting that God sees us as we truly are, that "there is no creature hidden from His sight, but all things are open and laid bare to the eyes of Him with whom we have to do" (Heb. 4:13). It is comforting in that it assures us that divine judgment of our lives takes into account all the idiosyncrasies of our personal stories: our hurts, struggles, misunderstandings, and weaknesses. God need not judge us according to some abstract ideal, for He knows each of us thoroughly as individuals and can judge our lives accordingly.

There is a story told about an 18th-century Jewish rabbi, Zushya—and retold very often by both Jews and Christians since—that powerfully communicates this truth of divine judgment. As he lay on his deathbed, Zushya lamented to those gathered around how little he had accomplished during his lifetime. One of his students asked him if the rabbi feared the divine judgment awaiting him. Zushya began to reply, "Yes," but then stopped himself. "No. For when I appear before the

---

1. Wiley, *Christian Theology* 3:342-43.

Almighty, I will not be asked, 'Why were you not Moses?' or 'Why were you not David?' I will only be asked, 'Why were you not Zushya?'"

God's thorough knowledge of us, and His demand of answerability on our part, can of course also be discomforting, for it means that He knows when we have chosen the lesser road, when we have consciously been and done less than what was possible for us, considering the gifts and graces that were ours in this life. God knows when we have not been our truest selves! One of the truths of Jesus' many parables is that much shall be required of the one to whom much has been given (Luke 12:48). Yet this discomforting aspect of the inescapability of "the eyes of Him with whom we have to do," the thorough and complete knowledge of our lives that God possesses, should never blur the essentially good news that He is just and fair. This is particularly so since, according to the witness of the Gospels, Jesus demonstrates and teaches that divine justice is first of all gracious and forgiving in nature. Jesus' willingness to forgive when others were ready to condemn and destroy (e.g., John 8:2-11) reveals God's own desire to receive us unto himself even in spite of our transgressions. But that willingness, even anxiousness, to forgive is nonetheless tempered by a profound sense of justice.

Probably the finest illustration of these two elements of forgiveness and justice in divine judgment is found in Jesus' parable of the king who wished to "settle accounts" with his slaves (Matt. 18:23). When one subject who owed millions was ushered into his presence, this king "felt compassion and released him and forgave him the debt" (v. 27). *That is divine grace!* But when it reached the king's ears that the subject had immediately turned around and treated a fellow servant harshly over a debt of approximately one day's wage, the king summoned him back into his presence. "Should you not also have had mercy on your fellow slave, even as I had mercy on you?" he asked. "And his lord, moved with anger, handed him over to the torturers until he should repay all that was owed him" (vv. 33-34). *That is divine judgment!* Jesus concludes this parable of judgment with the words, "So shall My heavenly Father also do to you, if each of you does not forgive his brother from your heart" (v. 35). The inherent justice of divine judgment, as it is revealed in this parable, is that God is anxious and willing to offer us grace, but also requires us to respond to that grace by living out of its bounty in our relationships to those around us.

The *second* basic conviction of a Wesleyan theology concerning divine judgment of our lives is that *God has committed final judgment into the hands of Jesus.* This second principle can readily be understood as an extension of the first; divine justice and fairness in judgment is manifested in the fact that God entrusts our judgment to a fellow human being, One who has walked in our shoes and shared in our human lot—and not one who, in the words of Hebrews, "cannot sympathize with our weaknesses" (4:15).

Jesus, the divine Son who shares fully in our humanity, and who fully exemplifes what it is to be truly human, is thereby fully qualified to be the Standard or Judge by whom all people are measured. This was apparently one of the primary emphases in the Early Church's proclamation of the resurrected Jesus. Thus Peter preached to the Gentile Cornelius and his household, "And [God] ordered us to preach to the people, and solemnly to testify that this is the One who has been appointed by God as Judge of the living and the dead" (Acts 10:42). And thus Paul later preached to the learned Athenian philosophers, "God is now declaring to men that all everywhere should repent, because He has fixed a day in which He will judge the world in righteousness through a Man whom He has appointed, having furnished proof to all men by raising Him from the dead" (17:30-31). We find, then, in this early layer of Christian proclamation the idea that it is precisely as the Resurrected One that Jesus is revealed and appointed by God to be the One through whom divine judgment shall be meted to His fellow human beings.

John's Gospel states essentially the same truth on several occasions, most notably 5:22: "For not even the Father judges anyone, but He has given all judgment to the Son." This theme is explored further in this Gospel, and even qualified in an interesting way, when Jesus says, "And if anyone hears My sayings, and does not keep them, I do not judge him; for I did not come to judge the world, but to save the world. He who rejects Me, and does not receive My sayings, has one who judges him; the word I spoke is what will judge him at the last day" (12:47-48). What is fascinating about this is that the accent is placed upon God's intention to save, not to condemn or judge. If the Father has entrusted judgment to the Son, the Son in turn (like the Father) is not nearly so interested in judgment as in grace (3:17)! True, there is a judgment that will be allotted to all, but it is not so much Jesus himself as the word He has spoken that will act as judge.

Once again, however, this idea that Jesus' spoken word is itself the criterion of judgment raises the question concerning those virtually countless people who have never heard that word. How can those people be judged by that word?

This important query leads to the third basic conviction in a Wesleyan theological understanding of the doctrine of final judgment, which is that *God, in Christ, will judge each person according to his or her light or extent of understanding of God's will and gospel.* The Pauline text with which we opened this chapter moves to a consideration of this issue when Paul speaks of "Gentiles who do not have the Law" (i.e., revelation), who nonetheless "do instinctively the things of the Law." Such people, says Paul, "not having the Law, are a law to themselves, in that they show the work of the Law written in their hearts, their conscience bearing witness" (Rom. 2:14-15). The apostle to the Gentiles here speaks of the possibility of heathen peoples who, responding to the light of prevenient grace as it impinges upon them in their own culture and circumstances (cf. chapter 4 earlier), live according to God's will to the extent that they perceive and understand it. Thus John Wesley, in his sermon titled "On Faith," referred to the faith of heathens and Muslims as lacking not sincerity but light. "It cannot be doubted," Wesley wrote, "but this plea will avail for millions of modern Heathens. Inasmuch as to them little is given, of them little will be required. As to the ancient Heathens, . . . no more therefore will be expected of them, than the living up to the light they had."[2]

Indeed, this principle of divine judgment according to the light received is yet another dimension of our first principle that God is an eminently fair and just Judge. It means that He does not hold a person answerable for what he or she has never heard or comprehended (cf. John 15:22, 24). This has important implications for the way we understand God's judgment even of people who seem to have heard at least a minimum of gospel truth; only God, who judges the hearts, knows the extent to which any given individual has received the light of the gospel in the sense of having understood and grasped it sufficiently in order to make a responsible decision. No wonder Wesley, in the same sermon already cited, wrote, "It is not . . . easy to pass any judgment concerning the faith of our modern Jews. It is plain, 'the veil is still upon their hearts' when Moses and the Prophets are read. . . . Yet it is not our part to pass sentence upon them, but to leave them to their own Master."[3] There are indications in Wesley's thought that he understood that people can and often do reject what they believe is the gospel, on the basis of its misrepresentations in either the words or deeds of Christians.

Given this consideration, for example, it is likely that God, the just Judge, takes into account the centuries of the church's anti-Judaism and actual persecution of Jews when he measures a modern Jew's rejection of Christ. But we cannot speculate far on this issue; finally, we are left with the basic primary conviction that all of God's judgments are fair and just, since He, in the words of John 7:24, judges

---

2. Wesley, Works 7:197.
3. Ibid., 197-98.

not "according to appearance" (e.g., not simply whether or not a person has "accepted Christ"), but "with righteous judgment" (i.e., the inner heart and motives of a person).

It may be objected that the doctrine of salvation by faith in Christ implies that a person is judged solely by whether or not she or he has confessed Jesus as Savior and Lord. But Jesus himself places a sobering qualification upon such thinking when He says, "Not everyone who says to Me, 'Lord, Lord,' will enter the kingdom of heaven; but he who does the will of My Father who is in heaven" (Matt. 7:21). And it is possible for any person to do God's will only to the extent, and in terms of, their understanding of that will. In this connection, one is reminded of Jesus' well-known story of the sheep and goats, in which He paints a fascinating scenario of final judgment where the criterion of judgment is not conscious faith in Him but quite unconscious deeds of mercy ("Lord, when did we see You . . . ?") toward the hungry, the thirsty, the stranger, the naked, the sick, and the prisoner, all of whom Jesus identifies as "these brothers of Mine, even . . . the least of these" (25:31-46, esp. 40, 45). Thus, this third principle of judgment, that God judges each individual person according to his or her light, means that His judgment of us finally is in terms of *what we have done with our lives in the light of what we believed to be divinely required of us in our lives.*

Does such an understanding of divine judgment lessen the Christian impulse to preach the gospel? In other words, it might be argued that the suggestion that God judges people according to the light they have received means that we really have no obligation to give more light to them than they already have. But this need not be our conclusion, and indeed should not. There are, in fact, three readily identifiable reasons why this is so: (1) because our primary motivation for spreading the gospel is not to save people from hell, but to fulfill Jesus' Great Commission to His disciples to evangelize every nation, and thus it is a matter of discipleship to Jesus; (2) because if faith in God through Jesus Christ truly has brought love, peace, and joy in the Holy Spirit into our lives, then it is the outflow of that new life to desire to share it with all people; and (3) the fact that people are judged by the light they have received does not by any means guarantee that many have lived up to that light—indeed, the doctrine of original sin leads us to serious doubt about the human capacity, let alone willingness, to live up to our ideals—and so we can be certain that people everywhere need to hear of the gospel of grace and forgiveness.

It is important to remember from our first principle that a crucial dimension of God's just judgment is His absolute willingness to forgive our sins, to offer us grace. Many people of various religions through-

out the centuries who have striven to please God have known only duty, not grace; only obligation, not forgiveness and acceptance. The
gospel of Jesus Christ, on the other hand, is a proclamation not only of
what God requires, but also, and more importantly, of how He loves us
and offers His rich and costly forgiveness in Christ. Truly, in the words
of the hymn "We've a Story to Tell to the Nations"—

> *We've a story to tell to the nations*
> *That shall turn their hearts to the right,*
> *A story of truth and mercy,*
> *A story of peace and light.*

> *We've a message to give to the nations*
> *That the Lord who reigneth above*
> *Hath sent us His Son to save us,*
> *And show us that God is love.*

> *We've a Savior to show to the nations*
> *Who the path of sorrow hath trod,*
> *That all of the world's great peoples*
> *Might come to the truth of God.*

> —H. Ernest Nichol

30

The End of God's Story

What will the end of God's Story be like? Hopefully it is clear by now that one of the hallmarks of a Wesleyan approach to eschatological doctrine is its sense of reserve. When we attempt to speak of "last things" or of God's envisioned "end" (whether in terms of termination or of goal), truly we are treading upon mysterious ground. Paul cites themes from Isaiah's eschatological vision and puts them to good use to remind us that God's intentions for His created order are beyond our wildest imaginations:

> Things which eye has not seen and ear has not heard,
> And which have not entered the heart of man,
> All that God has prepared for those who love Him.
>
> *(1 Cor. 2:9)*

Of course, we have noted earlier the basic Christian conviction that the end God has planned will be consistent with the divine self-revelation in Jesus Christ. If it is indeed true that "God was in Christ" (2 Cor. 5:19), and that while no human has seen God, the Son in His life and words "has explained Him" to such an extent that to behold Jesus is to behold the One who sent Him (John 1:18; 12:45), then certainly Jesus already reveals to us the nature of God's final end for His creation. The details may elude us, but we are assured that the coming of the Kingdom will not be unlike what has been revealed in Jesus. In His words, "Let not your heart be troubled; [you] believe in God, believe also in Me. In My Father's house are many dwelling places; if it were not so, I would have told you; for I go to prepare a place for you" (14:1-2).

These words of hope were, to be sure, spoken to His disciples, to those who love Him and keep His commandments (John 14:20-24). But not all of Jesus' words concerning final destiny were words of hope. Jesus also spoke freely, especially in parables, about the reality of hell. This reminds us that our accountability before God, as explored in the previous chapter, is truly of ultimate significance. We cannot take lightly our answerability, for God does not.

For many people, both Christian and otherwise, the idea of eternal damnation is distasteful and, according to some, contrary to the biblical emphasis upon God's love. But if in fact love is about mutual relationship, then one could argue that *universalism,* or the idea that all people will somehow finally be saved, is in fact the perspective that is truly contrary to divine love. It is because the Arminian-Wesleyan position is so thoroughly insistent upon the importance of human *response* to divine grace that it cannot embrace universalism, as inviting as it might be. The doctrine of eternal damnation, or hell, is in fact the logical outcome of the biblical affirmation of human responsibility before God.

Hell, then, is the end result of sin, or the "final resting place" of the person who is wrapped up in himself or herself to the point that God is utterly rejected, and thus utterly absent from the person's "world"; it is the self-chosen absence of God, one's own loving Creator. C. S. Lewis is said to have called hell "God's greatest compliment to man," since it means that God finally and irrevocably respects each person's quality of response to His grace.[1] God will not override any individual's ultimate decision, made out of the fabric of his entire life, concerning her relationship to God. To the person whose life and words say, "Leave me alone, God, and let me live my own life," God will finally respond, "As you will." And this divinely loving act of giving people up to themselves, or wrath (Rom. 1:21-32), finally will issue in an experience Jesus often described as "outer darkness" and "weeping and gnashing of teeth."

We must remember that it is not God's "will that any should perish, but that all should come to repentance" and life (2 Pet. 3:9, KJV). But if we also maintain that God is committed to covenantal relationship or partnership with us, we are led to the conclusion that simply because He wills that all be saved does not mean that all *will.* Even more important to God than our salvation is our moral agency, our capacity for authentic response to Him. This means hell is truly a "live option."

But while hell is as clear a teaching of the New Testament as practically any other doctrine, whatever we might say about it must, in the words of Russell Aldwinckle, "be consistent with the view of God as holy love, where holy love is to be interpreted in the light of its manifestation in the life, ministry, death and resurrection of Jesus Christ."[2]

---

1. For C. S. Lewis' compelling, if grandly speculative, story of the final destinies of heaven or hell, see *The Great Divorce* (New York: Macmillan Co., 1946).

2. Russell Aldwinckle, *Death in the Secular City: Life After Death in Contemporary Theology and Philosophy* (Grand Rapids: Wm. B. Eerdmans Publishing Co., 1974), 118.

Hell cannot be thought of as eternal sadistic torture, or it is not worthy of our belief in God as revealed in Jesus Christ. At the same time, it must not be dismissed or taken lightly, because it underscores, again, our final response-ability before God. It must be taken in all its awful seriousness as the condition of horrid Godlessness, as the ultimate pain of having been severed from the very Source and Giver of life and love. One may hope that somehow even hell may serve a divinely redemptive purpose for those whose destiny it is, but that is to speculate beyond what we know. Finally we are left with our first principle of final judgment as offered in chapter 29—that God, who is love, is eminently fair and just in all His judgments—and leave the rest to Him

If it is true that God's intentions for creation are for *shalom* and the "healing of the nations" (Rev. 22:2), if there "shall no longer be any curse" and "no longer be any night" (vv. 3, 5), then one might wonder if the possibilities of human freedom will also no longer be. If God truly values our responses to divine love and grace, what are we saying of heaven and hell—that He finally will say "Enough!" to the project of creaturely otherness and freedom? Will responsibility have come to its end? Will no change of relationship be possible? Granted, these are speculative questions, only occasionally touched upon by theologians in the history of Christian theology, but they are interesting nonetheless.

John the Revelator, in his vision of the new heaven and new earth, includes the fascinating detail that "there is no longer any sea" (21:1). When we recall that the sea is a recurring biblical symbol for the chaotic elements that threaten the order and stability of God's creation (symbolized by dry land), John seems to be suggesting that all contingency, threat and danger shall be removed. It is difficult to comprehend such a scenario that would still make room for the possibilities of human freedom, but on the other hand it is difficult to imagine the God who is Love ever denying or removing from us our capacity for authentic love rooted in our experience of freedom. Perhaps a solution to this problem can be suggested in the possibility that the experience of God's love, light, and presence in heaven will truly liberate us to love in ways unknown to us now, and thus paradoxically to make us more truly *free* than we can ever experience in this life. (And precisely the opposite in hell.) For in the glory that is to be revealed, we shall be truly *free to love, free to serve one another in love;* and that, according to Paul (Gal. 5:1, 13), is what authentic freedom is.

In his classic chapter on the nature of resurrection, in fact, Paul strains at the edges of human imagination and language to speak of "the end" in a way that affirms both the overwhelming reality of divine presence and our own individual participation in and awareness of divine glory:

Then comes the end, when [Christ] delivers up the kingdom to the God and Father, when He has abolished all rule and all authority and power. . . . And when all things are subjected to Him, then the Son Himself also will be subjected to the One who subjected all things to Him, *that God may be all in all* (1 Cor. 15:24, 28, *italics added*).

Can anyone imagine what our experience of the end of God's story shall be like? Only if we know what it will be for God to be "all in all"! Perhaps it would be akin to a newborn attempting to return to the womb to explain the world "waiting outside" to a child yet unborn. There simply are not categories available to us for comprehending such a sphere of existence. When God creates "a new heaven and a new earth" (Rev. 21:1), will it preclude the creation of yet other universes, either after or alongside the new creation? What new adventures might God have in store for His loved ones? Will there be new stories to weave? We do not know, and we cannot imagine, but we can trust that whatever God does will be done in unfathomable love.

> *Lame as I am, I take the prey;*
> *Hell, earth, and sin with ease o'ercome.*
> *I leap for joy, pursue my way,*
> *And as a boundling hart fly home,*
> *Through all eternity to prove*
> *Thy nature and Thy name is Love.*
> *Thy name is Love!*[3]

---

3. This is the 12th and final verse—and so the "end" verse—of Charles Wesley's "Come, O Thou Traveler Unknown." An earlier verse of this classic narrative hymn was quoted in chapter 2 of this book.

Appendix

THE DOCTRINE OF CREATION
AND SCIENTIFIC THEORY
AS REFLECTED UPON
IN KEY THEOLOGICAL TEXTS
OF THE WESLEYAN-ARMINIAN HOLINESS TRADITION

The claim was made in chapter 6 that the dominant understanding of the Wesleyan tradition concerning the Scriptures—particularly in relation to scientific research, discovery, and theory—is such that the Bible's primary concern and function are to communicate theological truth. If this is the case, then Scripture should not be consulted in order to give us scientific information, but, in Wesley's words, "to show us the way to heaven."

What follows are excerpts from three important sources in the Wesleyan-holiness tradition. H. Orton Wiley's *Christian Theology* was for several decades *the* foundational theological text in the Church of the Nazarene and widely used also in other denominations of this tradition. *Exploring Our Christian Faith,* authored by several theologians, has been the mainstay text in Wesleyan-holiness circles as an introduction to theology. Finally, H. Ray Dunning's systematic theology, *Grace, Faith, and Holiness,* published in 1988, is the most recent work of its nature written by a Wesleyan-holiness theologian.

The following excerpts all demonstrate a nonliteralist understanding of the Scriptures, and particularly of the creation accounts of Genesis. This in no way compromises the powerful theological truths of the creation accounts and in fact may help us understand and appreciate those truths more fully.

1. H. Orton Wiley, *Christian Theology,* vol. 1 (1940), 442, 444-45, 449, 454-57, 460-61

THEORIES OF CREATION

The mechanical theory . . . holds that the world was formed in a purely external and formal manner. It stresses the thought of transcen-

238

dence and wholly disregards the divine immanence. This was never the theory of the early Church. It arose only in modern times, and came as a protest against the extreme rationalism of the critico-historical movement.

The theory of natural evolution . . . when presented by Darwin and his school . . . was received with great applause. However, it could hardly be expected to hold its ground against the Christian belief in creation. It does not solve the problem. It merely pushes it back into time and therefore must rest ultimately in either creation or emanation. . . . Only the creative activity of God could have originated vegetable, animal and personal life.

In recent times, the idea of creation as an event, immediate and complete, has been challenged in favor of creation as a continuous process. The theory is the outgrowth of the renewed emphasis upon the divine immanence, and due to the influence of the evolutionary hypothesis, took the form of theistic evolution. While closely related to the [flawed] theory of spontaneous generation, it regards the divine immanence as the basic reality in contradistinction to the eternity of matter. It insists that organic development is due . . . to divine power working within the organism. The divine activity is sometimes identified with the entire process, and sometimes limited to merely the points of crisis in development.

THE SCRIPTURAL DOCTRINE OF CREATION

The scriptural doctrine of creation maintains that the universe had a beginning, that it is not eternal in either matter or form, that it is not self-originated, and that it owes its origin to the omnipotent power and the unconditioned will of God. This is the Christian conception. . . .

THE HYMN OF CREATION

The Book of Genesis opens with an inspired Psalm, sometimes known as the "Hymn of Creation," and sometimes as the "Poem of the Dawn." By this it is not meant that the account is an allegory or fiction, but a true historical description, poetically expressed. . . . the balanced rhythm, the stately movement, the recurrent refrains and the blend of beauty and power, all indicate that it is of the nature of poetry. . . .

THE MOSAIC COSMOGONY

The Genesis account of creation is primarily a religious document. It cannot be considered a scientific statement, and yet it must not be regarded as contradictory to science. . . . The Hebrew word **yom** which is translated "day" occurs no less than 1,480 times in the Old Testament, and is translated by something over fifty different words, including such terms as *time, life, today, age, forever, continually* and *perpetually.* With such a flexible use of the original term, it is impossible to either dogmatize or to demand unswerving restriction to one only of those meanings. It is frequently assumed that originally orthodox belief held to a solar day of twenty-four hours, and that the church altered her exegesis under the pressure of modern geological discoveries. This . . . is one of the "errors of ignorance." The best Hebrew exegesis has never regarded the days of Genesis as solar days, but as day-periods of indefinite duration. . . . Only with the scholastics of the middle ages and the evangelical writers of the seventeenth and eighteenth centuries was this idea [of six 24-hour days] current. Previous to this a profounder view was taught by the acknowledged leaders of the Church. . . .

The Genesis account of creation establishes a distinction between the first production of matter in the sense of origination, and secondary creation, or the formation of that matter by subsequent elaboration into a cosmos. . . . The term mediate creation better expresses the thought, and conveys the idea that God creates through creation itself. . . . When, therefore, God created the vegetation He did not say, "Let there be vegetation" but "Let the earth put forth vegetation"; when He created somatic life He said, "Let the waters swarm forth swarming things," and again, "Let the land bring forth living soul after its kind." This is mediate creation. . . . Each of the new days was ushered in solely by virtue of the omnipotent word spoken by the Creator, and was therefore *creatura;* but each new day dawned only when the time was full and the conditions perfect, and was therefore, *natura.* There is here, also, a suggestion that the progress of the entire creation depends upon the progress made by the creatures in their natural development. . . .

THE ORDER OF CREATION

Deep as is the mystery of creation in the primary sense, it is no less so in the secondary sense of formation. God does not originate the material of creation, and then in an external manner form it into individual objects with no relation to each other, except that of a common fashioner or architect. He creates through creation itself. . . . Thus the world has both a supernatural and a natural beginning. It is a cosmos in which all the parts which compose one whole are arranged in order and beauty. They are not disconnected, but one emerges out of the other at the command of God so that all things are related both in nature and as a consequence of their supernatural origin. There is no place in the account for the theory of spontaneous generation. This is the fallacy of the evolutionary hypothesis. If now we note the various stages which are introduced by the creative fiat, *Let there be,* and concluded with the refrain, *And God saw that it was good,* we shall have before us the seven formative acts of God as found in [the] Genesis account. These will constitute the sevenfold series of natural beginnings or births out of pre-existent and prepared material which through the Divine Word or *Logos* transformed the world from chaos to cosmos.

2. Roy H. Cantrell, Chapter 10 ("What Is Man?") of *Exploring Our Christian Faith*, ed. W. T. Purkiser (1960), 207-8

. . . In considering the Biblical account of man's origin, today's student will need to keep in mind a simple but profound distinction. This is the distinction between science, properly so called, and philosophical and religious explanations of the universe.

Science is that human endeavor which seeks to find the unifying principles (or laws) which underlie the phenomenal world (the world of things and events). It is, properly speaking, analytical and descriptive, concerned with the orderly processes of nature. Philosophy is the attempt to "see life steadily, and see it whole," to seek for the ultimate purposes behind the whole of existence, the "whence? whither? and why?" of our being. . . .

When these distinctions are firmly grasped, it will be seen that science as such has nothing to say about ultimate causes and purposes, or about that which lies outside the realm of observable phenomena and their explanation. This does not mean that scientific men may not theorize about the beginnings of life or the origins of man, for the philosophic instinct is very strong in the human mind. But when they do so theorize, they are not working as scientists but as philosophers or, if their thought embraces the idea of God, as theologians. It goes almost without saying that the philosophic opinions of the scientific are of little more value than the scientific opinions of philosophers. . . .

It may readily be conceded that it is absolutely impossible to reconcile naturalistic evolution with the Biblical view of origins. But let it clearly be seen that naturalistic evolution is a philosophical theory, not a scientific finding, however much some of its proponents may seek to build upon the legitimate prestige of the natural sciences.

When each discipline remains within the bounds it sets up for itself, there can be no conflict between science and true theology. This is not to ignore the multitude of conflicts which have been generated across the ages by one or the other or both stepping outside their areas of concern and competence.

3. H. Ray Dunning, *Grace, Faith, and Holiness* (1988), 75, 235-38

. . . we may affirm that it is the theological content of Scripture that is its authoritative dimension, and the most critical step in biblical interpretation is bringing to expression the theological structure that informs the text. . . .

It is unfortunate that [Genesis 1:1—2:4] has so often been used to create a struggle between science and revelation. Such a conflict is the result of failing to recognize the nature of the account. "While the account of creation in the Bible is not mythological, neither is it intended to be cosmological or scientific." . . .

[Referring to Wiley], we must be very careful to understand what is meant when we say that an account is historical, though poetical. In order to see the significance of this distinction we must first differentiate poetic symbolism from myth. Myth, in ancient religions, was taken from the realm of nature where rituals celebrated repeatable phenomena such as the cyclical recurrence of the seasons. The creation story is not mythical, in that it was a once-for-all event and not a repeated event; thus it is historical. . . .

Against this background, we propose to focus on the theological exegesis of the biblical narratives of creation. The purely theological dimensions are most clearly seen when they are set in contrast to the Babylonian creation epic that antedates them. The cosmology is essentially the same but the theology is significantly different. . . .

In the Babylonian text, the universe as the ancients knew it was described as coming into existence out of conflict among the gods. Bel, the supreme god of Babylon, vanquished Tiamat, cut her body in two, and with one half of it made a firmament supporting the upper waters in the sky; the other half became the "waters below." The parallels to Genesis are obvious. But the inspired account attributes the origin of the universe to one God and thus is monotheistic . . . rather than . . . polytheistic.

The structure of the account of the process of creation in Genesis 1 is clearly set forth to emphasize the theological truth that the Sabbath principle is grounded in the creative activity of God. It ultimately makes little difference, for this point, whether the Hebrew **yom** (day) is interpreted literally as a 24-hour period or as epochs of time of indefinite duration. The point is that the seventh day is a day of rest. The very nature of the universe supports the principle, and thus to ignore it in practice is to flirt with the chaos that was driven back by the divine fiat.

Bibliography

For Further Reading

Narrative Theology

Fackre, Gabriel. *The Christian Story.* Grand Rapids: Wm. B. Eerdmans Publishing Co., 1984.

Frei, Hans. *The Eclipse of Biblical Narrative.* New Haven, Conn.: Yale University Press, 1974.

Goldberg, Michael. *Theology and Narrative: A Critical Introduction.* Nashville: Abingdon Press, 1982.

Stegner, William R. *Narrative Theology in Early Jewish Christianity.* Louisville, Ky.: Westminster/John Knox Press, 1989.

Tilley, Terrence. *Story Theology.* Collegeville, Minn.: Liturgical Press, 1985.

Part I—Foundational Doctrine

Langford, Thomas A. *Practical Divinity: Theology in the Wesleyan Tradition.* Nashville: Abingdon Press, 1983.

Outler, Albert C., ed. *John Wesley.* New York: Oxford University Press, 1964.

Thorsen, Donald. *The Wesleyan Quadrilateral.* Grand Rapids: Zondervan Publishing House, 1990.

Wynkoop, Mildred Bangs. *The Foundations of Wesleyan-Arminian Theology.* Kansas City: Beacon Hill Press of Kansas City, 1967.

Part II—The Doctrine of Creation

Buber, Martin. *I and Thou.* Translated by Ronald Gregor Smith. New York: Charles Scribner's Sons, 1958.

Farley, Wendy. *Tragic Vision and Divine Compassion.* Louisville, Ky.: Westminster/John Knox Press, 1990.

Giberson, Karl. *Worlds Apart: The Unholy War Between Religion and Science.* Kansas City: Beacon Hill Press of Kansas City, 1993.

Hick, John. *Evil and the God of Love.* San Francisco: Harper & Row, 1966, 1978.

Jewett, Paul K. *Man as Male and Female.* Grand Rapids: Wm. B. Eerdmans Publishing Co., 1975.

MacGregor, Geddes. *He Who Lets Us Be.* New York: Seabury Press, 1975.

Part III—The Doctrine of Sin

Buber, Martin. *Eclipse of God.* New York: Harper & Row, 1952.

Cherbonnier, E. La B. *Hardness of Heart.* Garden City, N.Y.: Doubleday & Co., Inc., 1955.
Niebuhr, H. Richard. *The Responsible Self.* New York: Harper & Row, 1963.
Pittenger, Norman. *Cosmic Love and Human Wrong.* New York: Paulist Press, 1978.

Part IV—The Doctrine of Covenants
Hartman, David. *A Living Covenant: The Innovative Spirit in Traditional Judaism.* New York: Free Press, 1985.
Knight, George A. F. *Theology as Narration.* Grand Rapids: Wm. B. Eerdmans Publishing Co., 1976.
Martens, Elmer. *God's Design.* Grand Rapids: Baker Book House, 1986.
Mussner, Franz. *Tractate on the Jews.* Philadelphia: Fortress Press, 1984.
Waskow, Arthur. *Godwrestling.* New York: Schocken Books, 1978.

Part V—The Doctrine of Christ
Aldwinckle, Russell F. *More than Man.* Grand Rapids: Wm. B. Eerdmans Publishing Co., 1976.
Aulén, Gustaf. *Christus Victor.* New York: Macmillan Publishing Co., 1969.
Baillie, Donald M. *God Was in Christ.* New York: Charles Scribner's Sons, 1948.
Borg, Marcus. *Jesus: A New Vision.* New York: HarperCollins Publishers, 1987.
Heron, Alasdair I. C. *The Holy Spirit.* Philadelphia: Westminster Press, 1983.
Johnson, Elizabeth. *Consider Jesus.* New York: Crossroad, 1990.
Lee, Bernard J. *The Galilean Jewishness of Jesus.* New York: Paulist Press, 1988.
Swider, Leonard. *Yeshua: A Model for Moderns.* Kansas City: Sheed & Ward, 1988.

Part VI—The Doctrine of the Church
Baillie, Donald M. *The Theology of the Sacraments.* New York: Charles Scribner's Sons, 1957.
Kung, Hans. *The Church.* Garden City, N.Y.: Image Books, 1976.
Moltmann, Jurgen. *The Church in the Power of the Spirit.* New York: Harper & Row, 1977.
Snyder, Howard. *Liberating the Church.* Downers Grove, Ill.: InterVarsity Press, 1983.
Staples, Rob. *Outward Sign and Inward Grace: The Place of Sacraments in Wesleyan Spirituality.* Kansas City: Beacon Hill Press of Kansas City, 1991.
Wesley, John. *A Plain Account of Christian Perfection.* Kansas City: Beacon Hill Press of Kansas City, 1966.
Wynkoop, Mildred Bangs. *A Theology of Love: The Dynamic of Wesleyanism.* Kansas City: Beacon Hill Press of Kansas City, 1972.

Part VII—The Doctrine of Last Things
Aldwinckle, Russell. *Death in the Secular City: Life After Death in Contemporary Theology and Philosophy.* Grand Rapids: Wm. B. Eerdmans Publishing Co., 1974.
Cooper, John. *Body, Soul and Life Everlasting.* Grand Rapids: William B. Eerdmans Publishing Co., 1989.

Gowan, Donald E. *Eschatology in the Old Testament*. Philadelphia: Fortress Press, 1986.

Moltmann, Jurgen. *Theology of Hope*. New York: Harper & Row, 1967.

Robinson, John A. T. *The Body*. Philadelphia: Westminster Press, 1952.

Thielicke, Helmut. *Living with Death*. Grand Rapids: Wm. B. Eerdmans Publishing Co., 1983.

Subject Index

adoption 188, 190-91, 196
adoptionism 150
anthropic principle 34-35
anthropocentrism 96
anthropology 67 ff.
anthropomorphism 86-87, 97, 103
apostolic succession 175
assurance 27, 41 ff., 190
atonement 156, 158 ff., 186

baptism 179 ff.
of Jesus 137 ff., 148, 180, 209
Bible
inspiration of 22 ff.
nature of 16 ff., 25, 31, 40, 65

Calvinism 53, 84, 186-87
Canaanite myth 57-58
ceremonial holiness 193 ff.
Chalcedon, council of 151
Christocentricism 94
Christology 125 ff.
"from above" 134, 144 ff.
"from below" 134 ff.
Christus victor motif 162-63
Church, doctrine of (see ecclesiology)
Church of England (Anglican) 26, 40-41
Church of the Nazarene 25, 65, 192
Communion (see Lord's Supper)
conscience 45
Constantinople, council of 150
conversion 187 ff.
cosmological argument 33-34
covenants 85, 88, 90 ff.
created order 63 ff., 87, 90-91, 225-26
creatio ex nihilo 52-53, 104

creation 14-15, 33, 51 ff., 105-6, 176-77, 189-90, 238 ff.
creationism 221, 224-25
crucifixion of Jesus 140-41, 148, 154, 157 ff., 179 ff.

Decalogue 104 ff.
deism 106
docetism 137, 149-50
dualism 52, 221

ecclesiology 166 ff.
ecology 71, 226
entire sanctification 196 ff.
eschatology 62, 95, 103, 205 ff.
ethical holiness 193 ff.
Eucharist (see Lord's Supper)
evolutionary theory 64-65, 239 ff.
exodus, Jewish 19, 58-59, 104-5, 181

faith 87-88, 187
foreknowledge 53
freedom, human 81 ff., 88-89, 128, 236
freewill defense 55, 73-74

genealogies of Jesus 128 ff., 138-39, 214
gnosticism 137
God
as Creator 63 ff., 88-89, 91, 128
as Sovereign 52 ff.
as Sustainer 115
God, suffering of 60-61, 140-41
grace 88, 104, 229, 232-33

hamartiology (see also sin) 75 ff., 84
heaven 208

246

hell   208, 232, 235-36
history   17 ff.
holiness   26 ff., 192 ff.
Holiness Code   193
holiness tradition   192 ff.
Holy Spirit   23, 43, 58, 119, 122 ff.,
       135 ff., 170 ff., 186-87, 189-90,
                                196, 218

idolatry   76-77, 108-9
image of God   68 ff.
imitatio dei   109
immanence   109
immortality of the soul   221, 225
immutability   88
Incarnation   66, 164, 176-77, 226
initial sanctification   190, 196
Islam   34, 52, 99, 231
Israel   126

Jewish people   99-100, 119, 126,
                                194, 231
Judaism   17, 34, 52, 99, 105, 125-26,
                                180, 223
judgment   223, 227 ff.
justification   153 ff., 188 ff., 196

kingdom of God   140, 212 ff.
kingship narratives   111 ff., 128,
                                213-14
koinonia   146-47, 191

Last Supper   181-82
laughter   100 ff.
law (see Torah)
liberation theology   109
Logos Christology   145 ff., 154, 159,
                                     176
Lord's Supper (Eucharist) 17, 180 ff.

marks of the Church   172 ff.
Methodism   26 ff., 181
mission   232-33
monotheism   52, 99
moral argument   37-38
moral evil   55

moral influence theory   160

narrative theology   13 ff., 22, 48, 51,
                 134-35, 151 ff., 194, 200
natural evil   55 ff.
natural theology   32 ff.
Nazi holocaust   81, 126
Nicea, council of   150-51, 164

omnipotence   53 ff., 60, 88-89
omnipresence   53-54, 61
omniscience   53-54, 60-61, 87 ff., 97
ontological argument   35-36
original sin   79 ff.
Orthodox tradition   26, 164

Passover   17, 181
Pentateuch   202, 222-23
Pentecost   169 ff.
predestination   83
predetermination   113-14
prevenient grace   44 ff., 82, 84, 91,
                                186-87, 190
problem of evil (see also
      theodicy)   54 ff., 73-74
prophecy   118 ff.
propitiation   159 ff.
Protestant tradition   26, 175, 177 ff.,
                                     218
Providence   62

Quakers   177

reason   31 ff., 40, 50
recapitulation theory   130, 162-63
reconciliation   159-60, 196
regeneration   188 ff., 196
reincarnation   220
religious experience   40 ff., 50
repentance   187
resurrection of Jesus   20 ff., 140-41,
            153 ff., 168-69, 179 ff., 226
resurrection of the body   156, 222 ff.
revelation
   general   32 ff.
   special   32

Roman Catholic tradition 26, 29, 175, 177, 218

Sabbath observance 105-6, 193
sacramental theology 177-78
sacraments 176 ff.
salvation (see soteriology)
sanctification 26 ff., 190
scandal of particularity 108
second coming of Christ 183, 205
Shekinah 138
Sheol 221-22
sin (see also hamartiology) 75 ff., 86, 196-97
soteriology 144, 184 ff.
soul 69-70
Spirit Christology 43, 135 ff., 190, 215
spiritual gifts 174-75
synergism 46, 92

table fellowship of Jesus 148, 181
teleological argument 34-35, 57
temptations of Jesus 131 ff., 139
theodicy 54 ff., 61-62
Torah 104 ff., 118, 123-24, 130, 194
traditions, theological 25 ff., 40, 50
transcendence 63, 108-9
Trinity, doctrine of 149, 168-69, 173 ff., 179

universalism 235

virgin birth of Jesus 136-37

Wesleyan quadrilateral 41, 49-50
worship of the Church 173 ff.
wrath 94-95

yetzer hara 96

Index of Persons

Abelard 160-61
Aldwinckle, Russell 235
Anselm 35 ff., 160-61
Apollinaris 150
Aquinas 35, 224
Arius 150
Arminius, James 44, 53
Athanasius 150, 164
Augustine 83-84, 91, 182, 218, 224
Aulén, Gustaf 162-63

Barclay, William 132
Barth, Karl 68
Barth, Markus 173
Bengel, Johann 211
Bonhoeffer, Dietrich 104
Bonino, Jose Miguez 110
Brown, Raymond 130
Buber, Martin 66, 90-91, 106

Calvin, John 175
Camus, Albert 54, 110
Cantrell, Roy 241
Cobb, John 113
Cox, Harvey 77

Davies, Paul 34 n.
Donne, John 80
Dunning, Ray 238, 241-42

Eutyches 151

Fackenheim, Emil 53
Fackre, Gabriel 135 n., 187
Fox, George 177

Gaunilo 36-37
Giberson, Karl 34 n.
Gregory of Nazianzus 150-51

Hankey, Katherine 17, 191
Hartman, David 96
Heidegger, Martin 33
Heron, Alasdair 141
Heschel, Abraham 120-21
Hick, John 224

Irenaeus 136, 162-63

James, William 43
Jewett, Paul 68 n.
Jewett, Robert 105-6, 116

Kant, Immanuel 37-38, 45
Kierkegaard, Søren 147
King, Jr., Martin Luther 120

Langford, Thomas 47
Lee, Bernard 48
Leo, Pope 151-52
Lewis, C. S. 235
Locke, John 47
Luther, Martin 42, 77, 83, 126, 175, 189

Macquarrie, John 60
Marcion 127
Marx, Karl 219
Meland, Bernard 43
Moltmann, Jurgen 121, 219

Nestorius 151
Nichol, H. Ernest 233
Nietzsche, Friedrich 100

Origen 221
Ott, Heinrich 38

Pascal, Blaise 31
Pelagius 83-84

Peli, Pinchas 81
Plato 33, 221
Potok, Chaim 22

Robinson, H. Wheeler 158
Robinson, John A. T. 225 n.
Russell, D. S. 221-22

Sanner, A. E. 23
Socrates 221
Sontag, Frederick 89
Staples, Rob 75 n., 178 n.

Tillich, Paul 33, 189, 219

von Rad, Gerhard 95

Wesley, Charles 26 ff., 142, 192, 197, 237
Wesley, John 21, 24, 26 ff., 31, 40 ff., 49-50, 66, 69, 76, 91, 159, 177, 181, 192, 196, 198, 204, 211, 231
Whitehead, A. N. 61
Wiesel, Elie 22, 54
Wiley, H. Orton 64, 140, 228, 238 ff.
Wynkoop, Mildred Bangs 29

Index of
Scripture References

Genesis

1	15, 63 ff., 106, 138
1:1	13 ff.
1:1—2:4	239-40, 242
1:2	135
1:3 ff.	51, 95
1:7, 9	58
1:16	64
1:21	64
1:26	77
1:27	68, 79
1:28	71
1:31	63, 76, 86
2:3	193
2:7	21, 69, 96, 135
2:18	80
2:19	72
2:22-25	79
2:25	78
3	75 ff.
3:1, 14	76
3:5	77
3:6	76, 78
3:7	78
3:9	70, 78
3:12-13	78-79
3:15	79
3:16	79
3:17-19	79
4:6-7	80 ff.
4:9	70, 81
5:1-2	67
6:5-7	94
6:6	86
6:12-13	95
8:1	135
8:21-22	96-97
9:3	96
9:6-7	96
9:9-17	107, 113
9:10	95
11:1, 4-7, 9	169
12:1	116
12:2-3	129
15:1-2	100
16:2	101
17:6	101
17:17	101
18:15	102
18:23, 25	71
21:1-6	102
22:12	87
38	129

Exodus

3:5	193
3:6	224
8:19	140
14:21	19, 135
15:6-8	19
15:8	135
15:11	193
17:6-7	132
19:5-6	108, 212
20:2-3	104
20:4	108
20:10	105-6
20:18-21	193
34:6-7	105

Leviticus

17—26	193
19	193 ff.

19:18	27
19:28	185
25:23	117

Numbers

19:11	184

Deuteronomy

4:10-20	108-9
6:4-5	27
6:10-12	132
6:13	132
6:16	132
8:3	132
10:17-19	109
17:18-20	118
26:5	116
30:11-16	118
30:15	105
30:19-20	105

1 Samuel

8:5	111
8:7-18	111
8:22	112
13:13-14	119
15:10-11	112
15:22	114
15:29	112

2 Samuel

7:2	114
7:5-7	114
7:11	115
7:16	111, 115

2 Kings

10:15	29

1 Chronicles

28:6	115
29:10-15	115

2 Chronicles

6:18	112

Job

1:6-12	56
1:19	57
2:1-7	56

7:9	221
38—41	56 ff.
42:1-6	193

Psalms

2:4	103
8:3-4	67
8:5-6	68
10:1	70
13:1	70
14:1	36
19:1	32
22:1-2	70
53:1	36
74:12-17	58-59
103:14	96, 103, 228
104:27-30	135, 189
115:7	222
139:1-4	61

Ecclesiastes

9:2, 5	221

Isaiah

6:1-5	192-93
11:1-5	213
19:24-25	123
25:6, 8	183, 216
42:1-4	123
49:6	123
54:7-10	97-98
58	107, 119
58:2-10	119-20
61:1	139

Jeremiah

1:18	119
23:5-6	213
31:31, 33	122
31:35-37	124

Ezekiel

36:25-28	122
37:28	123

Daniel

12:2	227

Hosea

1:2	121

3:1	121
4:1-3	121
11:1-3	131
11:1-4, 8-9	121
14:8	122

Joel

2:28-29	143, 171

Amos

5:24	120

Micah

6:6-8	119

Matthew

1:1	117, 128-29
1:1-17	137
1:3	129
1:5	129-30
1:6	130
1:16	129
1:18-23	136
1:23	136, 164
2:2, 16-18	131
2:11-12	130
2:15	131
3:2	187, 209, 212
3:7, 10-12	217
3:9	180, 209
3:12	180, 209
3:17	138
4:2-4	131-32
4:5-7	132
4:8-10	132-33
4:17	187, 212
5:1	194
5:43-48	194-95
5:44-45	178
5:48	194-95
7:21	232
8:11	216
10:5-6	130
10:20	140
10:29	178
11:2-3	208
11:4-6	210
11:9	211

11:19	210-11
11:28-29	148, 211
11:28-30	217
12:18-21	123, 139
12:24	215
12:28	140, 215
15:21-28	130
16:13-17	19, 23
17:1-8	193
18:1, 2-5	216
18:23-35	229
19:14	216
21:1-11	117
22:23-33	223-24
22:34-40	27, 200
25:31-46	226, 232
26:38	148
26:39	43
27:52-53	21
28:2	20
28:18	133
28:19	131, 179

Mark

1:4	180
1:9-13	137
2:1-12	215
2:27	194
3:1-5	194
5:1-19	184 ff.
5:20	191
11:9-10	214
12:28-34	27, 200, 216
14:32-36	43
14:36	128
14:51-52	20
16:5	20

Luke

1:34-35	136
2:49	137
2:52	137
3:23-38	137-38
3:38	139
4:1	139
4:14-19	139
4:36	215

6:20-26	215	15:22, 24	231
8:27	185	20:10—21:14	158
9:31	183	20:12	20
9:53-54	202-3	20:19	156
10:25-37	27, 200 ff.	20:21-23	168
10:36, 37	15, 203-4	20:22	21
11:20	139-40	20:26	156
12:48	229	20:27	142
17:20-21	217		
22	181 ff.	**Acts**	
22:15-18	183	1:6-8	218
22:16, 18	217	2:1; 1:14; 2:2, 4-6, 11	169-70
22:19-20	182	2:16-18	143
22:27	182, 217	2:22	134
22:27-30	217-18	2:22-24	155
22:42	43	2:32-33	143, 174
23:34	142, 160	2:33	168
24:4	20	2:44-45	171
24:21	214	4:9-10	155
24:31	156	4:24-30	123
24:35	21, 182	4:27	139
		7:4-5	116
John		10:34-35	46
1:1	51, 59, 117, 134	10:38	138, 200
1:3-4	176	10:38-40	155
1:9-10	45, 176	10:42	230
1:10-11	117	10:45	124
1:14	59, 134, 159, 176	14:16-17	46
1:18	146, 199-200	17:26-28	47
3:3, 7	189	17:30-31	155, 230
3:17	230	26:8	155
3:20	78		
4:9, 22	202	**Romans**	
5:17	107	1:3-4	141
5:22	230	1:18-26	94 ff.
7:16-17	38	1:20	32, 94
7:24	231-32	1:21-32	94-95, 235
8:2-11	229	1:23, 25	76
8:29	128, 200	1:32	94
12:45	234	2:5-8	227
12:47-48	230	2:14-15	231
13:1, 3-5, 13-14, 20	145-46	2:16	228
13:3-5	147	3:23	83
13:35	198	4	188-89
14:1-2	234	4:17	141, 155
14:20-24	234	4:18-25	99, 153 ff.
15:12, 13	198	4:24	155

5:5	189
5:8	27, 186
5:10-11	159
5:12	76, 80
5:12-21	163
5:17-19	128
5:19	80, 163
6:4	142, 179
6:8-11	163
6:10-11	165, 179
6:17-21	188
6:23	94
8:9	141
8:11	140-41
8:14	142
8:14-17	42, 190
8:15	46, 191
8:16	27
8:17	43, 190
8:19, 21-23	183, 225
8:22-23, 37-39	62
8:29	190
8:34	142
9:4-5	126
11:17-18, 24	125-26
12:1	175, 195
12:1-8	175
12:2—13:4	195
14:7	218
15:12	123

1 Corinthians

2:9	234
2:10-12	142, 146, 174
3:1-4	172
3:9	91
3:16, 17	172
6:14—7:1	195
8:6	59
11:26	182-83
12:4-6	174
12:7, 13	191
12:13	179
15:3-4	20
15:12-19	156
15:14, 17	20
15:20	142

15:24, 28	237
15:38	156
15:43-44	225
15:44-45	142, 156, 168
15:49	142
15:57	197

2 Corinthians

1:9	224
1:18-20	224
1:20	154
1:21-22	174
4:6	128
5:7	38
5:18-19	159
5:19	149, 174, 184, 187, 234
5:21	180
6:14—7:1	195

Galatians

2:20	44, 187
3:28	173
4:4-6	42, 46
4:6	190-91
5:1, 13	82, 236
5:14	83
5:22	190
5:23	197

Ephesians

2:1-3	188
2:8-9	136
2:11-13	123
2:11-16	171-72
2:14	173
2:17	173
2:17-18	174
2:18	173
2:18-22	171-72
2:20	175
2:21, 22	175
4:14	41
5:20	174

Philippians

2:1-5	146, 175
2:1-11	144 ff.
2:5-11	145-46

	162
	59
2:13-15	162
3:10	195

1 Thessalonians
5:24	103

1 Timothy
2:5	161
4:4	66
6:17	66

2 Timothy
1:7	197

Titus
3:3-7	188 ff.

Hebrews
1:3	51
1:10-12	206
2:10-13	190
2:14-15	164
2:18	163
4:13	87, 228
4:15	142, 230
5:7	44, 142
9:14	44, 140-41
9:27	220
10:19-22	161
11:8	116
13:8	211
13:14	117

James
2:21-23	87-88

1 Peter
2:5	172
2:22	180
2:23, 24	163
3:18-22	93

2 Peter
3:9	186, 235
3:12	206

1 John
1:6—2:1	198
2:7	198
3:2	190
3:11	198
3:16	165
3:16-17	198
3:24	28
4:8, 16	27-28, 60, 165, 195
4:10	161
4:10, 11	165
4:16-18	30, 195
4:18	29
4:19	27
4:19-21	198

Revelation
21:1	206, 236-37
22:2	207, 215, 236
22:2-5	206-7, 236
22:20	183, 211